Call Centers For Dummies®

D0536137

The Call Center Team and What They Do

Roles and responsibilities in a successful call center

Role	Core Responsibilities
Senior management	Establish the mission and vision for the call center
	Establish the annual business objectives for the call center
Call center manager	Work with senior manager to establish business objectives that support the mission
	Identify the key performance drivers that impact and control the business objectives
	Identify and assign the key roles and responsibilities to achieve the call center goals
	Create a culture that supports the mission of the call center
	Ensure that all policies and procedures support the mission, business objectives, and performance drivers
Resource analyst	Forecast customer demand
	Determine the resources required to meet customer demand within department goals
	Determine when those resources are required
	Ensure that sufficient resources are available when they're needed
Reporting analyst	Provide statistical feedback on business objectives and key performance drivers
	Conduct analysis to identify opportunities to improve call center results
Computer & Network analyst	Recommend the appropriate tools to meet the business objectives and improve performance
	Configure the tools to work properly and reliably
	Provide the appropriate maintenance and troubleshooting support
The agent performance team: Recruiter Trainer Supervisor Quality analyst	Hire the right people to do the job
	Tell them what to do, and why
	Show them how to do it
	Support them and give them feedback on performance
Call center agents	Handle customer contacts in a manner that supports the call center's objectives and their own performance goals, as outlined by their supervisor

For Dummies: Bestselling Book Series for Beginners

Call Centers For Dummies®

Cheat Sheet

The Primary Components of the Call Center Business Model

- Mission
  - Identifies how the call center supports the company's goals and strategy
  - Determines what the company needs from the call center in the long term
- Business Objectives
  - Are the short to midterm goals — perhaps one year in duration
  - Define what the company needs from the call center, right now
  - Are specific outputs that the call center is expected to produce
- Performance Drivers
  - Are processes and behaviors that influence achieving the company's business objectives
  - Are usually measurable
  - Can be used to model the call center objectives
  - Are affected by what's done in the call center — "the levers"

Top Tech Tools Your Call Center Needs

- Telephone network
- Data network/Internet
- Telephone system/Automatic call distribution (ACD)
- Interactive voice response (IVR) system
- Predictive dialer
- Web-enabling applications: e-mail, chat, collaboration
- Local area network (LAN)/Wireless area network (WAN)
- Computer workstations
- Customer relationship management (CRM) tools: calling-customer tracking, billing system, scripting, customer analytics
- Knowledgebase
- Computer–telephone-integration (CTI) software and hardware
- Agent performance dashboard
- Workforce management software
- Call recording equipment
- Data warehouse for data collection, reporting, and analysis

WILEY

For Dummies: Bestselling Book Series for Beginners

Call Centers

FOR

DUMMIES®

Call Centers FOR DUMMIES®

by Réal Bergevin

WILEY

John Wiley & Sons Canada, Ltd.

Call Centers For Dummies®

Published by
John Wiley & Sons Canada, Ltd.
6045 Freemont Boulevard
Mississauga, Ontario, L5R 4J3
www.wiley.ca

National Library of Canada Cataloguing in Publication

Bergevin, Real

      Call centers for dummies / Real Bergevin.

Includes index.

ISBN-13 978-0-470-83549-4
ISBN-10 0-470-83549-4

      1. Call centers–Management. I. Title.

HE8788.B47 2005   658.8'12   C2005-900901-2

Printed in Canada

1 2 3 4 5 TRI 08 07 06 05 04

Distributed in Canada by John Wiley & Sons Canada, Ltd.

For general information on John Wiley & Sons Canada, Ltd., including all books published by Wiley Publishing, Inc., please call our warehouse, Tel 1-800-567-4797. For reseller information, including discounts and premium sales, please call our sales department, Tel 416-646-7992. For press review copies, author interviews, or other publicity information, please contact our marketing department, Tel 416-646-4584, Fax 416-236-4448.

For authorization to photocopy items for corporate, personal, or educational use, please contact CANCOPY, The Canadian Copyright Licensing Agency, One Yonge Street, Suite 1900, Toronto, ON, M5E 1E5 Tel 416-868-1620 Fax 416-868-1621; www.cancopy.com.

About the Author

Réal Bergevin began working in call centers for the automotive, airline, and cable industries immediately after finishing university. He moved from agent to scheduler to technology analyst, and ultimately to call center manager.

In 1991 he founded his first call center consulting firm, which specialized in bringing a data-driven management method to call centers. Eventually, this firm grew into the NuComm Corporation, a company dedicated to helping its corporate clients communicate with their customers. Today, the NuComm Corporation provides a full range of services including outsourced call handling and business processes, management consulting, training, and application development. NuComm, an ISO 9001:2000–registered company, was named one of Canada's 50 Best Managed Companies in 2001, 2002, 2003, and 2004.

In 2001, Réal was honored by the National Awards Program (sponsored by The Caldwell Partners International, TD Bank Financial Group, and *The Globe and Mail*, among others) as one of Canada's Top 40 under 40. He holds a business degree from Wilfrid Laurier University and is the author of *23 Steps to an Effective Call Centre*.

Réal, his wife Anne, and their three kids live in Fonthill, Ontario.

About NuComm

Réal and his team at NuComm can help you communicate with your clients in a number of ways:

- Small business "pay as you go" customer care services
- "Virtual agent" automated interactive voice response (IVR) and Web solutions
- Call center consulting and training support
- Call center tools and application development that can increase efficiency, lower costs, and improve services for your customers
- Call handling and business process outsourcing with high levels of quality and service at varying cost points through near shore and offshore options
- Credit management, collections, and receivables management

Perhaps you're running a small call center and are looking for some guidance, or maybe you're in a Fortune 1000 industry-leading call center, and you're considering outsourcing or moving part of your call-handling offshore. Maybe you're somewhere in between. You might not even have a call center but are looking to automate some of your customer care services. Whoever you are and whatever your needs, if you're interested in any of the above, please contact Réal Bergevin at

NuComm Corporation
80 King Street, Suite 300
St Catharines, ON L2R 7G1
Phone: (877) 637-2615 Fax: (905) 641-1456
www.nucomm.net

Or, if *Call Centers For Dummies* leaves you with just as many questions as it does answers, or you'd like to explore further some of the book's ancient call center secrets, please contact John Dickhout at the same address.

Author's Acknowledgments

I'd like to acknowledge my friends at NuComm for their help in writing this book. First and foremost, I'd like to thank John Dickhout who helped me throughout and co-wrote this book. Without John, this book would not have happened.

I also want to thank John Trivieri, the President of NuComm International, for picking up the slack. John has made me look bad by doing a better job with my responsibilities than I did. And for that, he can keep them. Also from NuComm, Daniel Willis was instrumental in conducting our research, pulling together our charts, and making sure I hit deadlines. Both Daniel and John Dickhout were able to dedicate a considerable amount of time to the book while continuing to contribute to our consulting business.

I would also like to thank Sue Bogert for her critical eye and helpful suggestions, and the team at John Wiley & Sons, Canada Ltd. who helped us through this process: Robert Hickey, for keeping us on track, Lisa Berland for her developmental edit, and Kelli Howey for her copy edit.

Publisher's Acknowledgments

We're proud of this book; please send us your comments at canadapt@wiley.com. Some of the people who helped bring this book to market include the following:

Editorial

Acquiring Editor: Michelle Marchetti

Associate Editor: Robert Hickey

Developmental Editors: Lisa Berland

Copy Editor: Kelli Howey

Cartoons: Rich Tennant, www.the5thwave.com

Production

Publishing Services Director: Karen Bryan

Publishing Services Manager: Ian Koo

Project Manager: Elizabeth McCurdy

Project Coordinator: Pam Vokey

Layout and Graphics: Pat Loi

Proofreader: Susan Gaines

Indexer: Belle Wong

John Wiley & Sons Canada, Ltd.

 Bill Zerter, Chief Operating Officer

 Robert Harris, General Manager, Professional and Trade Division

Publishing and Editorial for Consumer Dummies

 Diane Graves Steele, Vice President and Publisher, Consumer Dummies

 Joyce Pepple, Acquisitions Director, Consumer Dummies

 Kristin A. Cocks, Product Development Director, Consumer Dummies

 Michael Spring, Vice President and Publisher, Travel

 Kelly Regan, Editorial Director, Travel

Publishing for Technology Dummies

 Andy Cummings, Vice President and Publisher, Dummies Technology/General User

Composition Services

 Gerry Fahey, Vice President of Production Services

 Debbie Stailey, Director of Composition Services

Contents at a Glance

Table of Contents

Introduction

. . . . .

*W*elcome to *Call Centers For Dummies*. If you work, have worked, or are considering working in the call center industry, you've probably experienced the sight of someone's eyes glazing over when you've tried to explain what exactly a call center is. On the other hand, if you don't currently have anything to do with call centers, perhaps you'd like to have a better understanding of this call center business that everyone seems to be talking about.

Either way, you've come to the right place. The purpose of this book is to define and demystify call centers, what they do, and how they do it, in a simple, straightforward way. Hopefully, we'll have a little fun in the process too.

When I started working in call centers sometime in the 1980s, call center management as a business discipline was still fairly new. For me, as with many others, the business of call centers was instantly appealing. Call centers were fast-paced, dynamic, and full of interesting people. They were fun!

As a newly minted graduate, I found that the call center world was the perfect place to use all of the skills that I'd just finished developing in business school. (In fact, I even wished that I'd paid closer attention during statistics and cost accounting classes!) What a great place to start a career and meet girls. (Did I mention that I met my wife at a call center conference? What a great industry!)

Over the next few years, I enjoyed some great call center management opportunities with some fantastic companies. One of the benefits of getting in at the beginning of a new industry or business discipline is that the opportunities for those willing to learn and experiment are tremendous. At the time, we were making a lot of it up as we went along. Some early call center newsletters and trade shows were springing up, which contributed to a basic skill set needed to effectively run call centers, but in general the business was fairly undisciplined.

I had the good fortune early in my career to be exposed to people and teachings that called for a "systems" approach to management. A systems approach calls for the creation of business models that seek to understand and explain the causes and effects of business process — take an action, get a result. I believe that nothing is more important in business than to understand the implications of your actions.

My goal when I started my management consulting practice in the early 1990s was to provide corporate clients with a simple system of call center management that would give companies a high degree of control over the outputs of their call centers. Rather than focus on any one task — such as staff scheduling, queuing theory, or the application of technology — I instead wanted to provide my clients with a complete package that considered these important issues in an overall model of operations. And simplicity has always been the key. A system that can't be understood by everyone in the call center has little chance of success.

My team and I learned early on that any system of management, however well intentioned, wouldn't work without a strong and supportive culture. We also learned that the easiest way — for us, anyway — to get a supportive culture was to define the culture we wanted and then aggressively work to create it. Any management system of high control must preserve dignity, integrity, and respect within an organization. Otherwise, the system can become harsh. Similarly, the organization needs to believe that the system of management is the best way to achieve the goals of all stakeholders. Values and beliefs are key controllables in this system of management.

This pursuit of a system of cause and effect for call centers has been the foundation of any success that we've had at NuComm, and it continues to be the beacon that drives our efforts to improve. Virtually all of our clients, whether in the consulting or call handling business, have been looking to increase understanding and control over their customer communications. This foundation of cause and effect has been integrated into *Call Centers For Dummies*.

I can't think of a better vehicle to share my vision for a model of call center management than *Call Centers For Dummies*. The *...For Dummies* books are known for their straightforward and simple approach to instruction. This is our life's work at NuComm — to create a simple and straightforward approach to call center management.

About This Book

Since Alexander Graham Bell invented the telephone, people have been using it to do business. The concept of the call center, however, is a relatively recent one. As recently as the early nineties, few people knew what a call center was. Now it seems almost everyone you meet either works in a call center, knows someone who does, or has at least heard of call centers, even if they don't know exactly what they do.

Many people have developed some pretty strong opinions about call centers. Executives and analysts alike realize more than ever that the call center can have a tremendous impact on their overall business in the areas of revenue, costs, market intelligence, and customer loyalty. Call centers have become a significant part of your local and world economy.

I started working as a call center consultant because I wanted to apply method and discipline to the management of call centers. With the emergence of worldwide competition in the call center, it's become increasingly important for call center professionals to work from defined methodology.

Certainly, much advancement in the sophistication and use of call centers has been made and a great number of people who are good at running effective call centers exist, but many are still looking for help in making the call center machine work.

You can find call center information in a variety of publications, seminars, and Web sites, but this book attempts to provide a broader, more holistic view. My goal — with my call center operations, my consultancy, and now this book — has been and continues to be to provide an overall framework for the operation of call centers.

Why You Need This Book

If you've ever contacted a company, whether to order a product, seek technical support, complain about service, or make an enquiry, or if you've ever been called by a telemarketer — by the way, we hope to dispel the myth that there is a worldwide conspiracy for outbound call centers to call you just as you sit down to dinner with your family — chances are high that your contact was with someone in a call center. So, this book will likely be of interest to you.

Those of you involved in the call center industry, however, will find this book an easy-to-use, and (we hope) an easy-to-read reference guide to the effective operation of a call center. It'll be of particular use to you if

- You're a hot-shot MBA tracking through your career and you find yourself running a call center,
- You're an experienced call center manager and you're looking for some new ideas and perspectives,
- You're a supplier to the call center industry and want to better understand your clients' management perspective,

- You're working in a call center and want to advance your career by unlocking the ancient call center secrets found in this book,

- You're considering a career in call centers,

- You're looking for new material to dazzle members of the opposite sex with, or

- You're my mother and you want to know, once and for all, what I've done with my life.

What You Don't Have to Read

When it comes to reading this book, we certainly invite you to curl up on a Saturday night with a nice cup of tea, hot chocolate, or whatever and read this book from cover to cover. We're sure you hard-core call center types will find it quite gripping — a real page-turner.

However, we suspect that some of you may not have the desire or need to do this. We encourage you to find the part that most interests you and start there.

How This Book Is Organized

Call Centers For Dummies is organized into six parts, each covering a different aspect of the call center. Chapters within each part cover specific topics in detail. Each part contains concepts and definitions, interesting facts and anecdotes, and, in most cases, practical how-to suggestions pertaining to the topic. Of course, any approach you take to tackling *Call Centers For Dummies* is fine. Most people, however, will get the most out of this book by first reading Part I.

Part I: From the Ground Up: An Overview of the Call Center

This part provides a good overview of many of the topics covered in more detail in the book. Consider it a call center primer, plus. It's especially useful for those who are just getting started or those who want a brief indoctrination.

This section is also for you if you're planning a new call center. We introduce a business model for building a call center and relate that model to the larger corporate mission and goals.

Part II: The Master Plan: Finance, Analysis, and Resource Management

This part looks at call center analysis, financial planning, and staffing. We provide a simple overview of how (and what) measures come together to drive call center operational and financial performance.

Also, in this part of the book we'll uncover some of the mysteries of how and why call centers perform the way they do, and explore everything from forecasting to schedule creation and workforce management automation.

Part III: Making Life Better with Technology

Part III reviews call center technologies, including basic requirements and valuable enhancements. We also cover a simple approach to recommending and justifying new technology. Many will find this part useful, as it provides a layperson's explanation of what the technology does.

Part IV: Ensuring Continuous Improvement

In this part we cover recruiting, job expectations, training, feedback, and support. You learn how to implement a simple five-step process that will guide you in managing the performance of your people.

We also explore the call center process and how to manage it, and examine policies and procedures and the effects of legislation and employment law on call centers.

Part V: Handling the Calls: Where It All Comes Together

Part V gets down to the basics of call handling. We share some vital tips and techniques to ensure agents can effectively handle this most important interaction in the call center.

Part VI: The Part of Tens

Here, we have provided tips and techniques collected from the call center industry. These quick hits will give a boost to your company's revenue and efficiency, employee morale, and customer satisfaction — even if you don't read this wonderful book!

Enjoy.

Icon Guides

These are real-world stories that have happened to me or that someone's told me about.

The Tip icon provides you with a general recommendation on how you can make your call center better, or make running your call center easier.

This icon flags any potential pitfalls we think you need to be careful of.

This is — you guessed it — the stuff we don't want you to forget.

This icon designates information you probably don't need to know but may find interesting.

Part I

From the Ground Up: An Overview of the Call Center

In this part . . .

In this part, I answer the question "What is a call center?",
provide a brief history of call center development, and
explore what makes a good (or bad) call center. If you just
want to know a bit more about call centers, are thinking
about working in one, or have ever had any aspirations to
start a new call center of your own, then this is the part
for you. Consider this a call center primer, plus.

If you build it, they will call. I introduce a business model
for building a call center and relate that model to the
larger corporate mission and goals. I examine the organizational structure — exploring the roles needed to
ensure the center performs to its business model and
objectives. Finally, I consider the logistics of building a
call center. Much of the information in the latter section of
this part can be used when expanding an operation or
reviewing the operation of an existing call center.

Chapter 1

A First Look at Call Centers

In This Chapter

▶ Defining a call center

▶ Looking at the evolution of the call center

▶ Differentiating the good from the bad

*F*or years my mom has been asking me, "What is it you do, again?" Well here it is, Mom. I work in a call center. In fact, I work in lots of call centers. I know, I know — you don't know what a call center is. Well, please keep reading.

What Is a Call Center?

Basically, a call center is the person at the other end of the phone when you call an airline, cable company, or telephone banking operation. Sometimes a call center is just one or two people sitting beside a phone answering customer calls. Often it's a very large room with lots and lots of people neatly organized into rows, sitting beside their phones, answering customer calls.

To the customer (that's you, Mom), the call center is the voice of the company. If you're angry, you often get mad at the person on the other end of the phone — after all, you're talking to the company, right?

To the company, the call center is many things — cost center, profit center, key source of revenue, key source of frustration, strategic weapon, strategic disadvantage, source of marketing research, source of marketing paralysis — it varies from company to company with the strategic alignment and capability of each one's call center.

Inbound/outbound

Call centers communicate with their customers in a number of ways. Inbound call centers are those where customers phone the call center.

Customers call inbound call centers to buy things, such as airline tickets; to get technical assistance with their personal computer; to get answers to questions about their utility bill; to get emergency assistance when their car won't start; or for any number of other reasons for which they might need to talk to a company representative.

In outbound call centers, representatives from the company initiate the call to customers. Your first reaction might be, "telemarketing, right?" Well, yes, telemarketing is a reason for a company to call you, but companies have lots of other good reasons to call their customers.

Companies might call because the customer hasn't paid a bill, when a product the customer wanted is available, to follow up on a problem the customer was having, or to find out what the customer and other customers would like to see by way of product or service enhancements.

Some call centers are called blended operations — agents in the center handle both inbound and outbound calling. As I outline in Chapter 7, blending done well can make call center operations very cost-efficient and can improve service to the customer as well.

Is all outbound calling bad?

Recently, and not surprisingly, outbound calling has taken a lot of heat. Calling people at home has been a very effective and very successful marketing tool. Done well, it can be a great mechanism for building customer relationships.

An example that I frequently use is my friend Susan and her local gardening center. Susan is a strong supporter of anti-telemarketing legislation — and an avid gardener. However, when I told her that I'd just answered a call on her phone from her local garden center to inform her they'd just received a shipment of some tulip bulbs she'd been trying to get, she wanted to know if I'd asked them to call back later. "No," I said. "I told them to put you on their *Do Not Call* list because you don't like telemarketing."

The point is, in any good relationship communication is two-way. You contact your friends and they contact you. The same can be said — *needs* to be said — of good business relationships. The problem is that, as with so many things, marketers and telemarketers got carried away with telemarketing. The call center industry took a highly successful and cost-effective tool and ramped it way up.

And, because it's easier to make calls with inexpensive agents and low-cost offers than it is to understand your customer and provide targeted one-to-one, high-value propositions, telemarketing became a numbers game and everyone got calls at dinner time — for everything.

So now call centers have rules — and rightly so. However, all is not lost. Sophisticated marketers can still build individual customer relationships; you just need to get permission to do so. Enter the age of responsible, one-to-one telemarketing!

The explosion in popularity of the Internet and wireless communications has changed the way people communicate. People still use the phone — although it's frequently a phone that goes with them — but, along with the phone, you have e-mail, chat, Web forms, and instant messaging as means of communicating with friends, Romans, and Wal-Mart — and call centers have responded.

Contact or call center: What's in a name?

Increasingly, call centers are being called *contact* centers to reflect the fact that they handle more than just phone calls. These facilities are, in fact, the *center* for customer *contacts,* in whatever way the customer wants to communicate.

Bottom line, it's up to the customer to decide how they want to communicate with the company, and it's up to the company to respond appropriately through its contact center.

As with inbound and outbound call centers, some companies choose to separate the handling of customer contacts by medium — a group for inbound calls, a group for outbound calls, a group for e-mail, and so on. Some, especially smaller operations, have opted to create "universal agents" who handle all contact types. Call centers create universal contact agents for the same reason that they blend inbound and outbound call handling agents — efficiency and service.

This book is called *Call Centers For Dummies.* It could just as easily be called *Contact Centers For Dummies.* Throughout, I refer to call handling and call centers. This is partially because of my bias (I grew up in call centers — well, not literally), as the phone call still represents the bulk of communication between customers and companies, and partially because it doesn't really matter. The concepts in this book can be universally applied to all types of contacts — phone calls, e-mails, chats, instant messages, or smoke signals.

Tripping Down Memory Lane: The Evolution of the Call Center

Call centers are a very efficient and effective way to do business. I can't really tell you when the first call center opened. It's easier to ask, "When did companies start doing business over the phone?" Call centers probably started around the time that the telephone became a common household device.

The evolution of call centers just makes sense. It is so much easier for a consumer to pick up a phone and call a company than it is to hitch up the horse, bundle up the kids, and go to town to arrange for extra channels to be added to the cable service. Subsequently, the phone has been used for a long time as a way to do business. However, as a formal business discipline it's not so old — maybe 30 years or so in development.

Before the mid-1970s, airlines and major retailers made use of *phone rooms* — the precursor to call centers — that were either located in sites spread across the country or kept in large rooms with lots of desks, phones with many extensions, and lots and lots of paper to track everything that was going on. I'm too young to have seen this, but people who have tell me that these rooms were very busy, noisy, and confusing places.

One of the fascinating things about call centers is their never-ending pursuit of improvement. Call center operators are constantly looking for better technology, better management processes, better people, and better training for those people. It's all part of the original charter for call centers: to find a more effective way of communicating with customers so the company can serve customers better and cheaper, while generating more revenue.

Automatic call distribution: A key factor

One of the most significant advancements in call center technology was the invention of the automatic call distributor, or ACD, by Rockwell International. Rockwell built this specialized phone system for Continental Airlines in the early 1970s. Airlines were one of the earliest and most enthusiastic users of call centers in their constant pursuit of a competitive edge.

The ACD took an already good business practice — the use of phone rooms or call centers — and increased efficiency by two or three hundred percent. I discuss the ACD and other exciting call center technology in Chapters 8 and 9.

In general, the ACD made larger, centralized call centers more practical and efficient by providing a way of distributing large numbers of incoming phone calls evenly to a pool of call center staff. With the implementation of the ACD, the call center industry and the call center as a business discipline were off and running.

More recent history

Today, the call center industry is an important part of the economy. More than 55,000 call centers exist in North America alone, employing more than 6 million people, or 6 percent of the workforce. More than $700 billion in goods and services are purchased through call centers every year, and that number is growing. Almost anything can be purchased or serviced from the comfort of your home, office, car, or wherever you can get to a phone (or log on to the Internet).

And call centers continue to evolve at a dizzying pace. In an effort to gain greater efficiencies, provide better customer service, and generate more revenue, call centers are using more sophisticated technology, including customer information databases with scripting and analytical tools that tell agents the best way to approach each individual customer.

Call centers are at the head of the outsourcing debate, as companies move their call center operations offshore to countries where the labor is well qualified but less expensive. Call centers continue to invest in human resources practices, such as employment testing, accelerated learning techniques, e-learning, scorecards, and others in an effort to find the best staff.

The call center community is a tightly knit and proud group — many hold their specialized knowledge of the industry as a badge of honor — who improve their network, knowledge, and skills through trade associations, industry publications, trade shows, and specialized training and certification programs. And in an effort to better manage people, processes, and technology the industry has latched on to any management approach or philosophy that will give it an edge, including ISO-9001, statistical process control, and Six Sigma. I describe these programs in Chapter 13.

The evolving views of the call center

Most important is that corporations have changed their view of the call center — from cost center and in some cases necessary evil, to profit center and competitive advantage. Today, entire companies are built around call center capability. For example, you can buy a computer from a company that doesn't have a retail store, or do your banking with a bank that doesn't have branches — they offer the telephone or Internet as your only options.

Not all of this change and evolution has been viewed as positive. Call centers and call center managers have faced their share of challenges as well. Partially because of the impact that call centers have had on everyone's daily lives, and partially because of some bad management and bad business practices, call centers have raised the ire of consumers and caught the attention of legislators.

Laying down the law

Overly aggressive telemarketing practices have resulted in laws governing telephone sales, who can and cannot be contacted, and how people can be contacted. Some industries are legislated as to how quickly they must answer incoming calls — a response to poor service and long delays that consumers have experienced in the past.

Additionally, privacy legislation has added a level of complexity to how call centers collect and use information about their customers. Other legislation that restricts how and where call centers can operate is being considered in a number of countries. See Chapter 12 for more on legislation that affects call centers.

Some of the legislative challenges faced by call centers have been brought on by poor business practices, some by the success of the industry — explosive demand for call center services, both from business and consumers, has taxed the discipline's ability to grow in size and capability while maintaining excellence. Still, on balance, call centers continue to advance in number, capability, sophistication, and excellence for two reasons — they are effective and efficient business tools, and they satisfy the increasing customer demand for convenience.

Making Call Centers Work

Managing a call center well is not easy, because call centers are complex places. It's not just the technology — that's the easy part! Call centers are a microcosm of business. To run a good one, call center managers need to effectively blend people, processes, and technology to produce a desired result.

Consider this fact: most call centers rely on people, and often lots of them. Wages and salary typically comprise 60 to 70 percent of a call center's budget. And because customers can ask almost anything of the call center, agents need to have, at their fingertips, information on just about all of the company's policies, procedures, products, and services. Add to this a huge volume and variety of customers, and you get a lot of activity — even with the best technology to smooth things out. When you're dealing with hundreds or thousands of calls each day, the slightest bottleneck in how things get done can add up to a big problem.

Adding it up

A one-second increase in call length in a company that answers one million calls creates an additional 280 hours of work for the call center, requiring approximately 380 additional hours of staffing. (I explain the math in Chapter 5.)

Identifying good call center managers

A good call center manager needs to be part analyst, part accountant, part engineer, part psychologist, and part cheerleader.

Good managers have a strong sense of purpose — they understand their role and job within the organization. They have clear and measurable targets and goals, and understand how to affect and drive toward those goals. They effectively blend human resources, process management, and technology — being careful not to limit themselves or indulge too much in any one discipline.

For more information on the call center manager, see Chapter 3.

Defining the culture

As call centers rely so much on people, defining and creating a supportive culture is critical to their successful operation. I like to think of a supportive culture as one that clearly defines the values and beliefs that support the call center's mission. (I talk about developing your mission in Chapter 2.)

Once management has defined the values and beliefs that are important to operational success, management will integrate these elements into every part of the organization: policies, procedures, communication, goals, rewards — everything.

Figuring Out What Makes a Good Call Center

Well, a good call center has a strong culture where people work from a common set of values and beliefs and are bound by a common purpose and a strong focus on the business objectives. The practice of management continually aligns everything the call center does with its business objectives and desired culture.

Generally, as Figure 1-1 illustrates, you should look for your call center to deliver in three areas:

✔ **Revenue generation:** includes everything that leads to revenue — sales, upgrades, customer retention, collections, and winning back previously lost customers (see Chapters 3 and 16).

✔ **Efficiency:** refers to cost-effective operations for the organization — whether this relates to the operation of the call center or to getting work done for the organization (see Chapters 3 and 5). Generally, the call center will be a much more efficient means of contacting customers about a new promotion than John, Betty, and Fred in the marketing department.

✔ **Customer satisfaction:** is really long-term revenue generation — build customer loyalty and keep them doing business with you (see Chapters 3 and 14). Call centers (should) make things easy for the customer. The call center is available when the customer needs it, and has access to all the information necessary to answer customer questions. Try calling a checkout clerk or even the president of your favorite sporting goods store — trust me, even if you do get through, you probably won't get the answers you need.

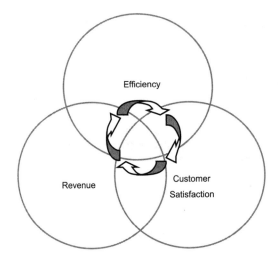

Figure 1-1:
Mutually
dependent
business
objectives.

It's a mistake to think that revenue, efficiency, and customer satisfaction are distinct goals. In fact, they're very much mutually dependent (Figure 1-1 illustrates this). Good revenue generation cannot happen without some level of efficiency, and only satisfied customers will continue to buy a product. And, for customers to remain satisfied, they want the same thing call centers do when they do business — an efficient transaction. For most customers, talking to your call center is not the highlight of their day!

When a call center fails to sell a customer on the first attempt, revenue isn't maximized because customers who really want your service/product must call back. This creates inefficiency by duplication of effort. It also represents poor service, as it makes customers do more work to get what they wanted when they initiated the first call.

The good

When the machinery is working, a good call center would exhibit the following traits:

- Focuses on its business goals
- Answers phone calls and e-mail messages quickly
- Has high employee morale
- Resolves a high percentage of customer inquiries on the first contact
- Measures customer satisfaction as a service indicator and has high customer satisfaction scores
- Is a significant source of revenue for the organization
- Has a good process for collecting and presenting data on performance: everyone knows where they stand monthly, daily, hourly, and even in real time
- Is efficient — little rework is required: calls are consistent in length, requiring a minimum of customer time for resolution
- Has everyone engaged and busy with a purpose, but with no one overly taxed
- Improves processes continually to make constant gains in service, efficiency, and revenue generation
- Is seen corporately as a strategic advantage — an ally to the rest of the organization

The bad — And the ugly

These are some things you'd expect to see in a call center that isn't working:

- Long delays for customers to get through to "the next available agent," and when they do, they are frequently transferred and/or put on hold
- Customer issues that frequently require multiple contacts before they are resolved
- Low employee morale and high turnover
- No way to measure customer satisfaction — or, if there is, scores are low
- A poor understanding of metrics or performance
- Harried staff running from crisis to crisis, putting out fires but not getting ahead

> ✔ A lack of improvement in working conditions
>
> ✔ The wider corporation grumbles about the call center, complains about costs, and questions the results; some talk about outsourcing

This book gives you the strategies, practices, plans, and skills to control what your call center produces. I talk a lot about objectives and alignment — with good objectives, when policies and procedures are aligned with those objectives, and when those objectives are achieved, the call center will have many characteristics of the good, few if any of the bad, and none of the ugly.

A well-run call center is not an accident. It's a result of good planning and good execution by good people.

What Does the Future Hold?

I expect that call centers will continue to improve in sophistication, capability, and service. Your call center will likely continue to evolve into a contact center — integrating all methods of communication into one quick and seamless channel, regardless of what language or device your customers are using.

I look for more call center services to be more customized to the needs of individual customers. There will be technological advancements, perhaps some "oos and ahs" in what call centers can do with automation. But the end of the movie will be that more call centers will provide better service. Great one-on-one service will become the minimum expectation for doing business over the phone. And as call centers improve in all aspects of their operation, they will look for ways to go beyond customer service — to make the experience of dealing with the company better. Call centers will do all of this because customers expect — and deserve — the best.

Chapter 2

Business Basics: Models and Drivers and Goals, Oh My!

*I*n this chapter I discuss business models and why they're important to the successful operation of your call center. A business model is a high-level description of how your business is organized and what things you're going to do in your business to produce results — profits, happy customers, whatever you want to achieve in your business unit. A business model is really no more complicated than a game plan or playbook. "Our goal is to win the game, so here's what we're going to do...."

Like game plans, business models change and evolve. Over time, your model will become outdated or you'll find better ways to do things, resulting in a need to modify the plan. The important thing is to *have* a plan.

Understanding the Call Center Business Model

A business model is a lot about understanding cause and effect — "do this, and this will happen." The better your understanding of cause and effect the better you can make your model. And the better your model, the better your results are bound to be. This pursuit of cause and effect is the basis for this book.

Business models vary in the amount of detail that they provide. Some are very general and provide only a low level of detail. Others can be incredibly sophisticated, including complex economic models that forecast business results. For a call center, I believe that a business model should include

- ✔ A statement of mission and vision for the call center

- ✔ Identification of the outputs that the call center is expected to produce in the next year (I refer to these outputs as *business objectives*)

- ✔ An economic model made up of the key variables that drive your call center performance (I call these variables *performance drivers*)

- ✔ An identification of the *business practices* that are used to affect performance drivers (these are frequently organized into the categories of people, process, and technology)

- ✔ The identification of a supporting culture

- ✔ A feedback mechanism

So why are business models so important? History is full of examples of a superior opponent falling to an underdog who had a plan. In 1974, the immensely powerful George Foreman lost to Muhammad Ali and his "rope a dope" strategy, handing over the world heavyweight crown.

In business, few companies would find investors if they didn't have a sound business plan. Oddly, we frequently find call centers in successful companies that don't have a well-thought-out game plan. As a result, their operations suffer from inconsistent service delivery, high costs, and less than optimal revenue generation. Typically, these operations have the necessary tools and talent to achieve their goals, all they need is a well-defined business model to greatly improve their results.

ANECDOTE

Lack of a model created lack of results for a retail company's call center

A while ago, my team and I had an interesting consulting assignment. The president of a successful retail company — I'll call it ABC Co. — approached us about his company's call center. For years the call centre had been producing terrible service with ever-increasing costs.

We conducted a fairly quick assessment. We interviewed management and staff, analyzed data, surveyed customers, and generally reviewed their entire process. What we discovered was a call center filled with smart people

and great tools. I should add that these were *frustrated* smart people, because they were only too aware that things weren't going the way they should.

Interestingly, the team had a very high level of sophistication around call center concepts and practices — they tracked all the measures, and then some; they had lots of training, and knew a lot about how call centers worked; and they had a lot of support from senior management — both financial and moral.

So why wasn't the call center achieving good results? The only thing lacking at ABC was a coordinated business model. And it was lacking in a big way. There was no focus among management and staff. Most management was crisis management. One important initiative was always quickly replaced with another. Priorities changed frequently, based on what senior management was focusing on. Few seemed to be on the same page. And the frontline staff recognized this — many sympathized with their managers, who were pulled in every direction. Results were inconsistent, and costs were high.

My team introduced a simple business model to ABC's call center. Within three months, results improved, costs were down, revenue was up, and customer satisfaction had improved. Equally important, the call center team was more energized and motivated.

I include a sample of a call center model blueprint in Figure 2-1.

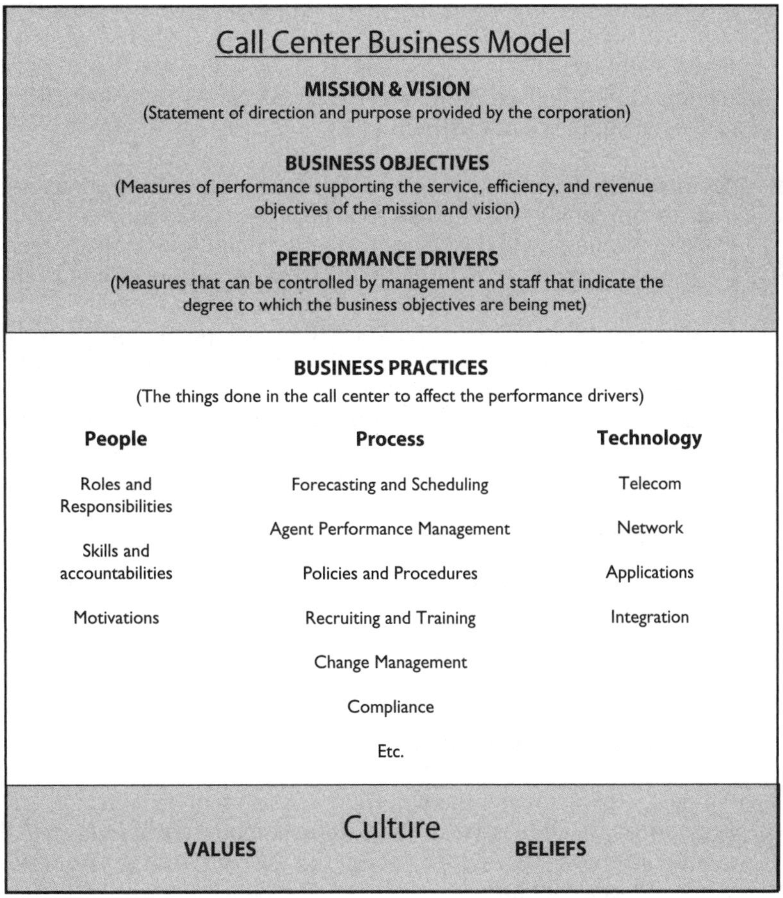

Call Center Business Model

MISSION & VISION
(Statement of direction and purpose provided by the corporation)

BUSINESS OBJECTIVES
(Measures of performance supporting the service, efficiency, and revenue objectives of the mission and vision)

PERFORMANCE DRIVERS
(Measures that can be controlled by management and staff that indicate the degree to which the business objectives are being met)

BUSINESS PRACTICES
(The things done in the call center to affect the performance drivers)

People	Process	Technology
Roles and Responsibilities	Forecasting and Scheduling	Telecom
	Agent Performance Management	Network
Skills and accountabilities	Policies and Procedures	Applications
Motivations	Recruiting and Training	Integration
	Change Management	
	Compliance	
	Etc.	

Culture
VALUES   **BELIEFS**

Figure 2-1: A call center business model.

Developing Your Mission and Vision

The mission statement is an articulation of your overall purpose — your *raison d'être.* It's your department's "elevator speech," which tells the world, in a sound bite, what you do and why you do it. Mission statements vary in length and what they include. I prefer brief, one- or two-sentence mission statements rather than more lengthy ones, because I believe that the mission statement is part of a bigger overall business model — the business model adds detail to the mission.

Mission statements share several key characteristics. They

✓ Are clear and to the point

✓ Identify your organization's uniqueness

✓ Are targeted to an audience of stakeholders that can include customers, senior executives, management, employees, or investors

Some people believe that the creation of a mission statement is a participative exercise involving senior management, call center management, employees, and even suppliers or customers.

My view is that senior management — those in the corporation to whom the call center reports — should deliver the mission statement, since the mission statement amounts to the call center's marching orders. Most organizations set goals and expectations at a senior level and filter those responsibilities down.

Creating a call center mission statement as a participative group exercise amounts to management by committee. If the resulting mission doesn't meet senior management's requirements, then the mission is doomed to irrelevance. It's powerless even before it gets printed on letterhead stationery and wallboards.

Mission statements may typically include the following:

✓ **A statement of purpose** — What are you here to do?

✓ **A statement of values** — What are your rules for behavior and corporate beliefs?

✓ **A statement of your competitive positioning** — What do you do really well?

✓ **A vision statement** — What does your future look like?

✓ **Stakeholder expectations** — What's in it for everyone involved?

Not all of these elements need to be included in the mission statement, but should be addressed in the business model. At a minimum, I like to see the mission statement address the statement of purpose, vision, and stakeholder expectations.

Dissecting a typical call center mission

An example of a call center mission might be:

"Our mission is to maximize value to XYZ, our customers, and our employees by providing the highest-value call center services available in our industry. We are a learning organization that constantly improves. This will result in our becoming a competitive advantage for XYZ, leading the industry in cost control, revenue generation, and customer satisfaction."

This mission statement has a few items of note:

- ✔ To "maximize value to XYZ, our customers, and our employees" speaks to stakeholders. Maximizing value suggests that you'll work to achieve what each one wants out of the relationship with the call center. From this, you'd expect that expectations are measured and understood. Value is a good word, because it allows us to define, through the business model, what is valuable to stakeholders.

- ✔ To provide "the highest-value call center services" does not suggest "cheapest," but instead suggests the most for the money, creating an opportunity to balance cost control, revenue generation, and customer satisfaction.

- ✔ "We are a learning organization..." is a vision statement identifying the long-term result of consistently following the mission and business model.

Overall, this mission statement is a nice way to launch into your business model and is a quick way to explain what your call center is trying to do.

The point is that the mission gives everyone an idea of what is expected of the operation. The mission describes the message that your senior management, both in the call center and in the corporation, should repeat constantly. If you say it enough, fairly soon you start to achieve your mission without a lot of specific micro-management, as people gravitate to your overriding purpose.

Mission statements should stand the test of time. It shouldn't be necessary to change them very often. When they do change, it's the result of a shift in corporate strategy — changing the call center's focus, for example, from a cost center to a profit center.

At ABC, our suspicion was omission of a mission

When we first began work with ABC, no one could articulate the call center's mission. How did we anticipate that this might be a problem? Well, in our initial interview with senior management we were told, "We don't have one."

It's no wonder that focus and direction was a problem. If you don't know where you're going, any road can take you there....

Determining Your Business Goals and Objectives

In the short term, the corporation will have goals and targets that it wants the call center to achieve. These are the more specific deliverables that the company needs — they generally relate to cost, revenue generation, and customer satisfaction, and they always support the call center's mission. These goals are frequently set once per year and coincide with the annual corporate budgeting process. I refer to them as *business objectives.*

Your mission is made more specific — and achievable — by defining the call center's specific goals and objectives. These goals are the inputs that go into your call center machine in order to get, as output, the results gained by achieving the mission.

Business objectives measure call center effectiveness and the organization's progress against the three broad areas of endeavor addressed by the mission: cost control, revenue generation, and customer satisfaction. Employee satisfaction is also included, as having satisfied employees is a requirement in meeting business goals.

Similar to the mission, these business objectives are provided by the corporation, or senior management, to the call center. However, in the case of specific objectives, ideally the call center has some input, if only to make sure that the objectives are realistic.

You shouldn't just pull the business goals out of the air, as they need to be well thought out and justified. When well defined, these goals are the gauges that tell you about the performance of your call center machine — like the gauges in an airplane. On the other hand, remember the old phrase "Garbage in, garbage out"? Well, it rings very true with operational goals — set bad goals, and you'll probably get equally bad results.

Unclear objectives were clearly a problem at ABC

In the case of ABC, when we asked company reps what their measurable goals were, they were able to produce lots and lots of measures — from cost per call to average speed of answer to call length — but they had a few problems.

First, no one could say which measurable objectives were most important. It seemed to depend on the day. Second, no one seemed clear on what the right targets were for many of the measurements. Overall, ABC lacked clear direction from senior management regarding which objectives to focus on.

Specific goals and objectives will vary by company, but examples of some that I like are illustrated in Table 2-1.

Table 2-1	Call Center Objectives and What They Tell Us	
Goal/Objective	*Measure*	*What It Tells Us*
Customer satisfaction	Post-call satisfaction scores	Are our agents providing good service?
	Call abandonment rate	
	Average speed of answer	Are we answering calls quickly enough? (Hanging up is one form of customer feedback!)
Cost control	Cost per contact	Are we handling contacts in an efficient manner?
	Cost per customer	
	Cost per case	Do customers have to call too often
	Cost per order	
Revenue generation	(Net) revenue per customer	Are we making money?
	Revenue generated per call	Are we maximizing sales and upselling opportunities?
	Total customers	Are we growing the business?
Employee satisfaction	Employee opinion survey	Do our employees feel valued and respected?
	Retention rates	
	Employee referrals	Do they like working here?

What makes a good objective?

Here are a couple of important characteristics of good business objectives:

⊯ They're measurable, and

⊯ They tell a complete story.

Ideally, a measurable objective will tell you as much about an area of the business as possible. For example, using total call center costs to measure cost control tells you something about what the call center costs to run, but it really doesn't tell you if it is expensive or not. A call center that costs $1 million per year but has only one customer is a lot more expensive than a call center that costs $50 million but has millions of customers. I believe the most valuable measures tell you about your success without having to refer to other numbers.

I like to measure objectives using the following parameters:

- ✔ **Revenue generated per customer:** the total revenue generated by the call center divided by the number of customers

- ✔ **Cost per customer:** the total cost of running the call center divided by total customers

- ✔ **Customer satisfaction:** how satisfied customers are with their call center experience

- ✔ **Employee job satisfaction:** how satisfied call center employees are with their jobs

There's really no end of measures that you can find or create. The key is that they tell you what you want to know about your operation.

Avoiding misleading measures

When establishing how to measure your business objectives, some common call center measures should be avoided. It's not that they aren't good measures; the problem is that they don't tell the complete story and, as such, can be misleading.

An example is the operating budget — how much we spend to run the call center. Most companies would like to minimize the total cost of running their center, but if the company is growing at 50 or 100 percent per year, then in all likelihood the call center is going to cost more. So looking at the call center budget can be misleading when considering cost control.

Another example is cost per call — a very common measurement and an easy one to understand. Cost per call is simply the cost of running a call center for a period of time divided by the calls answered for the same period.

Cost per call can be misleading because it doesn't consider the impact of poor quality and repeat calls. With an overemphasis on cost per call, the tendency might be to focus too strictly on keeping call times low — sometimes at the expense of good customer service. If agents don't do a good job of handling customer calls, making them too quickly and getting customers off the phone before their inquiry has been satisfactorily resolved, then customers are bound to call back. Although your cost per call will appear low, a large number of callbacks will increase your overall cost per customer.

What about service level?

Okay, you may be thinking, "What about that grand dame of call center measures, service level?" Service level — defined as the *percentage* of incoming calls answered in a specified amount of time — is probably the most talked about standard for inbound call centers. It actually refers to the measure of how fast we answer the phone, which has implications for customer satisfaction and total call center cost. Service level is a great measure, but, in my opinion, it's not a good high-level business objective measurement.

Satisfying customers, generating revenue, and managing costs are key business objectives. A well-thought-out service level considers all of these business goals and creates a balance that optimizes call centre and corporate performance.

Service level balances customer tolerances for waiting to speak with "the next available agent," the cost of providing service, and the revenue opportunity cost of customers who hang up, never to call again. So service level is a performance driver to the business objectives — a very good driver — but it is not an end unto itself.

Sticking to your mission

It's important that your goals be well defined and strong. Ask yourself, "If I achieve these goals or make constant improvements toward reaching these goals, will I be achieving my mission? Will my stakeholders in the corporation be happy?" If the answer is yes, then you are on the right track.

Flowing through the accountability funnel

Well-defined goals are important, not only to keep the stakeholders happy, but also because they involve the whole organization. Establishing, applying, and communicating appropriate goals to every manager, supervisor, department, and employee will increase accountability at every level and create a very focused organization — as illustrated in Figure 2-2. Your goals must keep everyone accountable to, and focused on, the right things. If you get it right, everyone is on track. Get it wrong, however, and everyone is headed in the wrong direction.

Figure 2-2:
The
accountabil-
ity funnel.

Measuring Progress with Performance Drivers

The business objectives are derived from your mission and are the goals and targets that you're trying to produce. Using them to manage your call center toward success requires a better understanding of how a business objective is managed and controlled. This comes through performance drivers.

Performance drivers are processes and behaviors — expressed as measures — that influence achieving your business objectives. For example, average call length (the amount of time required to fully answer a customer inquiry) is a driver of call center costs and has a direct impact on the business objective of cost per customer. So, average call length is a *driver* of cost.

Statisticians might think of the business objectives as dependent variables (y) and the performance drivers as independent variables (x), leading to the equation "y is a function of x," or "cost per customer is a function of call length."

Performance drivers are the building blocks of the operation, and with them you can mathematically model the business objectives, budgets, profit and loss objectives, and other aspects of operations — creating the economic model of your call center. You could say they're the levers that you push and pull to steer the call center ship toward its objectives.

Drop by a call center and you're likely to hear discussions about some of these performance drivers:

✔ **Service level:** refers to how fast you answer the phone, e-mail messages, and so on. It can be expressed in a variety of ways and is most commonly measured by the percentage of incoming calls answered in a specified amount of time. For example, if the call center answers 78 percent of all calls taken within 30 seconds of the calls entering the queue, the service level achieved is 78/30. Service level affects cost, revenue, and customer satisfaction.

- ✔ **Average call length:** refers to how long it takes, on average, to process one customer interaction.

- ✔ **Agent availability:** tells you how many of your agents are actually available to take a call — that is, they're not already busy on a call.

- ✔ **Agent occupancy:** availability's evil twin — refers to the percentage of time that agents are busy processing customer calls and not waiting for the next call.

- ✔ **Schedule adherence:** measures the percentage of time your agents are actually on the phones when they're supposed to be.

- ✔ **Conversion rates:** the percentage of contacts that are converted to sales, or customer saves.

- ✔ **Retention rates:** how many contacts that your company was at risk of losing as customers were saved by agents.

- ✔ **Customer satisfaction:** how satisfied your customers are with the level of service your call center's providing, often measured by way of a customer survey.

- ✔ **First-call resolution:** the percentage of callers who do not have to call back within a certain time frame (usually a day) to have their issue resolved.

I review other exciting stuff that can be measured in Chapter 5.

By managing the performance drivers, you can affect the outputs of your business objectives. Much of the information in this book is about how to effectively manipulate the drivers to get a desired result like the following:

- ✔ Wanna make customers happy and improve customer satisfaction scores? Answer the phone quickly, be nice to callers, and give them prompt and complete service to their needs. I talk about how to do this in Chapters 14 through 16.

- ✔ Wanna reduce the cost of handling calls? Reduce average call length, reduce the cost of your service, and make sure your agents are kept busier while they are on the phones. See Chapter 5 for more on how this can work.

Meanwhile, back at ABC Co....

In my ABC example, ABC tracked all of the necessary measurable stuff. The challenge was that management didn't see a clear relationship between the performance drivers and business objectives. As a result, they weren't working in a coordinated and consistent fashion to affect results through manipulation of the drivers. Instead, they were working at affecting some performance drivers one day and others the next. Because of this, results were mixed.

Categorizing the drivers

Generally, performance drivers can be grouped into four areas. There are drivers that affect

- ✔ cost control,
- ✔ customer satisfaction,
- ✔ revenue generation, and
- ✔ employee satisfaction.

Many call centers — including my own — add the fourth area, drivers that affect employee satisfaction, because we believe that employee morale and satisfaction contributes to all other areas of performance.

It's hard to say which driver is most important; it really depends on your organization's goals and the priorities you've established for the call center.

Cost-control drivers

Your call center is likely to come under the microscope for cost control often, even though call centers are on average a very efficient way to communicate with massive volumes of customers. Still, call center expenditures are frequently one of the larger line items for corporations, so it's no wonder their costs are scrutinized.

Items that affect the cost control of your call center include

- ✔ call length
- ✔ agent occupancy
- ✔ average cost of putting an agent on the phones (wages, benefits, management, etc.)
- ✔ repeat calls from customers who don't get an accurate or complete answer on the first call
- ✔ non-productive agent time (time away from the phone)

It's wise for your call center to scrutinize these items in great detail. Looking at the drivers of cost control is just a start.

Call centers with very good control over their outputs dig deep into these aspects of operations to better understand why they achieve the levels they do and how to affect them in the future. For example, call length can be further broken down into time spent talking with the customer and post-call work (time spent processing customer requests after the customer is gone).

Both can be still better understood when looking at what call lengths result from different types of calls — an information call versus a sales call, for example. Having a full-time analyst to research cost-control drivers would certainly be a worthwhile exercise — especially in a larger call centre.

Revenue drivers

It don't mean a thing if you ain't got cha-ching! Improvement in your call center's revenue generation can have a greater impact on margins than improvements in cost-control measures. In larger call centers, small improvements in *retention rate* (keeping customers who were calling to cancel service) represent hundreds of thousands or even millions of dollars in saved revenue. Similarly, small improvements in selling and upselling can represent many hundreds of thousands of dollars or more.

In addition to your retention rate, key revenue metrics you should consider include

- conversion rate (the number of sales made per contacts handled)
- revenue generated per sale
- cancellations per call (a variation on retention rate)
- revenue lost per cancellation (a measure of the degree to which individual agents are mitigating revenue loss)

Of course, it's only when you focus on cost control and revenue with equal dedication and discipline that you'll realize real improvements in profit.

Customer-satisfaction drivers

Some call centers are getting good — really good — at understanding what makes customers happy. Unfortunately, not all are good at actually doing what it takes to make customers happy.

For the most part, your customers want the same thing you do — an efficient and professional resolution to their call. It is primarily for this reason that the metrics you should use to measure and drive service include the following:

- How fast you answer the phone — including service level and average speed of answer.
- Call review assessments — are your agents being professional, courteous, able, and nice?

I talk more about call-handling skills in Chapter 14.

My advice is to use customer opinion scores at the end of inbound phone calls to tell you how the call center and agents are doing at serving customers. I talk more about this in Chapter 5.

Employee-satisfaction drivers

As I discuss in Chapter 5, your employees will tell you in your monthly employee opinion survey what the drivers to their satisfaction are. My advice is to start with general questions about employee job satisfaction, then ask open-ended questions about the greatest satisfiers and dissatisfiers. In subsequent surveys, you'll want to include questions on management's performance against the satisfiers and dissatisfiers identified in the previous survey. Some things that will definitely come up as key drivers to satisfaction include:

- ✔ **Supervisor support:** Am I getting the help that I need?
- ✔ **Feedback:** Do I know where I stand?
- ✔ **Training:** Did I get the training that I need to do the job well?

Why is employee opinion important?

I'm glad you asked. Of course, we all want happy employees. It's nice to live and work in a place where people get along and are happy. Mom always said be nice to the people you meet — she meant the people you work with, too.

Still, there are lots of good business reasons for treating people well. First, you're going to spend a lot of time and money attracting and training good people. It makes things difficult when those people leave your company to go work for nicer people. Even if they don't quit, unhappy people don't see the need to work hard to meet company goals. The employee who "quits" but stays on your payroll is very expensive.

Then there are the studies that suggest happy employees create happy customers — what's that worth?

It reminds me of the time my team and I consulted for two competitors in the same industry. Neither knew we were working with the other, and neither benefited from the work we were

doing with the other. Still, we took away some valuable learning. These companies had virtually the same products, priced approximately the same, with customers in the same geographic location. Customers had to communicate regularly with each company through the call center. In the first company, employees were very happy and rated their job satisfaction very high. Employee turnover was modest. In the second company, employees were not so happy, morale was rather dark, and employee turnover was high. As far as we could tell, this was the most significant difference between the two companies. However, when we looked at performance data, we were shocked. The second company had nearly double the rate of customer cancellations and a significantly lower customer opinion score. Not surprising, the average revenue per customer was much lower in the second company.

Now this is far from a scientific study, but it goes to show you ... just be nice. It's good for business.

The importance of balance

You'll need a sort of balance to maximize each component of performance and provide the best solution for achieving your goals based on your organization's priorities and what's more important to the call center. When you're attempting to strike this balance, keep in mind that overemphasis on one area can hurt performance in others. For example, too much emphasis on cost control can hurt service and revenue.

Don't go overboard on cost control

You've taken your quest for cost control too far if you

- ✔ Hire people unsuited for the job (perhaps because they'll work for less),
- ✔ Skimp on training and feedback, or
- ✔ Don't spend adequately on support services.

Offshore outsourcing is a hot topic. The benefit of taking a call center offshore to a far-off country such as India or the Philippines is greatly reduced labor costs. A company putting its call center in these locations can hire staff for a fraction of what the costs would be in its home country. General Electric helped to popularize this trend, and — as one would expect from GE — the move offshore was done in a well orchestrated and well planned fashion. Eager to capture similar benefits, many companies have moved their call center operations offshore without the same level of planning. In some highly public cases, the results have been less than ideal. Some of these companies have suffered more in terms of lost customers, lost revenue opportunities, and additional costs from repeat calls than they gained in reduced costs. In these cases, an overzealous desire to *cut* costs resulted in increased overall cost to the organization.

Avoid a surplus of service

Customer service is crucial, but making the customer like you shouldn't be your only goal. It's important to remember that customers want call center agents to perform a service, not be their best pals. Granted, it's true: people exist who want to spend extraordinary amounts of time on the phone with their favorite call center. But you have to admit — they're probably not quite right.

Ensuring that ten agents are always available, waiting for the next call, to answer every customer call inside the first ring might be overly expensive. Your average customer is probably okay with waiting an average of three rings before their call is answered.

Overemphasis on service can also turn into a belief that trying to sell the customer something is bad, or that keeping transactions quick and efficient will cause the customer to dislike you. This simply is not the case. As I've said before (and will likely say again), most customers want the same thing you do — an efficient and professional resolution to their call.

Killing 'em with kindness

Some time ago I was touring a call center and listening to agents on the phones. One fellow tried so hard to make the customer like him, he virtually held the customer hostage. Despite the customer's best efforts, he couldn't get off the phone with this agent. You could hear the pain in the customer's voice as he feigned interest — not wanting to be rude to this nice fellow — while the agent regaled him with information about everything from the weather in northern Alberta to the dietary habits of his Aunt Martha's cat. Interestingly, but not surprisingly, this agent had very high call times, only moderate customer satisfaction scores, and dismal sales results.

Resist revenue-generation mania

It can really turn off a long-term customer who calls with a service concern if an agent fails to resolve the issue but makes great attempts to close in for more sales.

Although an overall focus on revenue generation is vital, overemphasizing short-term revenue gain will probably lead to long-term service pain, as your call center loses the lifetime value of a loyal customer.

Don't focus on entertaining employees

When it comes to making employees happy, overemphasis happens when your management team attempts to turn the call center into a love-in. In an effort to ensure high employee morale, some companies live with the motto, "Try not to upset anyone." If you adopt that motto you'll probably end up hurting your call center's performance.

People need feedback, and sometimes feedback is a little negative. My experience has been that over time a fair, honest, and consistent approach wins as much or more in the morale wars as does a soft hand — and it has the added benefit of keeping the organization on track with its objectives.

As a company, you have to accept the fact that not everyone is going to be happy all the time. It shouldn't be a surprise that often the unhappiest employees are those who aren't doing a good job.

For a good operation you should attempt to strike a perfect balance between cost control, revenue generation, customer satisfaction, and employee satisfaction.

Table 2-2 provides a summary of the basic call center business goals and the corresponding key performance drivers that affect them.

Table 2-2	Call center business objectives and the performance drivers that affect them	
Objectives	**Measured By (Performance Drivers)**	**Driven By**
Cost control	Cost per customer	Call length
		Cost per hour of providing the service
		How busy the agents are while on the phone
		Percentage of time agents spend manning the phones
		Percentage of calls resolved on first attempt
Revenue generation	Revenue per customer	Percentage of calls resulting in a sale
		Dollar value of sales made
Customer satisfaction	Post-call customer	Accessibility satisfaction survey
		Agent professionalism, courtesy, ability
		Process — ability to service the customer
Employee satisfaction	Employee opinion score Retention rates	Management behavior and support — especially direct supervisor
		Adequate training
		Consistent feedback
		Other drivers identified by your employees

Understanding How It All Works: Call Center Business Practices

So, now you've developed (or been provided with) your mission — the reason why the call center exists in the corporation — and you've established what your business objectives are — what the corporation needs from the call center right now — and you've gained an understanding of the underlying variables or performance drivers of your economic model that directly affect your business objectives.

At this point, you should begin to see an alignment created in the business model. Sort of a "the leg bone is connected to the knee bone" arrangement: the mission is connected to business objectives. Business objectives are connected to performance drivers....

Finally, the performance drivers are connected to business practices.

Business practices are the procedures and policies — the specific things done by people in the call center every day — that affect the cost control, revenue, and customer service drivers of the operation and, in turn, affect your call center's business objectives and goals and help you achieve the desired results.

Any operation has many key practices, all implemented for the purpose of ensuring call center success (I discuss what makes a successful call center in Chapter 1). All of these practices and procedures — many of which I discuss in detail in this book — can be categorized under the headings of people, process, and technology.

To meet your goals, consider developing business practices as a continuous cycle:

1. **People**: Add better people and use the best performance-management methods to continue to make those people improve so they produce better results.

2. **Process:** Define, refine, and continuously better the process so that your business drivers are improved.

3. **Technology:** Automate good, well-defined processes through the use of appropriate technology, and driver performance will change for the better.

Indeed, much of your time as a manager will be spent doing and organizing things to make improvements in business practices, which will result in improvements in the outputs of the call centre — that's where the information in this book comes in. (I've always wanted to say "indeed.")

Unclear goals lead to confused practices at ABC

ABC followed many of the best practices in the call center industry. However, the company didn't follow these practices with a specific goal in mind: to affect drivers that would make improvements toward its business objectives. As a result, they weren't able to capture and build on improvements.

First people...

It all starts with folk: sometimes lots and lots of folk. You see, folk who want stuff often need to talk to folk who sell (or know about, or provide support for) stuff. If you have enough folk asking, seeking, or buying — like when Madonna concert tickets go on sale — you need *a lot* of folk taking their orders. Sure, tickets can be ordered and information can be sought through the Internet, but a great number of people still want to talk to real live people about buying their stuff.

Generally, those people doing the inquiring, ordering, or looking for help want to be dealt with in a courteous, professional, polite, and friendly manner. Making that happen is almost solely dependent on having great people.

You need to have the appropriate roles, responsibilities, skills, and account-abilities to meet your call center goals. Clearly defined job descriptions for all roles should be found throughout your call center's organizational chart. You'll also want the best folk you can find for the job. In Chapter 3, I discuss organizational design, the key roles, and the importance of culture in the call center; in Chapter 10, I talk more about hiring the right people.

No matter how impeccable your processes or tantalizing your technology, without the right people on your call center bus, you'll be headed down the road to mediocrity.

And process ...

"Someone has got to figure out how this is going to work!" Having the right processes in place to make stuff happen the way it's supposed to happen is important in any business, but it's absolutely imperative if you want to run an effective call center.

Process refers to how the work gets done — the organization of tasks for inputs and outputs. Call centers are very procedure-driven; in fact, some of the biggest success stories in call center management come from improvements in processes. A better way to schedule staff, a quicker way to service specific customer call types, or a better procedure for training new staff are all process changes that can have tremendous impacts on call center results.

That's why many call centers seek out quality-control programs such as ISO certification, and why call center–specific standards such as COPC (Customer Operations Performance Center Inc.) certification have been developed. Six Sigma, a process-oriented management discipline, is also gaining acceptance in the call center industry. I talk more about quality control programs in Chapter 13.

For virtually every business practice in the operation, you need to ensure your team has developed (and follows) a systematic methodology to make order from the mayhem that can at times be the call center.

Process is an area of call center business practice where you will always find room for improvement, and fortunately call centers generally respond well to an environment of continuous improvement, as I discuss in Chapter 12. In fact, due to the dynamic character of the call center industry, including a process for managing changes — sometimes called, appropriately enough, a *change management process* — in your defined business practices is a good idea.

I've got a hunch that call centers were actually born out of the need for better processes. Imagine, way back in the day, a ticket agency with just one agent answering a single phone, selling tickets for a Frank Sinatra concert. Eventually, someone likely realized that this was not the most efficient way to do business, and hollered "We need a better process!" A bunch of people were rounded up to answer a lot of phones and take a heap of orders, and voilà: the first call center. And we've been improving processes ever since. In Chapter 12 I discuss some process management concepts and methods.

Realizing the importance of defining things

The best-made processes are laid to waste, however, if people aren't speaking the same language. That's why definitions are critical — especially in call centers, where new buzzwords are created constantly. Agreeing to definitions can save much frustration. Something as simple as the definition of *call length* — the total amount of time it takes to complete a customer transaction from start to finish, including time spent talking to the customer and any post-call work time needed to fill out information in a database, for example — can make the difference between an employee meeting performance expectations and failing miserably.

To help you avoid that kind of costly miscommunication, I provide definitions and concepts throughout the book. Also, for your quick reference, I've included a handy-dandy glossary as an appendix at the back of the book. Read it now and amaze your friends with your astonishing grasp of call center terminology, or consult it later when you need a quick refresher.

Say what ya mean, kid! It sounds simple, but it's a basic truth — you've got to take great pains to define things clearly and communicate your definitions to your team. This is especially true with measures. Time and again I've visited operations, some of them my own, that are experiencing performance difficulties only to find that the lack of clear and universally understood definitions is creating a barrier to success.

> *In the opinion of many people in industry, there is nothing more important for the transaction of business than the use of operational definitions. It could also be said that nothing is more neglected.*
>
> — W. Edwards Deming

ANECDOTE

Make sure everybody's working from the same dictionary!

One of my supervisors approached me with a challenge she was having coaching one of her team members (I discuss the various roles on the call center team in Chapter 3). It seemed no matter how hard she tried to teach him how, this agent simply couldn't get his average call time down to the campaign's minimum requirement — and that meant he wouldn't receive a quarterly raise.

I agreed to help and took a look at the agent's stats. I found that, in actual fact, his average talk time (ATT) — the average amount of time spent on the phone directly talking to the customer — was lower than many others on the same campaign, but he took almost twice as long as most to complete his after-call work. In other words, his average after-call work time (AWT) — the average amount of time spent doing any post-call wrap-up work associated with the just-completed call — was twice as high.

When I spoke to the agent, I came to realize that he was rushing through his calls and saving all the database and other computer work until after the customer had hung up, because, according to him, his supervisor kept "hitting him over the head" with the "lower your call time!" stick (figuratively speaking, of course ... I hope!). He thought, mistakenly, that call time was the same thing as talk time.

The fact is, in most call centers the definition of average call time is the average time it takes to complete an entire customer contact transaction from start to finish — including talk time and after-call work. If the supervisor had simply picked up on the fact that the agent didn't fully understand this definition, a few months of frustration — for both of them — could have been avoided.

Try this: Ask your call center manager and a number of your call center agents to define after-call work. The manager might tell you that after-call work time (AWT) is a private state when agents can complete work related to the call they've just completed. The agents may give you a similar definition, but the agents and manager might differ on when after-call work should be used. Sometimes, even though it may seem like people are on the same page, when you get into the specifics they're miles apart.

TIP

Talk to your team to find out if your definitions are clear and specific enough to ensure that everyone is speaking the same language.

Enforcing an accurate definition for something as simple as AWT can be very important. Agents who are using AWT differently will create inconsistencies in the call length data, and that'll cause inaccuracies in performance measurements, coaching assessments, and staff scheduling. Ultimately, the call center will be out of alignment with its mission and goals, all because of one misunderstood term. (I talk more about goals in this chapter, and about missions in Chapter 3.)

... Then technology

In the simplest of terms, technology refers to the machines that help make the call center processes go faster, and make it easier for the people doing the work. What I'm talking about here is automation: computers, software, and networks that supercharge processes — or enable different processes — and speed everything up.

Imagine if, when you were ordering your Madonna tickets, all the agents taking all those calls recorded the pertinent customer information with pencil and paper only. What do you suppose would be your chances of ever seeing the concert? It could work, I suppose, but you'd need a whole lot of people and a whole lot of paper — and a whole lot more people to process the piles of paper.

Enter someone like Bill Gates and his team of process engineers. The addition of technology to a well-developed process can save you a great deal of time, errors, and back-end work.

If your process is poor, automating it with technology will simply add cost — in some cases a lot of cost — without driving performance toward your goals. Worse, poorly defined and applied technology can trap you in solutions that don't support the processes you need to maximize performance, taking you off track. Additionally, if you spend a lot of money on a piece of technology it's hard to justify not using it, so you may end up entrenching a flawed process.

The good news is that there is a lot of great technology that enhances call center processes. Just make sure that your process is sound, and you've done due diligence before investing in it. I discuss investing in new technology in Chapter 9.

Avoiding technology for technology's sake: Beware the magic in the box!

Technology can be expensive. You shouldn't implement a particular piece of technology unless you have a pretty solid idea of exactly what it's going to do for you, and what the return on investment is likely to be.

In my consulting, I still see organizations that feel inclined to invest in the latest and greatest technological tools on the market because they're *cool*. Don't fall into that trap. I've witnessed many examples of companies adding technology that doesn't serve any real purpose, and, lo and behold, those companies don't get the results they're looking for.

People, process, *then* technology

One call center implemented technology to collect sales data and deliver statistics to the agent's desktop within minutes of a sale being completed. The company used these sales statistics in a very aggressive incentive campaign it had recently rolled out. The idea was that agents could see their bank account grow in actual dollars before their very eyes with every sale they made, and this would drive them to make more sales.

It was great idea. Unfortunately, there was a problem. The process for collecting the sales data was flawed, and some sales were being double- or even triple-counted. The greater problem, of course, was that the company had implemented the technology to deliver the stats *before* recognizing the process issue. They ended up with a people problem, because they had to explain to agents that the large payouts expected (some very large) would not be delivered because of a management error. Ouch!

Technology can be dangerous, too. That's why I say "*Then* technology." While technology can lead to fantastic improvements in efficiency and speed, technology without a well-thought-out plan can be disastrous. It is my belief that even if you have good people, when you take a bad process and automate it you'll just arrive where you don't want to be, faster. It's like putting a Ferrari engine in an old lemon: chances are good it's still going to fall to pieces, it's just going to fall to pieces sooner!

Reporting: Providing Feedback

Call centers are data factories. Almost every tool that a call center agent uses collects, stores, and reports on something. When pulled together and analyzed, call centers are an Orwellian dream. Used properly, this information provides call center managers with tremendous intelligence to analyze performance, capture best practices that result in improvements in results, and discard practices that do not support the department's objectives.

Increasingly, call centers are hiring analysts with advanced degrees in statistics and engineering because their findings are so valuable in what they offer via improvements through the business model.

Reporting completes the call center business model. Information reports give managers the feedback they need about whether their business practices and performance drivers are aligned with the call center's mission and business objectives. In Chapter 5 I discuss analysis, and in Chapter 8 I outline many of the types of reports used in a call center.

Summarizing the business model

The call center business model I've laid out in this chapter attempts to create alignment among the call center's mission, objectives (goals), performance drivers, and business practices.

My experience is that good performance usually results when call centers are truly aligned with their mission and objectives. Add to this a strong supportive culture, and results can be great.

The call center's ability to collect and analyze data provides a great feedback loop to determine if the call center is aligned with its goals.

Chapter 3

Developing the Cast of Characters

• •

In This Chapter

▶ Developing the right organizational structure

▶ Creating and filling roles

▶ Finding the best people to fill the roles

▶ Creating a supportive culture

• •

*I*n this chapter, I discuss the people needed to run an effective call center — who they are, what their roles are, and how they're organized. Even with the development of self-help technology, call centers are still very much about people helping other people.

Organizational design — how the organization is set up in terms of roles and responsibilities and who reports to whom — is an important part of the call center business model. A coordinated effort is needed among numerous staff members for a call center to achieve its business objectives (which I discuss in Chapter 2). It doesn't take too many people working at cross-purposes to place a drag on results.

A key part of organizational design is having the right roles to manage the call center to its objectives. With the right mix of people and roles, the call center can operate in a highly coordinated fashion. When roles are missing, or a number of unnecessary roles creep into the organization, the call center can become overstretched or bureaucratic — either of which will slow down the march toward achieving your goals.

And because you're dealing with people, it's necessary to consider the culture of your call center workplace. A supportive culture will "grease the skids," even when the organization design is less than optimal. An unsupportive culture will sabotage even the best organization, making it difficult for the call center to improve.

Put together a good design and a great culture, and an organization can produce stellar results even when faced with challenges.

Designing an Organizational Chart

Organizational design is part of your business model. It's one of the things that the business does to create alignment with the mission. (See Chapter 2 for more information on developing a mission.) Done well, the design process gives you an organization that is flexible and scaleable — able to easily grow with the same design. With a good organization design, people can work together toward the same goals and objectives even though many will have their unique priorities.

When designed poorly, as it gets larger the organization becomes more bureaucratic, inflexible, and bloated.

The most senior person in the call center defines the structure of the organization. This person will have some responsibilities of his or her own in addition to developing the organization structure.

Some considerations in designing your call center organization include the following:

✔ **Begin with a clear mission and vision for the future.** It shouldn't be necessary to constantly change the organizational design. As the call center grows in size, the number of people supporting a particular function — say, scheduling — might increase, but it shouldn't be necessary to constantly change the structure.

✔ **Identify the broad critical tasks that need to get done to support the mission.**

✔ **Group functions around similar and related processes.** For example, accounting and payroll are similar and related processes that can report to the finance department.

✔ **Consider how the functions will work together to meet call center goals.** Introducing conflict can be a good way to build control (for example, the scheduler wants everyone on the phones; the supervisor wants everyone in a meeting), but it is important to keep in mind that in the end all the roles need to work together toward their common mission and business objectives.

Visit ten call centers and you're likely to find ten different organizational designs. The key to success in any call center is ensuring that all the necessary jobs are done — by someone.

Things that need to get done

A number of critical tasks need to be completed for the call center to function well. It's important to consider these tasks when designing the organization structure and when assigning roles and responsibilities (as I discuss in this chapter).

This is not a complete list of *everything* that needs to get done, but rather of critical items that should be handled in every call center. You will identify additional tasks that are important in yours.

- ✔ Determine the call center's mission. As I discuss in Chapter 2, the mission is more or less accepted by the call center, communicated, and designed into the department's business model.

- ✔ Work with senior management to determine the call center's business objectives.

- ✔ Identify the key variables — performance drivers (see Chapter 2) — that drive the call center's economic model and that directly affect the business objectives.

- ✔ Assign the roles and responsibilities required to achieve the goals. Create reporting relationships.

- ✔ Recruit, train, and support the management team.

- ✔ Create and maintain a culture that supports the mission.

- ✔ Create a process for documenting policies and procedures. Also create a process for updating policies and procedures as improvements are made.

- ✔ Create an audit process to determine if policies and procedures are being followed. Also develop a system of corrective action when policies and procedures are not followed or when existing policies and procedures are found not to optimize results.

- ✔ Recruit agents and support staff.

- ✔ Train agents and support staff.

- ✔ Manage and support agent performance.

- ✔ Assess and provide feedback on the quality of agent performance.

- ✔ Schedule staff and resources to meet demand.

- ✔ Analyze and report on performance and process. Identify opportunities for improvement.

- ✔ Implement and manage a telecommunications infrastructure.

- ✔ Implement and manage a computer network.

- ✔ Identify, build (or purchase), and support applications needed to support the call center.

- ✔ Ensure that the call center complies with all legal requirements.

- ✔ Provide frontline support to customers.

- ✔ Provide direction and support for the management team.

This list identifies the key tasks that need to be accomplished to manage a call center successfully to its mission and business objectives. Of course, you'll find lots of other tasks to consider, such as payroll and budgeting, facilities management, and others.

Introducing the Call Center Team: Roles and Responsibilities

The roles and responsibilities I describe here are intended only to identify the core call center work that needs to be done. Naturally, you may not organize your center in exactly this fashion. The size of the operation will have a significant impact on the structure of your organization. Figure 3-1 illustrates a typical functional organizational chart.

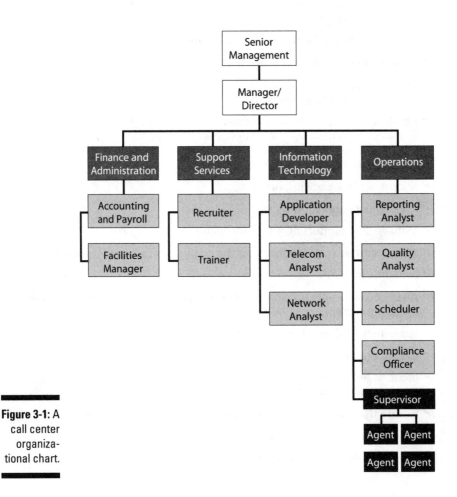

Figure 3-1: A call center organizational chart.

The other customer

It all starts with the "other customer." No, not the person on the phone wanting to know why *Lassie* was taken off the air — I'm talking about the person who signs the checks. In a corporate call center this is senior management — the boss who doesn't work in the call center, but tells you what you've got to do: generate more revenue, cut costs, do both, or make customers happier. If you run an outsourcing call center, then this is the client company. Either way, the other customer gives you your marching orders, and in your organizational structure they're at the top.

And this person has responsibilities to the call center, such as telling you what is expected from you. This includes giving the call center the general mission — "We are here to serve the customer in support of the product. Customers will never leave us for lack of support!" (I talk more about mission in Chapter 2.)

It also includes telling you exactly what your annual business objectives are — "The company needs the call center to acquire one million new customers next year, with an average revenue per customer of $100 and a cost per customer of $5. Oh, and customers must rate their satisfaction with the call center experience as excellent 95 percent of the time, with no more than one complaint per thousand customers." Hopefully, the objectives have been created with some input from the call center and are based on what is realistically achievable.

My view is that senior management should keep its direction to high-level business objectives — those that can be easily translated into corporate strategy and performance, such as customer satisfaction, customer growth, revenue per customer, cost per customer, and other measures that speak to customer satisfaction and corporate profitability.

"What about service-level objectives," you ask? Well yes, many — maybe even most — senior managers will dictate how fast the phone should be answered. Sometimes this is due to regulatory demands; other times, these objectives are based on very little critical analysis of cost and benefit.

Ideally, I like to see recommendations coming from the call center on the most appropriate speed of service. Any such recommendation would be based on the call center's unique understanding of customer tolerances and costs associated with various levels of service.

If senior management really wants to energize the call center it will set *base goals* — "We know we can achieve these, we just can't fall asleep at the wheel" — and *stretch goals* — "Okay, these will take some imagination and hard work, but we should be able to do it." Should the call center achieve the stretch goals, rewards should be given that reflect the value that hitting those goals represents to the organization. (No, a coffee mug won't do it.) If the call center fails to hit even the base goals, then it's "We need to talk."

Senior management works with the person who has the overall responsibility for the call center's goals, processes, and outputs — they work together to establish these parameters. Hopefully, it's a give-and-take relationship that results in realistic goals that support the organization.

And who is this wonderful person who has overall responsibility for the call center? This supporter of call center rights and freedoms? This champion of the little agent? It is none other than the wondrous, the celebrated, the awe-inspiring *call center manager!*

The call center manager

Okay, you might not call this person the call center manager. He or she might be a director, vice-president, AVP (assistant vice president), SVP (senior vice president), SDVP (super duper vice president), or "Janet over in the call center." It really doesn't matter what name the organization gives the job: when we say call center manager, we're talking about the person with overall responsibility for the call center's outputs.

In case you've never done it, it's a great job. Sure, there's the stress, the pace (the customer is on the phone RIGHT NOW!), and the uncertainty, but at the same time there's the people, the excitement, and the sense of control you have when you are responsible for an entire business process.

So, the call center manager (CCM) takes direction and goals from senior management, communicates them in the form of overall goals and the department mission, and then translates them into internal call center goals and measures. They do this by identifying the performance drivers that affect the business objectives — their department goals. For example, cost per customer is driven by call length, first-call resolution, cost per hour of agent time on the phones, and agent occupancy. (See Chapter 5 for more on these measures.)

The CCM tracks performance on these measures and ensures that each one is constantly improving to achieve the business goals. The CCM also analyzes and reports on performance, being sure to explain what happened (good and bad), why it happened, and how it might be different (especially if results are bad), and provides a forecast for future performance. (I cover this topic in greater detail in Chapter 5.)

Much of the CCM's time is spent ensuring that performance and all roles, accountabilities, and processes in the department are on track. Some of those responsibilities include

- ✔ Identifying, communicating, and managing to the call center's mission as directed by senior management
- ✔ Working with senior management to develop realistic annual business objectives

✔ Designing the organization structure of the call center and identifying roles and responsibilities

✔ Reviewing and approving all policies and procedures to ensure that each supports the department's mission and business objectives

✔ Recruiting, training, supporting, and developing the remaining management team in the call center, including people to handle all other support functions: recruiting, training, supervisors, quality control, scheduling, reporting and analysis, and technology

Finding a call center manager

A call center manager is a solid business generalist. He or she will have a well-rounded set of communication, interpersonal, leadership, and analytical skills. Business training, including accounting and organizational behavior, is also useful, and an understanding of call center technology will help.

You might find your manager in your call center working as a supervisor, as a trainer, or in another position. You might find him or her somewhere else in the organization running another business process.

You might even recruit externally; however, it is a mistake to think that you must hire people with call center experience. Call center skills, tools, and terms can be learned fairly easily. The combination of leadership and core business skills like statistics, finance, accounting, organizational behavior, and budgeting is a more difficult package to find.

The agent performance team

The recruiter

Okay, here it is — the ancient secret of call centers handed down by generation to generation of Bergevins. *You need people.* If they're good people, things work better. Getting enough people and making sure that they're good is the recruiter's job.

In many smaller call centers, the job of recruiting is absorbed into the supervisor's job. That's not such a good idea if your call center does a lot of ongoing recruiting, because your supervisor will spend all their time recruiting and your existing staff will lack the attention they need. Also, a dedicated, professional recruiter can improve the quality of recruits — maximizing the success of your recruits and operations. If you're hiring lots of people who just end up quitting in six months, then you're wasting time. If your call center does more or less ongoing recruitment, then you're best to have a dedicated, professional recruiter.

Being a good recruiter is tough. A good recruiter is part fortune teller, part researcher/psychologist/tea-leaf reader, part lawyer, and part super sleuth.

In some ways the recruiter needs to be a fortune-teller, working with the scheduling department to predict when new staff are going to be needed. He or she might have to go to the call center manager to get final signoff, but should ultimately know when and how many more staff are needed. He or she will then commence the process of finding people interested in working for the company. In this phase, the recruiter becomes an advertising and marketing specialist. The job includes communicating to potential employees the availability and desirability of jobs in the recruiter's call center.

Once the recruiter brings in a sufficient pool of candidates, he or she starts the process of comparing the candidates against the recruiter's criteria for success. (Nasty trick, eh? Entice people to interview with your company using all the power of advertising and promotion, then tell them that they still have to qualify!)

Now the recruiter becomes researcher/psychologist/tea-leaf reader — trying to determine who will be successful and who won't. Using the company's criteria for selection, the recruiter will determine what candidates, if any, are most likely to fit in and be successful in the job and within the company. This is the tough part, and includes two areas of investigation: first, does the candidate have the skills or aptitude to be successful in the job; and second, will the candidate value the job for a period that's sufficient to motivate them to better performance. The recruiter uses interviews, reference checks, and employment tests to predict a potential candidate's success.

When the recruiter finds people he or she believes will be successful in the job, he or she then makes offers to those candidates. This is where the recruiter becomes part lawyer — gotta make sure that the offer of employment is legal, promising the right things but not promising anything it shouldn't. It's got to be clear. Once candidates accept, sign the offer letter, and are scheduled for training time, the recruiter can become a couch potato — for a few hours.

Very good recruiters are also part sleuth. Recruiters will review the success of employees and look for patterns that can help with future recruitment. Employees that quit the company are interviewed to find out why they're leaving and how their departure might have been predicted during recruitment. (Don't be mistaken here: some turnover in your call center can be good, but you still want to understand it.) Recruiters will spend time looking at the employee's background, recruiting tests, and performance on the phones, trying to understand what makes someone a good long-term fit. With this knowledge, they can improve the recruitment process.

Finding recruiters
Recruiter is a great advancement position for agents in the call center because agents have an intimate knowledge of the job, which they can pass on to candidates. Still, it's important that new recruiters are trained in human resource practices and laws as they relate to recruiting.

The trainer

I once read somewhere that train*ing* is a place you go to practice your job; a train*er* is the person who shows people how to do their jobs. In the call center, trainers offer initial training for new agents, ongoing skill-enhancement training for existing agents, and management and leadership training for supervisors, managers, and other off-phone staff.

Along with facilitating training sessions, many trainers also develop course materials for training. Good trainers are skilled in adult learning, management, and motivation. They use a variety of techniques to develop the skills of those they train.

Being a call center trainer is a wonderful job. Things rarely go wrong in training. Unfortunately, things do sometimes go wrong in a day in the life of a call center agent — you should have a "when things go wrong" process and role-play to prepare agents for such events.

This book doesn't delve too deeply into the subject of training and trainers. However, it's important to know that the benefits of good training and great trainers are magnified in the call center environment. Call centers are about people — lots of people working the phones. Call centers are also about numbers, and small, consistent improvements in those numbers.

A call center with 1 million customers that reduces its contact rate by 1 percent because of effective training, cuts call volume by 10,000 calls. Or, imagine taking 10 seconds off call length through call-control training — that translates into about 4,000 hours in reduced staffing! These examples are modest and real.

Good training in sales, call control, anger diffusion, customer service, and other similar topics is one of the easiest and fastest ways to realize improvements in your call center. But it starts with a good trainer.

Finding trainers

You can certainly develop good trainers from your management team or even your agent group. A background in education, adult learning, and human resources is worthwhile. Barring this, a bright employee who's an excellent communicator and great problem solver will do nicely — but make sure you spend the time to have them trained in educational techniques.

The supervisor

Probably the most important management job in the call center in terms of driving operational performance is the supervisor. Core responsibilities of supervision include setting expectations, coaching, and support.

Good supervisors will drive agents and a call center to great improvements. Bad supervisors will quickly create poor morale and stagnating performance. In fairness, bad supervision is frequently not the supervisor's fault. Bad supervision can come from poorly designed supervisor roles — the supervisor is conflicted about his/her priorities, and as a result doesn't focus on the things that motivate employees and drive results. Also, bad supervision frequently comes from poor or lack of supervisor training. Many supervisors face the "You're a great agent, son — now get out there and supervise!" dilemma.

Great supervisors know their team members, what motivates them, and how they're performing.

I heard somewhere once that the number-one reason why employees fail is because they don't know what's expected of them. Amen to that! I'd go further and suggest that not only must employees know what's expected, it must be very simple, clear, and unambiguous. Expectations must be as clear as "this keeps your job, this gets you a raise, this gets you a big raise, and this loses you your job." The supervisor's job is to communicate expectations clearly and make sure that employees always know where they stand against those expectations.

Coaching includes providing feedback on performance, being careful to drill down to the specific kernel of performance that will result in the biggest improvement for the agent. It also includes providing the agent with ad hoc training and guidance in how to make changes for improvement. With some agents coaching will be minimal — these are the seasoned pros. Don't give them too much feedback, they know they're good. Maybe the feedback you give them is by way of asking them to help with coaching newer agents. For more on coaching and feedback, see Chapters 10 and 11.

Support is also a very important part of the supervisor's role. Whether providing job support or career support, it means being there for agents when they need help — clearing the way. This part of the job may not sound all that important, but it is. When roadblocks are erected that hamper agent performance, frustration sets in. If the supervisor doesn't remove the roadblock, then the agent will begin to direct that frustration at the supervisor. Support is the grease that moves along all your incentives and motivational programs.

Finding supervisors

The supervisor job is a great advancement opportunity for call center agents, but not everyone will be a great supervisor. Communication, interpersonal, and analytical skills are essential. A background in leadership and possibly some business education can be helpful. At a minimum, new supervisors will need training in leadership, coaching, and human resources practices.

Recruiter, trainer, and supervisor comprise the agent performance team. Together, they perform the core responsibilities that I summarize as the quick answer to agent performance management:

1. Hire the right people to do the job.

2. Tell them what to do, and why.

3. Show them how to do it.

4. Give them feedback on performance.

5. Make supporting them your number-one mission.

The scheduler

Okay, now here's a tough job. The scheduler (or in larger call centers, the scheduling group) is responsible for forecasting call volume demand and planning for sufficient staff, desks, and equipment to meet that demand within call center goals (service level, and so on).

The job includes multiple phases of forecasting and scheduling, including long-term ("Hey recruiter, we're gonna need 20 more staff next January"); medium term ("You know, we're going to have to add some people to the evening schedule next month"); short term ("We're going to be overstaffed Friday afternoon, let's schedule some training sessions"); and the present ("We're trending over forecast today. Noon to 2 p.m. will be busy; let's reschedule the team meetings until tomorrow"). It's all forecasting and scheduling in multiple time frames. If you want to know what's going on in the call center, ask the scheduler.

My first management job in a call center was that of scheduler. Oh, how I long for those days! Calculators, Lotus 1-2-3, graph paper, Erlang tables … and more hair.

A good scheduler can reduce expenses in a call center by 5 percent or more without any reductions in service provided. In many call centers, that's worth a lot of bananas. Chapter 7 is entirely dedicated to the process of call center scheduling.

Finding schedulers

Schedulers need to be analytical, and they should have a solid mathematical and problem-solving background. Without computer skills, they might have a hard time of it, too. Oh, and what a bonus interpersonal skills would be. Hmm … nah, it'll never happen.

Anyway, good schedulers might come from accounting, finance, or the reporting team, or maybe even from the agent group — especially if they have an educational background in accounting, business, or engineering. External candidates will also work, especially if they have the skills necessary to be a good scheduler. Past call center experience is good — particularly if it comes with good references. Expect to pay well for someone who has been a success in the scheduling role.

The telecommunications analyst

Yes, it's true; a call center isn't a call center without people, but it *really* isn't a call center without calls. Most phone systems are so reliable that we take them for granted. Still, the giant systems that work in today's call centers aren't phone systems as much as they are sophisticated telecommunications servers. Relax — they're still reliable, but they take some TLC to keep them that way. Oh, and there's the call center group — always asking for more sophisticated routing and data out of the system.

The telecommunications analyst maintains the phone system and network connection to the outside world's phone network. He or she changes configurations and assists with sophisticated applications that integrate with the phone system and network. Forecasting capacity within the phone network and phone system frequently falls to the analyst; however, they work with the help of the department scheduler, who tells the telecommunications analyst how much demand to expect.

Finding telecommunications analysts

Well, telecommunications analysts are special. Certainly you can find a person who has lots of analytical skills and some computer background and train them. You can also find them externally or working in other areas of the company.

The computer and network analyst

The computer and network analyst has a critical role to play. He or she is responsible for making sure that the call center workstations are functioning optimally as frequently as possible. I say, "as frequently as possible" and not "all the time" because they don't always work as they are supposed to, or as we'd like them to.

Most call centers today rely totally on the workstation to provide tools and information. When the tools are unavailable, the call center quickly grinds to a halt. Imagine a call center with 500 agents taking 4,000 customer calls per hour, and the network fails. Aside from the cost of having 500 idle agents, it doesn't take long to frustrate thousands of customers. You can bet that in this operation, downtime is taken seriously.

And it's not just downtime that concerns the computer and network analyst: when the workstation response time slows down call length, it creates an immediate bottleneck in the call center's work process. This bottleneck results in an increase in call length, which can create long holding times for customers and increase call center costs. Consider that a one-second increase in call length in a call center that answers 1 million calls per year can add more than $10,000 in annual costs — that's a *one-second* increase. When computers get slow, they can add a lot more than that.

So, keeping things working — and working well — is the job of the computer and network analyst. As one of these analysts once told me, "it's one of those jobs where you know you're doing a good job when you don't hear from anyone, but when you do...." But this masks the value of good computer and network analysts. Like Mr. Scott on the *Enterprise,* they can perform miracles, keeping things working and fixing them at warp speed when they don't.

Finding computer and network analysts

Computer and network analysts can be found in your call center — look for young people with a strong computer and network background eager for an opportunity to use their skills. They can be found in other departments, and they can be found outside the company. Good analysts have the required computer skills, are analytical, and are great problem solvers. Devils!

The applications developer

The sister (or brother) to the computer and network analyst is the applications developer. You need this person. Good ones pay for themselves many times over in a year ... but they tend to scare me. How can anyone stare into a computer screen for precisely 1.9 hours, get up, drink a diet cola for 14.5 minutes, and be back in their seat staring at a computer screen for another 1.9 hours? It's not natural.

Still, they create the tools that make the whole call center world work — and did I mention that *you need them?* They develop databases, troubleshooting guides, IVR (interactive voice response)applications — applications that provide automated services to incoming callers and that can interact with other computer systems and databases —, and scripting tools, and they link these tools together to make them work seamlessly.

They have superb development skills, can work unsupervised for months at a time, and drink amounts of diet cola that would make lab rats stand up and sing "Jailhouse Rock." They are analytical, have superb problem-solving skills, and I don't think they have any interpersonal skills. (Kidding — they *don't* have interpersonal skills.)

Finding applications developers

Sometimes you'll find developers in your call center — frequently, right out of school — and the smarter, the better. Don't look for them at night.

The reporting analyst

Historically, this role was performed by the person who produced department reports. The position of analyst has evolved a great deal. Reporting is still part of their job responsibilities, but now is a fraction of what the analyst should be doing. Today's analyst isn't just the kid who is really good with spreadsheets. Increasingly, he or she is someone with advanced skills in statistics and analysis.

Certainly, this person produces reports on how the call center is doing in meeting its performance metrics — business objectives and performance drivers. These reports are produced in almost any frequency that management wants — hourly, daily, weekly, monthly — and the task of producing this information should be largely automated. The analyst also makes sure that agent performance data are available so supervisors can provide feedback to their staff.

You might consider the reporting analyst the corporate scorekeeper for the call center — gotta have it!

A source of tremendous value in this position is in the opportunities that it identifies through analysis of performance. The analyst is the keeper of the economic models and the relationship between the performance drivers and the business objectives. By studying and researching the metrics, the analyst can identify and recommend improvements in processes and tools that will result in better performance for the call center.

Finding reporting analysts

Increasingly, the analyst is someone with formal training in statistics, analysis, and the use of computer applications including databases. People with advanced degrees in engineering, business, math, or statistics are worth considering. Experience with root cause analysis, Six Sigma, research, or other analytical disciplines is beneficial.

The quality analyst

It's the quality analyst's job to review the agents' work and provide assessments on how well each agent is performing against given call center standards. Their major focus is on monitoring calls for product knowledge and general call-handling ability, and reviewing data entries for accuracy and completeness. You've got to work hard to keep the role of quality analyst as positive as possible. If you don't, you might want to consider a locked room for them to work in.

In many call centers, the supervisor often performs this role. It's better to separate the responsibilities, however, so that the supervisor isn't collecting information, but rather is working with agents to use the information to improve performance.

Finding quality analysts

The role of quality analyst is a good training ground for agents who want to move up in the call center world as trainers and supervisors. You'll find lots of them on your call center floor.

The compliance and procedures officer

This is a relatively new and less seen role for call centers, but I believe that it's very important. The compliance and procedures officer is the keeper of process — what you do, and how you do it. This role is important for two reasons. The first is that call centers are subject to an increasing number of laws that govern their behavior. The compliance and procedures officer is responsible for making sure that the call center is aware of its legal requirements and that the work processes are adapted to meet those requirements.

Also, as I discuss in Chapter 12, managing call center processes is a powerful and important tool. This person is responsible for identifying existing processes, documenting those processes, and updating the processes as improvements are made. Finally, he or she will create an audit process to make sure that employees are following the approved work processes.

Finding compliance and procedures officers

This role requires someone who is well organized, detail-oriented, and a good communicator. It helps if this person has experience with documenting quality standards, such as ISO 9001.

The agent

Agents are the folks on the phones, talking to your customers. They're responsible for handling customer contacts in a manner that supports the call center's objectives and their own personal performance goals, which should be outlined to them by their supervisor.

Many call centers have other titles for their agents, including tele-service representative (TSR or REP), customer service representative (CSR), customer service person (CSP), or customer account executive (CAE) — and the list goes on.

This is the most vital role in the call center, whatever you choose to call it. The call center machine doesn't work without agents, and they can make or break the customer's experience when dealing with your company.

Finding agents

Agents come from a variety of backgrounds. When selecting agents it is most important to develop a profile of ideal candidates. I discuss agent recruiting in Chapter 10.

The precise structure of your organization isn't as important as ensuring that the major responsibilities all get assigned and the accountabilities are clear.

If your operation is smaller, one person might handle more than one of the roles and/or responsibilities I describe. For example, your supervisor might also do recruiting, or the analyst might also do some scheduling. On the other hand, if you're in a larger operation whole departments might handle one role. For example, in large call centers it's not unusual to find several people responsible for the scheduling or reporting functions. Similarly, the supervisor role might be broken up into finer areas of responsibility, with a group of supervisors handling coaching and feedback while another deals with disciplinary and human resource issues and other support.

Creating and Managing Culture

Lots of people recognize that culture is important, and I hear a lot about "understanding culture," but I don't see a lot of people *creating* culture.

Years ago, I was fortunate enough to spend some time with the president of a very successful company with an amazing culture. Everyone involved with this company said the culture was the reason why it was so successful. Employees loved working there, vendors loved supporting the company, and customers kept doing business with it. What's more, it was a very successful company, growing revenue and earnings year after year through both a recession and an economic boom.

"How do you do it?" I asked. "Is it superior planning, better financial analysts, what?" "The most important thing," the president told me, "is to create and maintain a supportive culture.

"You see," he told me, "if you don't design the culture that you need, create that culture, and manage to that culture, then you will get a different culture, one that you don't fully understand and therefore can't control. It will control you."

We then spent the best part of the next two hours talking about the impact of culture. I said, "I understand that culture is important, but what about other parts of the business, like marketing and finance. Aren't those important?" He answered, "Oh, if you get culture right, those things follow."

I can say that my own experience over the last ten years supports this claim. When we get our culture right, we can do amazing things. Even if other parts of the organization aren't quite right, a strong culture gives the team incredible confidence and power to overcome problems. When our culture is off, everything seems more difficult. I honestly can't think of anything more important in business in general, and in call centers in particular. Too bad it's not given enough attention.

This book isn't *Creating Culture For Dummies,* and it's not a book on leadership, so I won't go into it in too much detail. But you can have a positive influence on the culture of your call centre. Here are things I've noticed that work:

- ✔ **Make it a team exercise.** While I don't agree with consensus building when creating a mission, designing a culture is a great team exercise. Even if you can't involve everyone in the exercise, everyone will need to be involved in the communication and training that comes out of it.

- ✔ **Review the mission and vision.** The mission is the task ahead of you. The vision is what you're to become as a team. Both are assignments that you as a team have to complete.

- ✔ **Define what a culture is.** I like to define culture as the behavior that results from the beliefs and values that you share as a team. If you want to define certain codes of behavior, then you've got to define some values and beliefs that you want to incorporate into your work lives. The behavior, values, and beliefs should support your mission and vision — they certainly cannot contradict the mission or vision.

  - • **Values:** These are the stated rules of engagement. Values describe how everyone involved with your call center — management, staff, customers, clients, vendors, everyone — should treat each other and expect to be treated. Examples of values include honesty, dignity, respect, and so on.

  - • **Beliefs:** These are the ideas of how things work best. They describe your core, underlying strategies for how the work gets done. Examples might include continuous improvement, competitive learning, win-win-win.

- ✔ **Decide what you are going to do to turn the values and beliefs into a culture.** You'll need to ask the question, "How are we going to make this happen?" These values and beliefs will need to be incorporated into your management practices, your policies, and your rules of conduct. In my company, values violations are offences that result in discussions and, if continued, disciplinary action. Beliefs, such as competitive learning, are reinforced by continuing education and research. If enough threads are tied among values, beliefs, and the operation of your business, in time the fabric of the culture that you're looking for will be created.

You'll need to be steadfast and consistent. Many attempts at creating values and beliefs disappear with the flipchart paper that they're written on. Creating a culture takes lots of work.

The creation of a culture is a journey, not a destination

It happens: people drift off the cultural bandwagon. You operate outside your values, get frustrated, and challenge the corporate beliefs. This is where your peers and co-workers come in. "Hey Réal, do you really think that is respectful?" A question like that can stop me in my tracks. It's the team's job to remind each other of the values and beliefs. If violations happen, people need to call each other on them.

Over the long term, your culture will develop and take root. Thinking that "we have this culture and I never work outside of it" is a sure way to *prevent* a culture from taking root, and it amounts to pretending or faking it — then it becomes just a poster on the wall.

Sizing the Organization

The basic design of the call center organization shouldn't change depending on its size. The roles that are needed in a 20-seat call center are the same ones that are needed in a 500-seat center. The key difference is that in smaller organizations tasks might be grouped so that fewer individuals can handle them.

In a larger call center, tasks might be subdivided because several people are needed to complete a task. For example, in a small call center the supervisor might handle recruiting, training, and feedback, whereas in a large center there may be an entire department for recruiting, a separate department for training, and so on. The number of people required to complete any of these tasks is determined by the complexity of the task and the volume of work to be done.

How big a call center organization gets depends largely on how much work it has to do. In Chapters 6 and 7, I discuss how to determine the number of agents you are going to need. In most call centers, the agents will be the bulk of your workforce.

Your ratio of supervisors to agents (see the discussion in this chapter on span of management) will determine how many supervisors you need. If your call center has another layer of reports — supervisors, reporting to managers — then you'll need to determine the optimal ratio of managers to supervisors to calculate the size of the management team.

Remaining are the support positions, whose size is based on how much work is to be done in each function.

And as the organization grows...

As your call center grows in size and complexity, you'll find that some things don't work like they used to. In fact, you may find that some tasks fail altogether. For example, in some smaller call centers one person using some fairly basic tools — perhaps homegrown spreadsheets — can do the center's scheduling. As the call center grows in size and complexity, that person may find they can no longer get their job done in a day.

The increased workload that results from a growing organization can be handled in two ways. The first is to add more people, and the second is to change the work process.

The problem with automatically adding more people is that people grow roots, they like to stick around, and they are expensive.

In many cases, as a company grows its old work processes no longer meet the needs of the business, and what is necessary is a change in process or new technology and not necessarily more manpower. In the case of the scheduler, a new, fully automated scheduling package may have changed the work process enough so that the existing scheduler could again do the entire job of scheduling for the call center.

I'm not saying that you won't need to add people, but you should consider both options when the existing staff can no longer do the work.

Ensuring the Best Management-to-Staff Ratio

Call center managers spend much time discussing management *span* — how many agents can any one supervisor supervise, or how many supervisors can any one manager manage? Span of management for your organization should be directly proportional to the amount of support your agents require. It really depends on the complexity of the work in the center, the experience and capability of the staff, and the amount of support that is made available through technology and tools that help agents do the work.

Some prefer a lower span of management control, as it provides more time for the supervisors to spend with each call center agent — improving the quality of call handling, reducing the employee learning curve, and improving employee morale. The obvious downside is that lower spans of management cost more.

A span of 15 to 1 seems to be the de facto standard: "When in doubt, use 15 to 1." I'm not sure that this is such a good idea. Span isn't fixed. I've seen operations that work well with a 30 to 1 span; others work only with ratios as low as 5 to 1. It varies by operation. Most are in the area of 10–20 to 1 with an average of about 15 to 1. I encourage you to use some of these criteria to determine the right span of management for your organization.

Things that will allow you to increase the span of management control include

- ✔ Technology that supports call center agents, such as performance feedback to their desktop or knowledge bases with answers to even very difficult questions

- ✔ E-learning, which allows agents to take training right at their desktop

- ✔ E-mail, which allows supervisors to communicate more effectively with their staff

- ✔ Automated call recording, which increases supervisor productivity, making it possible for them to provide feedback to more staff in the same amount of time

- ✔ The creation of a dedicated call evaluation team that listens to agent calls and assesses them for the supervisor — essentially offloading some of the supervisor's tasks

- ✔ Highly tenured and mature staff who know the job well

- ✔ A movement toward self-direction in the workplace

Excellent support tools — A higher span of management

Imagine one of your supervisors coming in to the office to do her job of supporting and coaching her staff. To start her day she prints off a variety of reports from various systems that tell her about the team's performance. She then summarizes these reports in a spreadsheet so she can better understand each agent's strengths and weaknesses. Next, she spends a few hours remotely listening to calls being taken. (This takes a while, because there aren't many callers today.) After she hears some complete calls by a few of her staff, she reviews and scores the calls. Now, with reports and work samples prepared, she is ready to provide coaching. Unfortunately, the day's almost over and she needs to wrap some things up before heading home. Oh, well, I guess coaching can wait until tomorrow.

Now, imagine the same supervisor with better support tools. When she comes in to the office, she starts her computer and waiting there for her is a statistical performance analysis for each agent. This analysis is far more detailed, with more history than she could ever collect on her own, and includes identification of the strengths and weaknesses of each agent. Oh, and her agents have already seen these reports, which include their identified weaknesses and a list of coaching points for improvement.

Also available for her is a large sample of complete calls for each agent. The calls have been scored and the scores have also been sent to the respective agents. With all this work done, your supervisor can start her day by approaching agents and offering help in working on their already defined coaching areas. These tools are available today and are discussed in greater detail in Chapters 8 and 9. With the use of these tools, supervisors are freed up to spend more of their time supporting their agents through coaching and feedback. This promotes a higher span of management control.

Still, I can't tell you what the right span of management control is for your call center. Having too low a span of management is rarely a problem. Concerns over cost control, growth in the call center, and movement of management to new assignments place constant upward pressure on management span. However, it's important to recognize the signs of a span of management control that is too high:

- ✔ Call center agents complaining that they don't get enough time with their supervisor
- ✔ Quality of call handling decreasing or in need of improvement
- ✔ Inability of supervisors to get to everything they need to do

These are signs that the span of management is too high. Either the way the supervisor's work gets done needs to be changed (through the addition of new tools or processes), or the number of supervisors will need to increase.

No One Right Way

I'm not sure that there is one right way to design a call center organization structure. I am positive that it's important to give careful consideration to the roles and responsibilities within the call center. It's important to make sure that someone in the organization is responsible for completing all the critical tasks to operating a successful call center.

The best you can do with organizational design is to make sure that roles are coordinated in a way that splits up responsibility but ensures that everyone is working toward the same mission and business objectives. The most important thing to get right is culture. This is a people business, and like all people businesses it works best when everyone is engaged, working together in a healthy, supportive environment.

Chapter 4

Building a Call Center of Your Own

. . . .

In This Chapter

▶ Asking the questions to get things started

▶ Determining the type and size of your center

▶ Deciding where to locate

▶ Choosing an outsourcing partner

. . . .

*T*he implementation of a call center starts with a need — sometimes an urgent need. Okay, *frequently* an urgent need! An organization finds itself receiving lots of calls from customers — perhaps because business is booming — but there is no place for the calls to go, so someone decides "We need a call center!" Often, and particularly in the more urgent cases, the call center is built quickly to expand the company's existing customer contact capability.

At other times the call center is planned well in advance. For example, if your company is rolling out a new product or business and you expect to have lots of calls coming in, you're more likely to plan ahead to meet the need for more call handling.

In this chapter I provide some of the questions and answers to the why, what, where, when, and how of building a call center.

First Things First: Questions to Ask

You'll need answers to some basic questions to determine your call center's logistics:

✔ What outputs will the call center deliver?

✔ What kinds of services will the call center provide (inbound customer service, outbound collections)?

✔ What types of management support services will the call center provide (supervisors, trainers, schedulers, quality control, analysts)?

✔ What other customer support services (processing warranty claims, e-mail response) are required?

✔ What are the skill requirements for agents and management?

✔ What are the technological requirements?

✔ What will be the call center's size?

✔ What are the options for locating the call center?

Understanding these issues will help the planners create the list of requirements that will ultimately become a project plan for building the call center.

What are the demands of the business?

As I discuss in Chapters 2 and 3, senior management in the corporation sets the call center's strategic direction by defining its mission. Getting an early understanding of what's expected from the call center will help you begin to define future capabilities and requirements.

In Chapter 2, I provide more information about service level and other call center goals, along with a model for ensuring you're meeting those goals.

What types of services will the call center provide?

The types of services provided by your call center will dictate the skills needed to provide services to callers, and may also influence the call center's location. For example, if you're taking highly technical calls it may be wise to locate in an area that has a technical school. If a lot of your callers speak Spanish you'll need agents who do too, so you might want to locate in an area with a highly concentrated Spanish population.

Following are some typical services you might provide in your call center:

✔ **Inbound customer service:** providing general product information or service help to customers

✔ **Inbound technical support:** helping customers use their product or service and offering troubleshooting advice for technical problems

✔ **Inbound sales:** helping customers make purchase decisions

✔ **Inbound billing:** helping customers with their invoices and providing them with general account information

✔ **Outbound telemarketing:** selling new offerings to customers

- ✔ **Outbound service:** following up with customers on inquiries and problems; providing information, gathering opinions, or conducting surveys
- ✔ **Outbound collections:** attempting to pry payment from people whom you may no longer choose to call customers
- ✔ **Inbound collections:** receiving payment from people whom you probably do still call customers
- ✔ **Back office:** processing customer requests and orders for new products or services

How big should the call center be?

The size of your call center will depend primarily on the number of resources (agents, specifically) it's going to take to manage all your customer contacts. It will be necessary to predict the workload handled by the new call center. When doing this, it's a good idea to conduct a long-range forecast — say, five years out, so some room is planned for growth. In Chapters 6 and 7 I discuss forecasting and staffing and explain how to determine how big a call center will need to be.

Determining your future call center's size tells you a lot, including which community it needs to be located in (one with a sufficient labor pool that has the skills you need) and the type of building it needs to located in (one with sufficient space, utilities, telecommunications infrastructure, and parking!).

Will it be a standalone or part of a network of centers?

As part of your sizing discussion, you'll want to know if the call center is a separate entity — a standalone facility that does all the work itself — or part of a network of call centers that perform similar functions. A new operation will require more planning and research, as a blueprint may not exist on which to base decisions. On the other hand, adding to a network of call centers may be an easier task because the new operation can rely on the model developed by the existing operations.

What support services should be included?

In addition to call-handling services, call center planners need to ask what additional services will be performed. Some of these will be obvious, such as management support functions — supervisors, schedulers, trainers, and the other roles that I discuss in Chapter 3. Others might not be so obvious and must be identified in advance of starting the call center design.

Depending on the services that the call center is providing, additional work may be required in addition to handling calls. For example, a customer support center may also provide e-mail support for customers who prefer to use that method of communication.

Some product and service support functions that might be required and that must be considered when determining the center's requirements include

- ✔ Communicating with customers via fax, Internet, e-mail, or chat
- ✔ Processing mail
- ✔ Provisioning customer orders on company systems
- ✔ Reviewing and approving (or denying) customer requests for claims, credit, and so on
- ✔ Distributing the product
- ✔ Processing warranty claims

Answering the questions

Answering the questions in this chapter will tell planners a lot about what the call center will be like.

Because a call center's requirements cross a number of disciplines, it's a good idea to have people with a variety of skills on the planning team. Necessary expertise includes specialists in project management, human resources, and facilities, technology, and staff planning, along with someone who has experience running the type of call center that you're building — perhaps the future call center manager.

With these skills on the project team, it becomes less likely that important requirements will be missed.

X Marks the Spot: Situating Your Call Center

The major factors — the core criteria — influencing your center's location are

- ✔ the availability of reliable telecommunications,
- ✔ the availability and skill of the workforce, and
- ✔ the overall cost of running the operation in the location.

Some companies might also argue that it's important for their call center to be located close to other corporate locations or to their customers. Simply add whatever criteria are important to your company to the core location factors listed above and you have a great basis for comparing operations.

You should consider each criterion when deciding on the best location for your new center — and you have a lot of location options. With the worldwide availability of the Internet and telecommunications services, new labor markets all over the world have opened up to call center operators. Every market has its benefits and, everything else being equal, a call center can be located anywhere in the world and still achieve the operation's mission and business objectives. The options have never been greater.

Setting up virtual call centers

In fact, you don't even have to limit your call center to one location: you can create virtual call centers, with agents working in different locations around the world while serving the same group of customers.

In a virtual operation, the fact that locations are separate is irrelevant. The technology makes the separated groups appear as one. In fact, call center agents don't even have to be in an office; they can work from the comfort of their own homes. Multiple agents working from home can be tied together into a virtual call center using the Internet and a telephone network.

Virtual call centers are useful for companies that have very large call center needs. Rather than one mega call center, the company can build multiple call centers and link them virtually.

Linking multiple offices also provides a large measure of disaster preparedness — if one office is closed due to an emergency or bad weather the other centers will likely continue to operate without interruption, keeping the company's call center open. Some companies virtually link home agents as a way to secure a large workforce of part-time labor, or to reduce facilities costs, or as a perk for top agents. I discuss some of the specifics of these technologies in Chapters 8 and 9.

Testing an area's labor market

To test whether a market has sufficient qualified labor, call center managers will place newspaper recruitment ads and review the volume and quantity of candidates who come forward. A good response will make the market a candidate for the new call center.

My company has developed a recruiting application using interactive voice response (IVR). (I talk more about IVR in Chapter 8.) When looking for new sites we advertise in several communities, giving each a unique number to call. Candidates call our IVR, which prescreens applicants. The IVR then gives us an indication of volume of interest and an initial indication of quality of applicants.

We've also used IVR to determine very specific locations. Recently, we were faced with the need to add a new call center on a short timeline — *really short* — to satisfy a client's urgent demand. Our problem was that we had not yet identified our next geographic location. We had a short list of six cities, but had not reduced it to one. Our biggest concern was selecting a location that had the labor pool necessary to satisfy our long-term demand.

We decided to place ads with local radio stations and newspapers in each city. In each ad we provided a unique phone number linked to our recruiting IVR. The IVR was set up to prescreen qualified applicants: respondents called the number advertised in their community and were prompted by the IVR to answer questions about their qualifications, such as Do you have previous call center experience? What do you understand the job to entail? and Please describe a situation where you've provided exceptional customer service. The IVR recorded and categorized the applicants' responses. After less than a week of running ads and reviewing the IVR results, we had sufficient information to select the best city. I doubt this would have been possible had we not automated the prescreening of candidates.

Locating near other facilities in the corporation

How integrated is your call center with your organization's other functions? Is it necessary for corporate management to have an ongoing presence in the call center? If the answer is yes, you'll want to locate your call center close to the corporate head office.

Could a call center job be considered an entry-level position to other roles within the company? If so, staying close to home makes sense because the call center can become a labor pool for the organization.

Building the call center near existing corporate facilities and capabilities — data processing, human resources, recruiting, training — can provide cost advantages. You can save on personnel costs, since you may not have to fill certain roles that are duplicates of those in place at head office, and the availability of facilities space (like training rooms and meeting rooms) can help to avoid the increased costs of extra buildings for the call center.

On a more warm and fuzzy level, it may be important for your organization to promote a strong sense of corporate community and teamwork, and keeping the call center close to the home office will certainly contribute to that.

Setting up shop close to potential employees

The availability of enough people with the required skills to do the job is vital, especially if your call center does complex work that requires a specific skill set or advanced qualifications. A poor decision regarding location can escalate recruiting and training costs if the right people are not readily available.

Also consider the cost of available labor. It's cheaper to staff a call center in Upper Rubber Boot than it is in Lower Booming Metropolis. When you consider that labor will account for more than 60 percent of your costs, this is obviously a serious consideration.

I like to see call centers in the middle of large residential communities. This tells me that the employee base is close by — a prime consideration for people to come work for you. If a call center is inaccessible, that's a roadblock to attracting the greatest number of highly qualified staff.

Getting close to your customers

Are there important advantages to serving your specific customers? Does your product or service require a significant degree of local area knowledge? If so, your organization may be one of the many for which understanding the customer's business environment at a very intimate level is vital, and this can be reason enough to locate the call center close to your customer base.

Customer: *I'm at 123 Happy Valley Drive.*

Agent: *Hey is that near Herb's Pierogi Emporium? Yeah, I know that area really well. As a matter of fact, we have a store just down the street from you...*

As the world of commerce becomes increasingly cosmopolitan, however, this type of customer service intimacy is less important or expected.

You'll certainly ensure cultural familiarity by keeping the call center in the market that serves your customers. However, by locating within your own country but out of the state or province, you may not lose much in the way of customer service while gaining the advantage of lower costs and increased capacity — particularly if your market is one with relatively high labor costs, such as Los Angeles, New York, Toronto, or London.

Being far, far away from your customers

By far the least costly alternative on a purely operational basis is to move your call center operations offshore. Locating in places like Central America, the Caribbean, South Africa, India, the Philippines, or China can greatly decrease labor costs.

There is significant risk associated with such a move, as you'll likely find there are fewer skilled people available, your control is minimized, and cultural differences can create communication and operational challenges.

Of course, moving your call center offshore is not going to be cheap in the short term. A lot of front-end work and support is needed to make sure that an offshore center is a success. Just as there are a lot of success stories, there are horror stories as well; many of these are the result of a poorly planned and hastily executed move.

If you're going to genuinely consider the offshore option, you have to do substantial research and project planning — don't forget to factor in the local levels of efficiency when comparing to a call center closer to home. I would also recommend that a home office management presence be permanently stationed on-site to assist in alleviating potential control and communication issues.

A Home Away from Home

Wherever you locate, you should be looking for ways to simultaneously cut costs and improve quality — your customers simply want high-quality products and services at competitive prices, and your company's investors like to see good returns on their investment.

If being close to your customer base or to other corporate facilities are not important criteria for your organization, you are afforded certain cost advantages that come with this freedom. However, when building *green field* — in an area perceived as greener pastures, away from the corporate head office — there are still other site location criteria that you need to consider.

Primary considerations

Whether you decide to build close to home or not, you always have to consider the availability of sufficient labor with the appropriate skills your center needs.

Additionally, you must ask yourself, "What are the average labor rates in the target area?" To justify locating your center away from home it only makes sense that you should be gaining an advantage — preferably a significant advantage — in labor costs. You need to also factor in the percentage of staff turnover in a year, as well as call center growth. The population base of your target area has to be able to sustain more than just your immediate needs.

Are there educational institutions in your target area? If so, do they offer programs that support your business's needs — that is, the skill requirements that you will be hiring for? Additional training is a significant call center cost, so it pays dividends to locate your center in an area where there is an abundant supply of educated employees. Remember, too, that communities with university or college campuses provide a great source of part-time and summer replacement employees.

It sounds odd, but make sure you can get a qualified management team in your new location. Trust me, it's happened that planners have built a call center in a great remote location only to have a tough time placing a qualified management team there. Sure you may be able to train a manager from the call center agents, but that takes time.

Naturally, it will be vital for the area that you select to be equipped with the latest and greatest telecommunications infrastructure. Other utilities, such as power, will also be important.

Technological advancements mean it doesn't really matter if you're locating your call center out of the city, county, region, state, or province — today's telecommunications will link everything back to your other operations seamlessly.

This *geographic outsourcing* — locating away from the home office or customer base — has been going on for a long time and is a common business practice. Companies that moved all or part of their operations from New York to Iowa, for example, were taking advantage of geographic outsourcing.

Urban vs. rural locales

While locating your call center in a big city will increase the availability of labor, the competition for labor will also be increased; and, although utilities are likely to be better, wages will also be higher in urban centers.

Small communities, on the other hand, often have a strong culture of support for customer-service operations. Often, a new call center will be a significant employer in a smaller community, reducing unemployment and building immediate company loyalty within the entire community.

Call centers work well if they are located in or near the communities where people live — that is, near the skilled target labor you require. A great way to attract staff to your center is to make the commute easy for them.

Exploring near-shore vs. offshore options

Near-shore refers to locating call centers in a neighboring country. A common example is U.S. corporations locating call centers in Canada or Mexico, or a firm in England locating a call center in Ireland.

Locating near shore

Locating your call center near shore is an easy and often viable alternative because the center is close to the company's home country, so language, education, and cultural issues tend not to be significant problems.

A near-shore location is essentially just an extension of the geographic diversification within your company's own country, and you can gain some significant advantages in available labor pools, cost of labor, education, and skill level of interested labor.

Locating offshore

Locating offshore is the next logical step in geographic diversification, and it offers even greater savings in the cost of labor especially. Also, continuing advancements in data communications, telephony, and the Internet have virtually eliminated technological distance issues — it really is a small world after all!

A consideration for locating your call center offshore is that some countries have a huge number of highly educated and skilled people looking for work. (In India, for example, millions of people graduate from university every year.) In many of these countries the availability of jobs is lagging well behind the country's ability to produce a skilled workforce.

You might also consider that, contrary to the stigma sometimes attached to working in a call center in North America, call center jobs are actually coveted in many offshore countries. Where an MBA grad in Canada might not give much thought to a call center job, an MBA grad in Manila will jump at the chance.

When an affordable and abundant labor pool that is interested in and values call center work becomes scarce in your home country or near shore, moving your center offshore makes sense. As I discuss in Chapter 10, motivation is at least half of what makes up agent performance. Finding a location where qualified people truly value the work might be the single most important criterion for call center location.

Locating offshore is just a logical extension of the geographic outsourcing practice — something that has been going on for some time with the expansion of the global, international economy.

Implementing a combined option

If you're seriously thinking about pursuing an offshore location, you may wish to consider moving your call center operations in two steps.

First, move a portion of your operations to a nearby location in a less expensive labor market. After your organization gains experience running a remote location, the offshore project can begin.

You can then either run the two operations simultaneously — perhaps sending less complex or overnight work offshore — or you can begin the process of moving all operations offshore to take advantage of very low labor costs.

Some large companies send part of their workload to a nearby location, gaining efficiencies and benefits from an abundant, cheap workforce that highly values the work. Once the company has learned how to manage that, then the company sends work offshore, gaining even more cost advantages and an even larger motivated labor pool.

Perhaps the company will keep its most complex calls onshore, send some less complex calls near-shore, and send the simplest calls offshore. The company benefits from multiple labor pools, redundancy in the event that any one call center needs to be shut down (say, in a snowstorm), and a blended labor rate that is lower than what they have onshore but higher than their lowest rate. For some, this provides a nice mix of cost-control and capability.

If you're not sure about taking your call center to a far-off land, consider testing the waters by sending some of your simpler calls or other work offshore. By creating a blend of your local call center — doing the more complex and valuable work — and the offshore call center — doing the simpler and less valuable work — your company can test the offshore option and lower its overall cost. It might be all you need.

Other location considerations

Other factors also weigh in to the decision of where to locate a call center. Items on the list below may not be the first things you consider, but they can affect your final decision:

- ✔ Interest and support from the local government
- ✔ Availability of tax breaks and subsidies for locating in the community
- ✔ Proximity of colleges, universities, and other training institutions that provide the skills you need
- ✔ Number of other call centers in the community that may compete for labor
- ✔ Availability of an existing building to house your call center
- ✔ Reliability of local utilities providers, such as power and water
- ✔ Availability of public transportation
- ✔ Tax considerations
- ✔ Labor laws

Setting Up Shop: What Needs to Be Inside the Call Center?

Regardless of where you decide to locate your call center, you'll need to think about what it will look like and what special circumstances you should consider.

Beyond bricks and mortar: the facilities

So, once you've settled on a location for your call center, what will you actually put there? The term *call center* describes the operation quite well, actually. *Calls* are answered, and the operations are *centralized* — handled in one place, either real or virtual.

Most call centers have one or more large rooms with lots of grouped *workstations* — which include desks for the agents, an electronic terminal, phone, headset, chair, and so on — making it easier for the agents to work together. Some call centers look quite nice — comfortable, modern, aesthetically pleasing — some, not so much.

Workstation layout comes in many different designs, including the everyone-wedged-in-together "I can hear your heart beating" style, or the everything-exposed-to-the-all-powerful-corner-office "I've got an eye on you, son" style. Somewhere in the middle exists a nice place to work, which is spacious, quiet, and pleasant.

The call center is designed with a major purpose — to answer calls. So, good design should focus on the actual call center — the big room with all the people. Everything else that's added to the facility should be set up so that it supports the call center.

For example, washrooms should be easily accessible, not requiring agents to make long walks. Similarly, the washrooms should be large enough to avoid the lineups that can result in agents missing time from their shifts. All other rooms in the facility should be designed in a similar fashion that ensures convenience.

Usually, your call center will include specialized rooms, such as those listed below, set up in different areas of the building:

- ✔ **Data center:** This is a separate room that holds the computer servers and telephone equipment.

- ✔ **Training room(s):** A room or rooms where training sessions are conducted can be very useful. Many include whiteboards and audio/visual equipment, and some have workstation setups for simulating and role-playing call-taking scenarios. Training rooms need to be large enough and plentiful enough to accommodate the multiple classes that come with anticipated expansion or skill enhancements.

- ✔ **Meeting rooms:** As you'd probably guess, these are rooms for conducting meetings. There are any range of sizes of meeting rooms — from the small room with a desk and a couple of chairs, which could be used for conducting interviews or one-on-one meetings, up to the lavish boardroom with leather high-back reclining chairs and — for the executive bigwigs — an expensive polished mahogany table that could seat a small country.

- ✔ **Lunchroom:** Another obvious one: a room where staff can eat lunch. Generally, there is some kind of cafeteria-style tables and chairs, and there may be a kitchen, cafeteria, and/or vending machines for staff use. The lunchroom needs to be especially accommodative to the call center. Too few seats will frustrate your staff, and a lack of amenities, such as microwaves, will result in lineups and agents being late returning from lunch. Some call centers have on-site hot/cold food services. This can work great, especially where outside facilities aren't available.

✔ **Offices for various other high-falutin' officious types:** Most centers will have offices for executives, directors, and any managers who require more privacy than the typical Dilbert cubicle world affords.

You may want to go further, as some operations do, and add some nice amenities for the staff. These amenities aren't strictly necessary, but they make the call center environment a little more fun and a slightly nicer place to work.

✔ **Games room:** The job of a call center agent can be stressful, so some companies provide their employees with a room in which to unwind and enjoy their break time. Some include video games, TVs, table tennis, air hockey, and the like.

✔ **Quiet room:** Similarly, quiet rooms offer a place to unwind after or in the middle of a hectic day. These often include reclining chairs or sofas, a place to put your feet up, and books or magazines to read.

You can go a lot further than this. Some companies have put health centers, massage therapy facilities, and even a basketball court in their call centers. These ideas aren't as crazy as they might sound. Retaining your workforce and keeping them happy has a tremendous return.

Designing the ideal space

The layout of your call center is very important. A good design is vital, as you want to build the center for maximum efficiency — from a cost reduction standpoint, of course, but also for efficiency in operations. You don't want to have supervisors hunting for agents, agents hunting for supervisors, or *anyone* hunting for the tools they might need to do their job.

Average workspace depends largely on the specific demands of the agent's role. A customer support center in which agents may be required to access printed manuals, for example, will require more desk space than a simple information-providing campaign. Make sure your agents have ample room to do their work and also have some privacy.

When designing the layout for your center, make sure that all your staff have ample room to work, yet not so much room that everybody has their own corner office. The area of workspace per call center desktop can vary substantially — from as little as under 50 to upward of 150 square feet per desk.

The look of different call centers tends to vary greatly. You've got your Taj Mahal call centers and you've got your fixer-uppers. Both can produce good results and happy employees. Figure 4-1 shows a possible call center design layout.

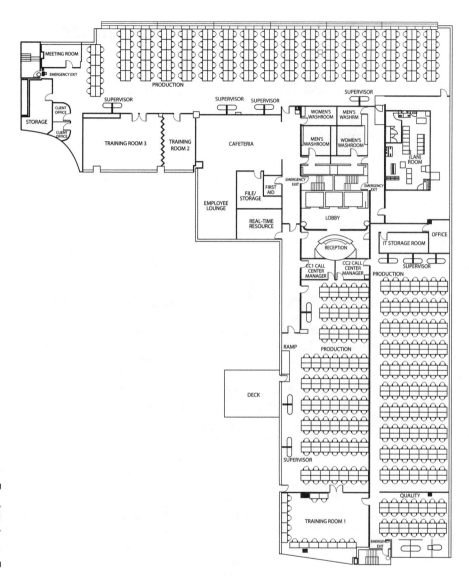

Naturally, for cost control your aim will be to maximize the use of your space, but if you try to cram too many desks into one operation noise control will be a concern. No bunk stations, please!

Your highest design consideration is to ensure that everything is *centralized*. Otherwise, I suppose it wouldn't make much sense call it a call *center*.

Understanding environmental issues

The environment created by your management team — how people are treated, and whether they feel valued — has greater impact on employee morale than creature comforts and paintings on the walls. Still, there are some things that can go a long way toward making your call center a great place to work:

✔ Natural light

✔ Noise control

✔ Comfortable desks and chairs

✔ Cleanliness/neatness

✔ Ample eating and resting areas

✔ Conveniences such as a hot-food cafeteria, relaxation rooms, and lockers

Taking special needs into account

Your call center can open doors to people with a variety of special needs, because of technology that makes it possible to overcome many disabilities in the workplace. Some special-needs concerns include

✔ Increased wheelchair access: wide aisles, wheelchair-accessible desks, offices, and elevators

✔ Amenities for visually impaired employees: reader software, which reads text information from computer systems to the employee, or special monitors that expand the size of text on a computer screen (you may also want to consider assisting visually impaired employees with navigation around the call center)

Creating accommodations for employees with special needs is not only a socially responsible thing to do, but also good business as people with disabilities are a large source of underutilized, highly skilled labor.

Building a Call Center: One Step at a Time

Lots of things need to get done when building a call center. As I discuss earlier in this chapter, the first thing you should do is assign a project manager — the person responsible for keeping the call center project on track. The project manager will track tasks and accountabilities and will hound anyone who falls behind.

Be sure to select someone who has experience with project management. I'll also repeat that it's important to pull together a team of people with expertise in human resources, facilities management, technology, staff planning, and general call center management.

Table 4-1 summarizes some of the steps that my company follows when building our call centers. There are probably other considerations for your call center, but this is a good start. I review the important steps in the table next.

Table 4-1	Steps to Building a Call Center
Step	**Miscellaneous Details**
Establish site goals/reason for build	Mission for the call center
	Likely business objectives
	Standalone or part of a network
Determine the capability requirements of the call center	Identify the types of services that the call canter will provide to customers —inbound, outbound, support, sales, e-mail, etc.
	Identify the support functions needed in the call center, supervisors, trainers, schedulers, etc.
	Determine specific skills agents will need to perform the work
	Determine the technology requirements
Determine the call center	Size of the facility based on seat requirement and of the size planned space per seat
Select a location for the center	Identify target regions: Are there time zone considerations, for example?
Criteria: cost, available labor, telecommunications, and others	Assess availability of physical locations in each region
	Assess the government and business environment
	Select a region
	Identify potential markets in the region that meet size and skilled labor requirements
	Advertise for applicants in each market
	Measure response rate in each market

(continued)

Table 4-1 *(continued)*

Step	Miscellaneous Details
	Develop a shortlist of markets with sufficient response
	Assess candidates in each market
	Determine each market's ability to support the center's capacity and growth
	Assess telecommunications and utility availability in each market
Decide on renting, buying, or building	Contact Economic Development Office, area real estate agents/search companies for guidance
	Consider zoning within municipalities: commercial/industrial
	Investigate government subsidy/support programs: H/R, skills training; facilities-related subsidies; tax reductions or deferrals, etc.
	Look for abundant selection of suitable properties for lease
	Depending on availability of suitable space, purchasing may be an option
	Design/build may suit immediate concerns
	Conduct comparative analysis of leasing, buying, or building
	Develop plan
Create an implementation plan	Create budgets for building and running the center
	Create build-out plan
	Define initial work processes
	Hire and train staff
	Install furniture, equipment, and technology
	Establish timelines
Approval	Present plan to senior management
Implement plan	Execute and launch

Managing the project

Someone in senior management will sponsor the project, probably the same person who creates the mission for the call center and works with the call center to establish annual business objectives. As sponsor, this person provides the mandate to build the call center and makes the final "go/no go" decision, including commitment of capital.

Once senior management has blessed the project, the project manager assembles the project team and they begin to go through the planning process, which resulted from answering the questions listed earlier in the chapter.

- ✔ **What is the call center's purpose?** The team starts by deciding whether the center is to support existing customer demand or to handle new products and services. In doing this, they gain an understanding of the call center's mission and what types of outputs the corporation expects.

- ✔ **What are the call center's capabilities?** From the purpose, the team calls upon its collective experience to identify services that the center will provide — inbound support, outbound collections, or e-mail support — and the necessary agent skill types, such as sales or technical skills and language requirements.

- ✔ **Should it be a standalone center or part of a network of call centers?**

- ✔ **What technology is needed to support the services that the call center is to provide?** With this knowledge, the team will determine the staff support requirements, such as supervisors, schedulers, and trainers.

- ✔ **How big must the facility be?** Size can be determined by forecasting annual demand for the next five years. The team must consider the total space requirements, starting with the number of workstations, the space required per workstation, and the supporting rooms and facilities. (I review sizing requirements in Chapter 7.)

- ✔ **Where should the call center be located?** Using the criteria that are important to the company and including, at a minimum, the associated costs, the availability of labor with the required skill set, and the availability of a suitable telecommunications infrastructure, the team will search for and identify potential locations for the new call center. Ultimately, the team will settle on one location as the best candidate.

Considerations will include how to finance the new call center, whether to build a new center or renovate an existing facility, and whether to purchase a building or to rent one. Some locations may offer government subsidies for locating your new call center in their community. Zoning requirements will need to be verified before work can begin on the new center. At this point, the team may be tasked with creating budgets for how much the call center will cost to build, and how much it will cost to run.

Creating the plan

Once the building and budget details are arrived at, the team can create an implementation plan. This plan will identify all the steps necessary to launch the new call center, including creating budgets for how much the center will cost to run and how much it will cost to build; defining and documenting initial work processes; hiring and training staff; installing furniture, equipment, and technology; and answering the first calls. The implementation plan will include timeframes and deadlines for launching the call center on time.

When the implementation plan is completed, it can be presented to senior management for approval. Giddy up!

Instituting a Disaster Recovery Plan

Disaster recovery is all about ensuring that you can continue to do business should something, well, *disastrous* happen to your call center's location, people, or tools.

Every call center needs some form of disaster recovery plan. The sophistication of your plan and the protection it offers depend largely on the impact to the organization that the loss of the call center — even for a short time — could have.

Some companies cannot function without their call center, and therefore would consider them critical to their functioning. An airline's ticket and reservations center might be an example.

Disaster recovery plans may range from ensuring that all call center data are backed up daily to having a complete mirror backup of the call center and its tools on standby just waiting to be used.

Multiple locations

Disaster recovery provides good reason to have multiple sites in separate cities, if possible. This way, your system requirements can be duplicated, building in some redundancy. Having multiple sites also provides some security against temporary localized issues, such as severe weather, power interruptions, workforce fluctuations, famine, a plague of locusts...

Standalone centers

If you're in a standalone operation — where multiple sites are not an option — you should consider the following:

- **Remember your A-B-C-D's.** Always Back Up Critical Data! Your operations should include a backup of critical data at least daily.

- **Have redundant services.** For telephone and data, especially. You might want to make your data center redundant *and* locate it off-site.

- **Utilize a disaster-recovery site.** Disaster-recovery services offer sites that sit empty, with the capabilities your call center needs (telephone systems, computers, and operating systems) just waiting to be used. They can also include data backup capabilities.

- **Engage an outsourcer.** Splitting work with an outsourcer is a great way to balance workload, benchmark operations, and provide a level of disaster recovery. There are many ways to work with an outsourcer. One is to send the outsourcer a consistent percentage of your overall volume. In this case, the outsourcer gets the same call types that you do. It's also useful to use your outsourcer to benchmark against your internal organization. Further, should your call center ever have a weather-related power failure, you can route all of your volume to the outsourcer. Sure, the outsourcer could become overwhelmed with the additional volume, but at least you're not out of business. If you outsource work that can be stopped at a moment's notice, such as outbound collections or telemarketing, then the outsourcer may be able to temporarily increase the number of calls it can take. I discuss outsourcing in more detail at the end of this chapter.

Disaster preparation might include provisions for quickly accessing:

- **Backup batteries and generators**

- **Your manual (paper-based) processes:** You'll need to access customer information and call tracking in the event that the data network fails.

- **Your telephone network:** For a fee, you can have control over your phone network so that customer calls can be quickly routed to another center.

- **The services of a disaster recovery center:** This is basically a call center that's ready to go when you need it, using your own staff.

- **The services of a third-party outsourcer:** It's a good idea to keep an overflow agreement in place so that the outsourcer becomes familiar with your business and customers.

Of course, if your call center is part of a network of call centers, you already have a degree of disaster recovery built in. In this case you'll need to consider

- ✔ **Whether your network has a single point of failure:** Is there one thing that can bring down the entire network if it fails?
- ✔ **Whether the remaining center(s) can handle the additional volume:** If so, for how long?

Almost anything can be planned for — at a cost. When planning for disaster recovery, you have to balance the cost with the risk of loss. You're likely to spend more time and money protecting a 911 call center than one that answers customer inquiries from people who dial the number on the side of their toothpaste tube. (No offense intended to all you dedicated dentifrice employees.)

Should You Run the Call Center or Outsource it?

Here's another question to ask before the call center is built. Should you do it yourself or let someone else do it? The decision whether to outsource the call center work or to keep it in-house has been, is, and is likely to continue to be a hot topic. Some organizations simply want to keep their call center work in-house because they believe they risk losing control over their operations when using an outsourcer.

An outsourcer is a company that you can hire to handle a portion of your business on your behalf. You would hire an outsourcer that specializes in call center work.

A good outsourcer will handle call center operations better than most in-house centers. After all, running call centers is an outsourcer's sole focus: they are very good at pulling the levers that result in cost control, revenue generation, and customer satisfaction.

Reducing costs through outsourcing

In the majority of cases it should be cheaper to run your call center through an outsourcer, while getting the same quality work. Many in-house call center people argue that this isn't true. They say, "I pay my staff $12.50 per hour, while the outsourcer wants $29 per hour."

The problem with that statement is that it's like comparing apples and gorilla feet. The outsourcer's $29 is a rate that includes everything from the agent's pay to the supervisor's pay, the trainer's pay, the cost of the desk and phone system, the cost of having the carpet cleaned when a visitor drops a cup of coffee on it, and so on.

Most in-house, corporate call centers would be well advised to look at their true hourly costs. Add up all your operating costs and divide by the total number of hours that agents actually staff the phones: you might be shocked. My research and experience suggests that outsourcing typically reduces a company's call center operating costs by more than 30 percent.

Building your own call center will cost in excess of $10,000 on a per-seat basis. Using an outsourcer can avoid this capital cost — turning it into a variable cost.

The use of an outsourcer also allows your company to focus on your core business. Let's face it: your shareholders don't care that you run your own call center — they just want to know that you are managing their investment well. If your core business is making ice sculptures, you might want to focus on that and let others focus on call center excellence.

On the other hand, the call center outsourcing market also includes an abundance of companies doing poor work. The profit motive causes some outsourcers to do things they shouldn't — like cutting corners in technology, recruiting, and training costs, or taking on more clients or campaigns than they can effectively handle. Using a bad outsourcer can be very costly and damaging to your corporate image and customer relations.

You want your outsourcer to seem like an extension of your own business — one with particular call center expertise. It comes down to setting objectives and working closely with the outsourcer to ensure that these objectives are achieved. Clarity is vital — clarity of purpose, expectations, communications ... the works!

The final decision is a matter of considering

- ✔ Can you do the job as effectively as the outsourcer in terms of cost, revenue generation, and customer satisfaction, and

- ✔ How badly do you want to run your own operation?

When choosing to outsource, keep an eye on your outsourcer. When choosing to keep it your call center work in-house, keep an eye on your competitors.

Part II
The Master Plan: Finance, Analysis, and Resource Management

The 5th Wave   By Rich Tennant

Brenton Call Center

"I tried calling in sick yesterday, but I was put on hold and disconnected."

In this part . . .

*T*his is where the call center business model comes to life — analysis, financial planning, and staffing. I provide a simple overview of how (and what) metrics (things you can measure) come together to drive call center operational and financial performance to achieve good results.

Staffing is probably the biggest mystery and frustration to most call center professionals. In this part of the book I also explore everything from forecasting to schedule creation and workforce management automation. I'll help to uncover some of the mysteries of how and why call centers perform the way they do.

Chapter 5

Analyze This!

● ●

In This Chapter

▶ Understanding the important role of finance and analysis

▶ Knowing which business objectives and performance drivers to concentrate your efforts on

▶ Creating models to analyze the numbers

▶ Ensuring the alignment of measures throughout the call center

▶ Tracking the numbers and setting appropriate targets

● ●

*O*kay, to some of you just the thought of call center analysis may seem a little boring, and for others it might even hurt a bit, but trust me — it really isn't that difficult, and it's very important.

Call centers can be complex beasts and they run very much by the numbers, so analysis plays a significant role in operating them effectively. Call centers can get very big, and while they offer a cost-effective way of doing business, they can require a lot of dollars from the parent organization to make them go.

Miniscule changes in procedures can make an enormous difference in results, including — and especially — in performance and financial results. Increasingly, call center managers are turning to the analysis team to identify opportunities for improvement. A good analyst is an essential ingredient to a successful call center.

Analysts in your call center primarily do two things:

1. Track and report results, and

2. Analyze the results and report on opportunities for improvement.

Good analysts help to ensure that your call center departments are hitting their targets and constantly improving on all business goals, and they provide the feedback that your call center management needs to steer the course — similar to way the gauges on an airplane provide feedback to the pilot.

As I mentioned in Chapter 3, the analysts in call centers are getting increasingly sophisticated. It's not unusual to find an analyst with an advanced degree in engineering, business, or math. Call centers are also investing in programs and training, such as Six Sigma, for their existing analysts. (I talk more about quality programs like Six Sigma in Chapter 13.)

Understanding and improving performance isn't the concern of just the call center analyst. Ideally, everyone in the call center is concerned with performance and the numbers. This chapter includes basic information that should be understood and practiced by as many people in the call center as possible — certainly by all management.

Adding It Up: Call Center Math

I'll keep this simple, I promise. As a matter of fact, most of the math that you'll use in call centers every day is very simple. Sure, you can get real fancy, using all sorts of sophisticated techniques like multiple regression, but I've found that not only are these not needed very often, but when they are our egghead analyst is only too excited to do the work and translate the results into English.

Most call center analyses and mathematical models can be done with some fairly basic concepts. You'll need to have a basic understanding of

- ✔ Percentages and cumulative percentages
- ✔ Averages and weighted averages
- ✔ Standard deviation
- ✔ Simple charts, such as bar charts and pie charts
- ✔ Charts that illustrate variation, such as control charts and run charts

I'll discuss these tools in greater detail, as needed, whenever they come up throughout the book.

Using mathematical models — Look what I can do!

Once you've established your objectives and understand what is needed to achieve them, then you can use mathematical models to figure out what levels to aim for, or to create and analyze "what if" scenarios in costs per contact, cost per customer, the call center budget, and other measures.

Being able to model call center outputs is very powerful. Ultimately, if you can use the drivers to create an economic model of your operation, you will have gained a lot of valuable insight into how your call center works.

Calculating contacts per hour

For example, contacts per hour is easily modeled using occupancy and average call length with the following formula:

Contacts per hour = Occupancy × 3,600 ÷ Call length (in seconds)

Note: 3,600 is the number of seconds in an hour. So if your call center's occupancy is 75 percent and the call length is 360 seconds, then contacts per hour will be 7.5:

75% × 3,600 ÷ 360 = 7.5

You can see from this model that to increase contacts per hour, you simply have to reduce call length or increase occupancy.

Analyzing the Appropriate Objectives

Your call center's business objectives are generally grouped into four areas of business need: revenue generation, cost control, customer satisfaction, and employee satisfaction.

In Chapter 2 I discuss the call center mission and how it is a function of what the business needs from the call center. I also discuss how concrete, measurable business objectives flow from the call center mission. In this section I review various ways to target and measure these business needs, and the variables that have a direct effect on your call center's performance — the performance drivers. Table 5-1 summarizes the relationships among the four areas of responsibility, the business objectives that measure performance in these responsibilities, and the performance drivers that affect results.

Table 5-1	Business Objectives, Measures, and Corresponding Drivers	
Business Objectives	*Business Measures*	*Performance Drivers*
Revenue generation	Total revenue generation	Conversion per contact
	Revenue per contact	Dollar value per conversion
	Revenue per customer	
Cost management	Department budget	Occupancy
	Cost per contact	Cost per agent hour
	Cost per customer	Call length
	Cost per resolution	Contacts per customer
		Agent utilization
Customer satisfaction	High customer satisfaction survey scores	Accessibility
		Agent call quality
		First-call resolution
Employee satisfaction	High employee satisfaction survey score	Valuing the work
		Supervisor support
		Recognition
		Environment

Business-Objective Measurements

As I discuss in Chapter 2, business objectives are the desired outputs of the call center — what the corporation needs from the call center by way of revenue generation, cost management, and customer satisfaction.

Many organizations add employee satisfaction as a business need. Some because they believe that it's part of their obligation as a socially responsible employer to provide a quality work environment; others because they believe that maintaining high employee satisfaction is a good business practice — happy employees are productive employees. This makes a lot of sense, particularly given that recent research tells us there is a link between happy employees and satisfied customers. I guess happiness is contagious!

Here, I outline some common ways to measure whether your call center business objectives are being met.

Call center operating budget

As with most business units, the operating budget is a critical business planning mechanism. The message is fairly simple when it comes to budgets — "Don't exceed it, and if you can beat it, that would be great!"

The operating budget is the sum of all the costs associated with running a call center for a given period, usually a year. The largest cost in the call center budget is typically labor. Budgets are based on assumptions about the number of calls that the call center will receive, how long those calls will be, and how fast the phone is to be answered. These assumptions are used to determine how many agent, management, and support staff are needed. In Chapters 6 and 7, I discuss how to calculate labor requirements.

Companies need operating budgets, and managing to a budget can help the company achieve its goals. Very effective call center managers have a great deal of control over their costs and can generally tell you how much they'll spend in any month — long before the finance department produces an expense report.

Budgets do, however, have their limits. Meeting or beating an operating budget doesn't tell you if you've been very efficient or if your general business activity was lighter than planned. In a growing company, operating budgets for call centers generally go up. An increasing budget doesn't tell you much about whether you are running the call center more efficiently than you did last year.

Also, managing strictly to an operating budget isn't always a good idea. I think most people would agree that if demand for your product greatly exceeded the demand that your call center budget planned for, and as a result your call center was swamped with people who wanted your product, then exceeding your budget to accommodate these purchasers might be a good thing.

Modeling the call center budget

Modeling the call center budget is very useful. It gives you the opportunity, through "what if" scenarios, to see the real impact changes to various drivers will have on the bottom line. The following formula is a simplified version of the call center budget model. It also provides an easy way for everyone in the operation to do a simple cost–benefit analysis.

Call center budget = Customer base × Forecasted calls per customer × Average call length ÷ Planned occupancy at service level × Cost per hour

For example, assume the following:

✔ Number of customers (customer base): 1 million

✔ Forecasted calls per customer (annual): 1.0

✔ Average call length: 360 seconds

✔ Planned occupancy at service level: 75%

✔ Cost per hour: $45.00

Call center budget = 1 million × 1.0 × 360 ÷ 3,600 ÷ 75% × $45.00 = $6.0 million

Assume for a moment that you were able to reduce call length by 30 seconds. Your new calculation for the department budget is

Call center budget = 1 million × 1.0 × 330 ÷ 3,600 ÷ 75% × $45.00 = $5.5 million

In this case, reducing call length by 30 seconds translates into a $500,000 savings. Perhaps management is planning to make some significant changes to the call-handling process, or introduce call-control training, or perhaps introduce some new software that streamlines how information is retrieved. Either way, being able to do a quick calculation on the impact of changing the drivers goes a long way to motivating management to find ways to make improvements.

The tricky part is in knowing what occupancy levels will be when you hit service-level targets. (I talk more about occupancy earlier in this chapter, and I talk about forecasting in Chapter 6.) This is easier than it may seem.

Look at your results over time and determine what occupancy level you typically hit when you're at the service level target. This gives you a benchmark that you can improve upon. It's simple, but effective.

It also helps to know what your optimal occupancy is. I discuss this in Chapter 7.

Cost per contact

Cost per contact is a useful measure because it tells you how much it costs every time a customer contacts you or you contact a customer. It tells you something about your call center's cost control, and if cost per contact is getting lower your boss is probably happy.

It doesn't tell the whole story, however. If your call center's cost per contact is low because your agents are rushing off calls to keep their call length low, or if you have a very high percentage of repeat calls, then cost per contact can be masking a problem.

Cost per contact is calculated by dividing the total costs to run the call center for a period of time by the total contacts responded to in the same period. Remembering the concern about short calls and repeat calls, this is one of those measures that you want to see get better over time. Figure 5-1 illustrates a run chart of cost per contact over a period of time.

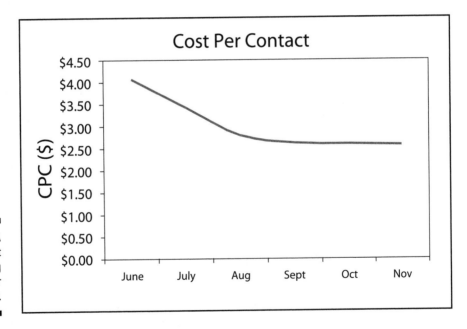

Figure 5-1: A run chart illustrating cost per contact.

Run charts

A run chart is one of the simplest statistical tools to use and understand. It is a line graph that shows data points plotted in the order in which they occur. Run charts are great because they illustrate trends — hopefully good trends. Ahhhh, yes ... I could stare at run charts all day.

Simply chart any data point, such as how long your new agent Sally's calls are over a period of time, and voilà — instant analysis.

Although it's not a common practice for run charts in general, you'll find it helps to illustrate control limits on a run chart when tracking an agent's performance. When the control limits are included, it's much easier to compare the individual's performance to the trend of the group, and to see exactly how much variation has changed over time.

Determining cost per contact

Using the formula for contacts per hour, and taking it a step further provided you know your cost per hour, it is easy to calculate cost per contact:

Cost per contact = Cost per hour ÷ Contacts per hour

For example, if your cost per hour is $45.00 and your contacts per hour are 7.5, then your cost per contact is $6.00. To reduce this, you have to reduce your cost per hour (maybe by improving agent utilization, as I discuss later in this chapter) or increase calls per hour (perhaps by improving occupancy).

Models are powerful, in that they provide a simple but effective way to create and experiment with "what if" scenarios. Models provide an exceptional way for doing cost–benefit analyses, and in many cases for helping you get what you want — like that corner office and key to the executive lunchroom. Nudge, nudge, wink, wink!

Cost per customer

Cost per customer is a good measure that addresses the problems with cost per contact, as long as you have a finite customer base. It's more telling than cost per contact as it takes into account repeat calls. Cost per customer is calculated by dividing the total cost of running the call center for a period of time by the average number of customers for the same time frame.

If your cost per customer is constantly getting lower it means your overall call center costs are going down — and you can bet you are definitely being talked about in the executive lunchroom.

Cost per resolution

I recently came across this measure, and what a great business objective measure it is! Cost per resolution recognizes that sometimes customer issues are not satisfied in a single contact. It also recognizes that customers sometimes call back because of new issues.

Cost per resolution can be difficult to calculate because it's difficult to track unique issues, but with customer management software, which tracks customer contacts and unique issues, it can be done. If you have these data, divide total costs for the period by the cases resolved. Again, what you're looking for is improvement over time.

Total revenue generation

Total revenue generation is similar to the call center operating budget in that it is included in the regular, probably annual, planning process. If yours is a revenue-generating call center, then you may think of it as a profit center. Like an operating budget, total revenue generation lacks in clarity. Certainly, as a company grows you'd expect the call center to generate more revenue.

Your finance or marketing department will calculate total revenue generated. They'll probably make an estimate about the number of sales inquiry calls that you're going to get for the period. They'll also estimate the percentage of these inquiries that your agents convert into sales, and the average value of these sales.

Beating the revenue generation target is a good thing, but you don't know how good until you put it into the context of how many customers called the call center. If customer calls exceeded your plan by 100 percent and revenue generation exceeded plan by only 50 percent, then the outlook on revenue generation might not be so good.

Revenue per contact

This is a fairly good measure of how much revenue your call center agents are bringing in per contact — the higher the better.

Again, this is simple to calculate: divide total revenue generated by the call center for a period of time by the number of contacts for the same period.

Revenue per contact is a nice activity measure in that it offsets cost per contact. I like to include the impact of customer cancellations in the revenue per contact measure to arrive at net revenue per contact. When measuring revenue per contact at the agent level, you get an understanding of who's doing best at maximizing all revenue opportunities, including sales and retention opportunities.

Include all calls when you're calculating revenue per contact. Don't make an attempt to qualify which calls to count ("Well, if you take calls made to wrong numbers out, my conversion rate goes way up!"). In the world of call centers, everyone gets the same percentage of misdirected or non-revenue opportunity calls. Qualifying which calls count and which ones don't introduces subjectivity, interpretation, and error into the measure. Use all calls — it's the same for everyone.

Revenue per customer

Revenue per customer provides a nice comparison to cost per customer, giving your call center a good visible contribution to the organization on a per-customer basis. Like cost per customer, revenue per customer is calculated by dividing total revenue generated for a period of time by the average number of customers over the same time frame.

If you can manage to constantly reduce cost per customer and constantly increase revenue per customer, then you're looking the good life right in the eye — corner office, parking space, key to the executive lunchroom, it's all yours.

Customer satisfaction scoring

Yes, yes, of course customer service is important, but not just because your mother, or the President of the United States, or the Queen of England plans to call. Customer satisfaction is a driver of future business.

At the very least, a *lack* of customer satisfaction is a primary cause for loss of future business. You certainly don't want the call center to be the reason why customers stop doing business with your company, so at a minimum delivering good customer service will keep you out of trouble.

In some cases, call centers provide such great service that callers say, "Wow, thanks!" If you can do this often enough that the call center actually increases the number of customers your company has, then you can forget the executive lunchroom — you'll be able to afford to eat out ... a lot.

Measuring customer satisfaction can be a challenge. Many call centers rely on supervisor assessments of agent calls. Here, the supervisor listens to recorded phone conversations between agents and customers. I'm sure you've heard the recorded message, "this call may be monitored for quality purposes" — this is what that recording is referring to.

This type of assessment — or call monitoring, as it is frequently called — has a number of challenges. First, supervisors can't possibly assess enough calls to get an accurate view of call quality. In most operations, supervisors might listen to three to five calls for each of their agents in any month. That's not a lot. Secondly, even if the supervisor could listen to enough calls, the assessment of the quality of these calls is usually based on management's subjective idea of what makes a good call. It's hard to get two managers to agree on these criteria. Only the customer knows if he or she was happy.

Employee satisfaction scoring

Employee motivation is a complex topic, which I'm not going to dive into too deeply here. Suffice to say that it's important to give it a lot of attention, make it one of your business objectives, and do lots of things to make it better.

A good place to start measuring employee satisfaction is with regular surveys. I like to see these surveys done once per month.

Some will suggest that a quarterly or semi-annual survey is more appropriate. I can't agree with this. You certainly wouldn't measure cost-per-call performance semi-annually. So why measure employee satisfaction any less often than your other business objectives? More frequent measurement of employee satisfaction gives the call center the ability to track not only progress but also the impact of initiatives that are designed to improve employee satisfaction.

I suggest that you include a few consistent questions in the monthly survey, like, "Do you like working here?" or "Do you find your supervisor to be helpful?" In addition to these, you can add a few "questions of the month" to drill down into issues.

In our call centers we use a Web-based survey that can be edited and launched on a moment's notice. The survey includes room for employees to write in their recommendations and concerns. Participation is confidential, something that I think is important to foster open dialogue. The application automatically tabulates results and produces trend data on overall satisfaction and satisfaction relative to the individual questions.

Like all other measures, you're looking for a high level of performance in employee satisfaction. A bad score can, and should, be cause for concern and quick action.

Improvement — graphs that go up — is what you're looking for.

Affecting employee satisfaction

A lot has been written on employee satisfaction and how to improve it. I'm not going to rehash that discussion here, except to identify some of the basics.

Here are some things that will keep your employees happy:

- ✔ **They value the work.** It makes a big difference if you hire employees who like the job and want to continue doing it. No job is for everyone, and if you hire someone because they need some quick cash, then you run the risk of having an employee whom you can't motivate. I discuss recruiting in Chapter 10.

- ✔ **They get the supervisor support they need.** One of the biggest turnoffs in call centers, or anywhere, is not being able to get help when you need it. Time and again I've been struck by the importance to employee satisfaction of having a competent staff of supervisors.

- ✔ **They get recognition for doing a good job.** This is part of valuing the work. If they do something truly good, employees want someone to notice it.

- ✔ **They feel that the environment is positive.** This can include so many things, like culture, having friends to work with, clean carpets, adequate lighting, and so on.

All of these drivers, and others, can be measured on your employee opinion survey.

It's a good idea to also ask open-ended questions on your survey to determine what in your operation is important to your employees. Once you have a good idea of what's important and what isn't working, you can make changes.

Performance Drivers: Managing the Results

As I discuss in Chapter 2, performance drivers are variables that have an impact on your call center's business objectives.

They're called performance drivers because, like a person who manages the controls of a car, or like the programs that make computer equipment work, drivers are things that make other things go. In this case, performance drivers make business objectives go.

Statisticians might think of the relationship between business-objective measurements and performance drivers in terms of dependent variables (business-objective measurements) (y) and independent variables (performance drivers) (x), giving rise to the relationship $y = f(x)$ — y is a function of x. For example, budgets are a function of call length, among other things.

Determining who has influence over the performance drivers

The models I discuss in this chapter show that the measures you identify really do drive results, especially in the very measurable goals of cost and revenue. Understanding this is just the beginning, however; it's making results happen that counts!

A key component to controlling and manipulating outcomes is to designate responsibility throughout the organization — most importantly to the call center agents, because each agent is a microcosm of the operation.

Table 5-2 shows how to track and improve results on the agent level. Individual agent improvement pulls up improvement in overall average agent performance, which in turn drives overall improvement in the call center.

Table 5-2	Measures at the Agent Level
Call Center Drivers	*Agent-Level Drivers*
Cost per hour of agent time	Wage rate
Agent utilization (L/P)	Schedule adherence
Call length	Call length
Contacts per customer	
First-call resolution	First-call resolution
Occupancy	N/A
Conversion per contact	Conversion per contact
Dollar value per conversion	Dollar value per conversion
Accessibility	N/A
Agent professionalism and ability	Agent professionalism and ability

One of the first things you'll notice when viewing the table is that some measures — the ones that cannot be influenced or controlled by the actions of agents — do not correlate with agent-level measures, since they're not considered agents' responsibilities. For example, occupancy and service level are group measures that individual agents cannot control. Nor can agents directly control company policies and procedures.

You'll also notice that cost per hour becomes wage rate at the agent level, because apart from their wage, which directly correlates to them, agents cannot generally control any other costs.

Lastly, the call center driver agent utilization is measured as schedule adherence at the agent level. *Schedule adherence* is the percentage of expected phone time that agents are actually on the phones. A low schedule adherence basically signifies unexplained absences during an agent's phone shift.

When agents have a low schedule adherence it means they were on the phones less than expected, directly impacting agent utilization (L/P) — the percentage of time agents were on the phone compared to their paid time.

The goal is to work to help agents achieve continuous improvement in the areas for which they are responsible.

Wherever possible, break the drivers down into the smallest unit of measure that you can stand. For example, break call length down into talk time and after-call work. If you can break these down further, say, by contact type, that's even better.

Tracking them at an agent level is just another way of breaking down the data so you can understand the driver better.

There are probably hundreds of performance drivers that impact a call center's results. A big part of an analyst's job is to identify these relationships and gain a better and better understanding of how the relationships between business objectives and performance drivers work. What I look at in this section are the big ones, the variables that have the biggest impact on call center results. Master these, and you'll develop a great deal of control.

Occupancy

Occupancy refers to how busy call center agents are while they're logged in to the company phone system. It is one of the most important performance drivers in the call center and has a large impact on cost control.

Occupancy is calculated as the percentage of call center agents' *logged time* — the time agents spend logged in to the telephone system — where the agent was busy and unavailable to accept customer calls. It's the opposite of idle percentage — time that agents spent waiting for customer calls.

What is logged time?

It's very important that everyone in the call center is very clear on and in agreement with what it means to be logged in to the phone system. Agents should be logged in whenever they're handling customer calls. This includes all work states associated with handling calls: talking to the customer, having the customer holding, doing after-call work, or waiting for the next call.

When agents are at work but not handling customer calls, they should not be logged in to the phone system. Agents should log out for breaks, meetings, training, and so on.

Reserving telephone logged time exclusively for time spent handling customer calls makes it much easier to keep the data associated with call handling clean. Some disagree, arguing that the phone system can track many uses of agent time. I've found that, invariably, when agents stay logged in to the phones for non–call handling reasons, it becomes unclear what time was for call handling and what time was for breaks. You can find other ways to track agent time. Keep logged time pure.

Agents can be doing a number of things to be considered occupied. This includes talking to customers, researching customer issues while the customer is on hold, and working on customer files after the customer has hung up. This final occupied state is referred to as after-call work and is tracked by a button on the agent's phone that tells the system the agent is temporarily unavailable to accept calls.

One of the most important relationships to understand is that between occupancy and how fast you answer the phone. A general rule is that the faster you answer (you have lots of agents waiting for customer calls), the more occupancy decreases. If you answer the phone more slowly (customers have to wait for "the next available agent"), occupancy increases.

The other key relationship is between occupancy and the size of your call center. The rule here is that the larger the call center, the higher the occupancy is at any service level. Pick a day when you come close to your service level earlier or later in the day — when volumes are low. Then compare this to a busy time of day when your service level was approximately the same. You should note that the occupancy was higher during the busier part of the day. Cool, huh? Many strategic call center location and amalgamation decisions are made based on this dynamic.

Dealing with random call arrival

Why isn't occupancy 100 percent? Wouldn't that be more efficient? Unless your call center is getting swamped with calls — making customers wait a long time before getting to a live agent (at least you hope they're still alive), occupancy will never be 100 percent. In fact, often occupancy is nowhere near 100 percent.

Occupancy of 65 to 75 percent is not uncommon. The reason for this is, as we say in the business, the random nature of call arrivals. To put it simply, customer calls come in bunches.

This probably won't come as a surprise, but customers do not contact each other before calling your call center to arrange themselves in a nice sequential order. "You call at 9:00 and be done by 9:04, because then Betty will be calling...."

As I discuss in great detail in Chapter 7, the call arrival pattern in a typical call center is spikey, random. Imagine if this were a chocolate factory and the spikes represented chocolates coming off a conveyor belt, which it's your job to wrap. If you were left alone, you'd probably miss a lot of the chocolates, especially during the spikes in chocolate arrival. If it were important that you didn't miss any, you'd call for a few friends to help you catch and wrap all the chocolates. Now, you and your friends don't miss any chocolates, but for the most part you're not very busy. In fact, it's very slow on the chocolate wrapping line during the valleys in chocolate arrival.

It's exactly like this in call centers. Calls arrive in bunches. Too few people, and you miss calls. Add people so you don't miss calls, and your staff spends time waiting around.

Each caller makes a decision to contact the call center independent of other callers. As a result, the calls arrive randomly, often in bunches. The impact of this call arrival pattern is that you can't just staff the phones to handle the average number of calls arriving in any time period — the peaks will kill you, just like in our chocolate example. To answer all calls reasonably quickly, you must staff above the average number of calls and closer to the peaks in caller demand.

The difference between the workload represented in the calls you receive, and the actual amount of staff used to answer those calls, is waiting (idle) time for your call center agents.

If you want to answer customer calls quickly, you have to have some agent idle time. Conversely, if you want your call center agents to be more productive (increasing occupancy) you need to staff fewer agents, reducing idle time and making your customers wait for an agent.

Oh, and don't let anyone tell you that you can't set an occupancy target. You can! As I discuss in Chapter 7, there is a difference between optimal occupancy (what you'd achieve with perfect scheduling) and expected occupancy (what you get with the imperfect schedules we humans work). Getting closer to optimal is a goal of every scheduler and is achieved through better, more flexible schedules. In large call centers even a 1-percent improvement will add up to significant savings.

Occupancy as a driver of cost

So, how does occupancy affect your cost objectives? For any given caller demand, you can easily determine how much work the demand represents. For example, if you're going to get 10 calls in a half hour and each takes an average of 3 minutes to handle, some quick math tells us that we have 30 minutes of work to do. In half an hour, that's one person. But this assumes that our worker will be 100-percent occupied. If calls arrive at all randomly — and you know they will — some callers won't get an immediate answer. If it's very important that you answer calls quickly, you'll have to add another person. The second person should make sure that calls get answered quickly enough, but with only 30 minutes of work and two people, your occupancy has fallen from 100 to 50 percent, and your cost of answering these calls has doubled.

You can't get away from it: you have to consider occupancy when planning the call center. But you can manage it and maximize it — that's what makes it such a powerful driver of cost.

Cost per agent hour

Cost per agent hour is another very powerful variable, and an important one for call center managers to know and understand. It amounts to the total cost of operating your call center for an hour of telephone-logged time. It's calculated by dividing total call center cost for a period of time by the total hours logged in to the phone system for the same period.

You'll need to track cost per agent hour over time, as it fluctuates with call volume. However, this is a measure that you can control, and if you do you'll gain a great deal of control over the cost-management objectives in your call center.

Once you've calculated your cost per agent hour there are a number of things you can do, the first of which is to gain a better understanding of the result. A better understanding of your number will come from breaking the total cost per hour down into component parts. How much is agent labor, how much is benefits, how much is management, how much is rent, and so on.

Next, you may want to benchmark against other organizations if you can. By benchmarking, you'll get a feel for whether your results are high or low, keeping in mind that you may not be in the same industry or may not provide services comparable to the company you are benchmarking with. Through benchmarking, you may find that you're doing well or you may find that you can improve — if you do find others who are running good operations with a lower cost per agent hour at least you'll have an idea of what's possible. It's a good idea to benchmark with outsourcers, too. They know their cost per agent hour number only too well and have it squeezed down tight.

Most of the variables that I discuss here are influenced by variables of their own. Cost per hour is no exception. Some of the key variables that impact cost per agent hour are average wage rate, benefits, and something I call "logged hours over paid hours" — "L over P" for short; "L/P" for even shorter.

Logged/paid (L/P)

L/P refers to the total logged time by all call center agents divided by the total payroll hours for the same period. If you aren't familiar with L/P, you should be. Some might call this agent utilization. It's a ratio that illustrates the overall productivity of your call center. I've seen L/P ratios in call centers range from below 50 percent to more than 80 percent.

In a large operation that I recently helped, a 1-percent increase in L/P reduced total call center expenditures by approximately $1 million, or approximately 2 percent of total budget — something worth considering.

The best way that I know to manage L/P is to account for all the time that does not end up as time spent on the phones — the difference between L/P and 100 percent. If you haven't looked at it before, I'll bet you find there are savings to be had.

Call length

Call length is a major building block in the call center. Together with call volume and service level (speed of answer) desired, it tells you how big to build your operation, how many people are needed, how many desks are needed, how large a phone system is needed, how many phone lines are needed, and so on.

Call length is also one of the most powerful measures in the call center. It's a little controversial in that some believe too much focus is put on call length without appropriate attention to other measures. The concern is that an over-focus on call length will lead to agents feeling pressured to reduce call times, which will result in reductions in customer service.

I agree that too great a focus on hard and fast benchmarks for call length can be harmful and inappropriate; but I also believe that no other measure can tell you as much about your operation as call length — it's a mirror of process.

One thing that our internal research has told us is that customers want the same thing that call centers do — a quick, accurate, and complete resolution to their problem or inquiry. Very long call times cause me concern because I have to wonder if customers are getting what they want. Frequently, you find that very long calls are the result of very complex problems.

Your efforts to improve call-handling processes and reduce call length not only save the call center money, but also make for more satisfied customers — provided that the lower call length is accompanied by equal or better service and call resolution.

Short call length also worries me. Again, I wonder if we are fully serving the customer. Usually short calls are the result of simple problems, but sometimes the call-handling process does not allow agents to fully support customers. In these cases I'd like to see call length go up — along with customer satisfaction and call resolution.

Calculating call length

Call handling is a complex process. Phone systems need to accommodate the many varying preferences different users have for specific call-handling processes. As a result, call-length calculations that come out of phone systems can sometimes be over- or under-stated.

Here's a calculation that I've used for years that makes for a nice consistent measure of call length — one that you can use with confidence for analysis and scheduling. Take all the time that your agents are logged in to the phones, subtract the time that they are waiting for calls, then divide this by the number of calls answered. Express this in seconds. I call this "call service time," or CST. You may find that this is slightly different from the average handle time (AHT) reported by your phone system because of the different ways that phone systems calculate AHT.

Bar chart/histogram

Bar charts are great for showing you how one thing compares to another, or how frequently something occurs. In your call center, you could chart calls received by day of the week, or types of calls received by day, as shown in this handy bar chart.

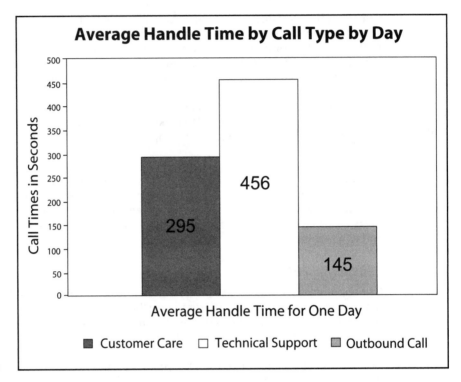

Figure 5-2:
Tracking average call length by call type.

Track your call times by the different types of calls you take. Once you know what the longest call type is, map out the flow of a typical call of that type. After you've done that, try to map out a different way to handle this type of call that wouldn't take as long. When you've done that, continue to track the length of this call type — hopefully, you'll see some improvements. Then move on to the next call type. Over time, you'll definitely increase cost control and customer satisfaction.

Contacts per customer

Contacts per customer is another useful measure for forecasting and tracking call center cost control over time. Tracking the number of contacts per customer on a monthly or daily basis and then multiplying that by the current number of customers gives a very useful forecast of call volume demand.

Reducing contacts per customer is a primary goal for driving cost control for many service or support call centers, because the more times a customer calls, the more total calls you have to take and the more agents you need to schedule to handle the calls. Of course, if customers buy something from you every time they call, you may not be too concerned if they call a lot.

Reducing or eliminating errors and unnecessary callbacks plays a major role when you're striving for improvements in cost control. *First-call resolution* — the percentage of callers who do not have to call back within a certain time frame (usually a day) to have their issue resolved — is a useful measure that I talk about in this chapter.

Conversion per contact

Let me make sure I'm clear here. A *contact* is any time you say hello (via the phone, e-mail, chat, whatever). A *conversion* is any time you generate or save revenue on a contact.

When it comes to conversion, higher is better. Period. Full stop. I don't care if the customer just called to ask you what time the store in Upper Rubber Boot is open, if you managed to sell him something when he called it's a good thing. Conversion is always good — more is always better.

In most call centers, the opportunity associated with improving conversion per contact is big, big, big! A lot of time in call centers is spent finding ways to improve this variable. Conversion per contact affects total revenue generated and other revenue objectives.

Dollar value per conversion

Would you like fries with that? It's one thing to make lots of sales, given the total universe of opportunities. It's another thing to make lots of *big* sales. The terms "upsell" and "cross sell" address this variable. If we can make bigger sales, or tag on more cross sells, then this variable will increase, increasing total revenue generated, revenue per customer, revenue per call, and so on.

Accessibility

I'm using the term *accessibility* here because the call center industry is so messed up. It has 100 ways to describe how fast you answer the phone. Accessibility means how easy it is for callers to get through — it's how fast you're answering the phone, and it's important because it has an impact on customer satisfaction and cost control.

Accessibility is also a planning consideration for call centers. A well-selected accessibility target will balance customer satisfaction with the cost of providing that level of accessibility. Accessibility affects cost by influencing how many agents will be needed for any particular level of demand. As a result, accessibility has an influence on cost through occupancy.

Here are three common measures, of the many, used to calculate accessibility:

- ✔ **Service level:** Service level is probably the most common term used to define accessibility. It refers to the percentage of callers whose calls are answered or who hang up within a defined time. For example, if your time threshold is 20 seconds, you may have a service-level objective of answering 85 percent in 20 seconds. Meaning, your objective is to answer 85 percent of all calls within the first 20 seconds of the calls arriving at the center.

Just to keep you on your toes, service level is sometimes referred to as *telephone service factor* — TSF. When this term is used, the target number of seconds — the 20 in 85/20 — is referred to as the TSFT — *telephone service factor threshold.* Oh, boy.

The nice thing about service level is that you can get a very specific measure, which can be especially useful when you take the time to research the cost and benefit of service-level objectives.

- ✔ **Average speed of answer:** Also known as ASA, this refers to the average amount of time your customers waited in queue before an agent greeted them. Generally speaking, lower is better.

- ✔ **Abandonment rate:** Abandonment rate refers to the percentage of callers that hung up before an agent answered their call. This isn't really a very good service-level measure; it's more a measure of customer satisfaction. If your customers are hanging up a lot, guess what? They don't like the speed of your service. If they aren't hanging up much, then you're probably okay.

Be careful, however, with this guideline. If customers are not hanging up in circumstances where they normally would because they absolutely *must* speak with you, then making them hold through a long delay can result in some nasty exchanges between frustrated customers and overworked agents.

Agent professionalism and ability

Agent ability is a little harder to nail down, but it's probably the most important requirement in achieving customer nirvana. Whether calling a contact center or shopping for new shoes, most customers expect the same thing of the customer-service people they deal with: know what you're talking about, and be nice!

The customer satisfaction surveys that we discussed earlier will certainly help you find out how capable your agents are. Customers will tell you about the agents who aren't nice or who can't do their job. When you ask the right questions, customers will also tell you specifically what your company needs to improve at. This learning can make for excellent training material.

As I mention earlier in this chapter, many call centers will have people listen to agent calls to determine if their agents are professional and capable; this is frequently referred to as "call assessment" or "call monitoring." When listening to these calls, the evaluator will score the agent calls against a template of key call behaviors. I discuss call monitoring a little more along with general call-handling tools in Chapter 15.

Call monitoring and scoring is a good practice, but it's a really good idea to survey customers first to determine what's important to them. Saying the customer's name three times, as per Dale Carnegie, might not be as important as giving the customers a quick, courteous answer and allowing them to get off the phone and get on with their lives. The customer rules. Long live the customer!

First-call resolution

First-call resolution (FCR) refers to the percentage of customer inquiries that are completed on the first attempt. If customers have to call back once or many times because the call center did not resolve their inquiry or concern the first time, then FCR will decline.

It's somewhat difficult to track this driver, because the call center must keep track of everyone who called, and why they called. This may sound easy enough, but with hundreds or thousands of calls arriving every day it can be a challenge.

Tracking first-call resolution is made easier through the use of customer tracking software.

The benefits of tracking first-call resolution are large. Improving this measure has an impact on customer satisfaction — customers want the same thing we do, namely quick and accurate resolution to their problems and needs. It also improves cost control — improving first-call resolution will have an impact on calls per customer, reducing it as the number of repeat calls decreases. As you can see, the needs of the call center and the needs of the customer are frequently intertwined.

Company and call center policies and procedures

The drivers listed in this chapter aren't the only ones that influence your operation. A large part of your analyst's job will be learning how to identify and manipulate these and other drivers of call center performance. Once she has identified the variables that contribute to performance, she'll look to your company and call center policies and procedures to understand the process behind each driver.

Ultimately, process is where your call center will find the answers to how to control and improve your performance drivers. This is one of the reasons why it's wise to have detailed documentation of company policies and procedures — right down to how processes work. If your processes are well documented, then when you want to review the process you don't have to spend a lot of time researching it. In fact, the act of documenting a work process is an improvement exercise. As a work process is laid out on paper you or others might look at it and say, "Wow, that doesn't make any sense!" and change the process for the better. There's a lot more on process management in Chapter 12.

Setting Performance Targets

Setting performance targets is extremely important. People work better with very specific targets, while vague targets create vague results.

Unfortunately, my experience is that the setting of performance targets is generally poorly done (or not done at all) in many call center operations — probably because it's not easy to set effective targets. Oh sure, it's easy to say, "Hey, tomorrow I want you to answer 25 calls and I want you to make all the customers happy," but knowing if those targets are effective is another matter.

First, you have to figure out what's the right thing to target. After you've selected the thing to target, you've then got to determine what level of performance to expect for that target.

Setting a target that is too low will result in your operation underachieving. Setting a target that is too high will frustrate people in your operation. A big part of the challenge is in understanding that call centers (or any other business, for that matter) are the results of thousands of different inputs and processes.

Sorting out this mess and selecting the perfect performance targets requires a very big brain. I don't happen to have one of those, but here are some ideas that can help you use yours to set appropriate targets for some of the most important call center drivers.

Accessibility/service level

Here are some examples of methods you can use to set performance targets for service level.

Do what everyone else does

The default level of service for answering phone calls tends to be 80/20 (80 percent of calls are answered or hung up in 20 seconds or less). In most operations this will result in a relatively short average wait time for customers (8 to 18 seconds), and most customers will hang in there for that long.

While 80/20 is *good enough* for a lot of operations, you should note that the wait time on the other side of the "80" in 80/20 (that is, the 20 percent of people who wait more than 20 seconds) can be a long time — as much as one or two minutes or longer. That's not too bad if you're calling to claim your lottery winnings, but it probably doesn't satisfy the guy who calls 911 because his house is burning down.

E-mail and chat don't seem to currently have the same generally accepted default standards, perhaps because of their relative infancy.

Go with the industry direction

A number of industries are self-regulating or even government-regulated in terms of how fast call centers must answer the phone — cable TV comes to mind. Some regulated targets are aggressive; some are passive, depending on the industry and service. Choosing your service level this way is kind of like just going with the de facto standard — c'mon, get a spine!

Develop a business case

Do a cost–benefit analysis to determine your service-level objective — then you can claim you've got game. Actually, it's pretty simple. Work out the cost of providing faster service through a broad range of service levels: 50/20, 60/20, 70/20, 80/20, 85/20, 90/20 — you get the idea. Next, work out the benefits of providing faster service.

For example, more customers will get through to your call center (meaning they won't hang up and call the competition); when they do get through, they aren't grumpy; your agents aren't fraying at the edges from taking one call after another for eight hours (so, they don't call in sick, and don't take extra breathers between calls); and you aren't paying additional toll-free (800-line) costs for your customers to listen to a repeating loop of elevator music.

If you do this analysis well, you can find the break-even point between the cost of providing faster service and the benefit of providing that service.

In some cases you might have to make some assumptions, but even so, the target you come up with will have a strong business foundation that will help you justify your call center budget.

In Table 5-3, I illustrate a simple analysis you can use to determine your ideal service level. Here's an explanation of the information in the table, column by column.

To increase service level you need more agents on the phone, so staffing costs rise (staffing costs were estimated based on staff requirements calculated using an Erlang C calculator, as I discuss in Chapter 6). At the same time, abandonment rates decrease, because customers don't hang up due to a long delay. Additionally, fewer lost customers means less lost revenue. And, as you're answering the calls more quickly, the total length of customer wait time is decreased, so your telephone (800-line) costs decrease — another benefit to you.

So, incremental cost is simply incremental staffing cost associated with raising your service-level objective. The incremental benefit is measured by costs avoided — you take the incremental lost revenue avoided and add the incremental 800-line-delay costs avoided.

For example, look at the first two rows of figures in Table 5-3, representing a change of your service-level objective from 50/20 to 60/20. Staffing costs go from $200,000 to $220,000, an incremental cost of $20,000. Lost revenue (due to customers abandoning calls) goes from $180,000 to $120,000, an incremental benefit of $60,000. Additionally, 800-line-delay costs decreased from $2,100 to $1,733, an incremental benefit of $367. Adding these benefits together gives you a total incremental benefit of $60,367.

Analysis, then, is a matter of finding that sweet spot where the incremental cost is balanced by the incremental benefit. In this example, we'd probably recommend something along the lines of an 85/20 objective.

Table 5-3			An Analysis of Service-Level Targets			
Service Level	Staffing Cost	Abandonment Rate	Lost Revenue	800-Line-Delay Cost	Incremental Benefit	Incremental Cost
50/20	$200,000	18%	$180,000	$2,100	-	-
60/20	$220,000	12%	$120,000	$1,733	$60,367	$20,000
70/20	$244,000	8%	$80,000	$1,281	$40,452	$24,000
80/20	$270,000	5%	$50,000	$851	$30,430	$26,000
85/20	$290,000	3%	$30,000	$508	$20,343	$20,000
90/20	$320,000	2%	$20,000	$336	$10,172	$30,000

Call length

Ah, the age-old question that's been posed by call center mystics, gurus, and shamans for eons: "What is the correct benchmark for average call length?"

Answered honestly, I don't know. You can't know! *Way* too many variables, all of which are changing all the time, go into determining call length. Here are a few to consider:

- Product complexity
- System capabilities
- Responsiveness
- Availability
- Working environment
- Temperature
- Noise level
- Training
- Competitive environment
- Policies and procedures
- Work distractions

All of these, and many more, affect call length. Add to this the individual difference brought by each of your call center agents and you have a very complicated process. Identifying the one *right* call length is nearly impossible.

What you can — and should — do is try to understand as much about your own center's (or, more accurately, each of its own individual campaigns') call length as possible. Of course, you should also attempt to make call length as consistent as possible.

Gaining control by eliminating variation

Consider what would happen if your call center produced exactly the same call length day after day, and every agent produced the same call length as the others day after day. Then you could be fairly certain that the call length produced was the product of your defined work processes. You'd be certain that all agents were following the same processes day in and day out. You could then experiment with making changes to the work processes and measure the impact of those changes on the resulting call length. Do this enough and you'd have a great deal of understanding and control over call length, and the task of making improvements would be greatly simplified.

Unfortunately, it doesn't happen that easily. Most call centers see a great deal of variation in call length from one agent to another. Day after day — often, even hour after hour — your call center produces very different call lengths, making planning and process improvements difficult.

Using variation analysis

Start by plotting whatever it is you wish to analyze (usually, one of the drivers) on a control chart (Figure 5-3 illustrates an example). Next, identify those agents who are *out of band* — the ones who are above the upper control limit or below the lower control limit — and target them for coaching and follow-up.

The first step of your actual analysis is to look for differences. What are the things causing these agents to be statistical anomalies in this driver (metric)? If the differences are good things, teach them to others on the team. If they're bad things, beat them out of the agents (figuratively speaking, of course!). Remember, the overall goals of this analysis are to reduce variation and increase your understanding.

Note: This approach should be used with all agent metrics — first-call resolution, conversion rate — not just call length.

This doesn't mean you should throw in the towel, however. For planning purposes, like scheduling resources or creating your budget, simply use your call center's historical average call length. In Chapter 6, I provide details on how to do this.

To increase consistency and to help you reach your performance targets, use a process of variation analysis, understanding, and control to identify exceptions in overall operation performance and individual agent performance.

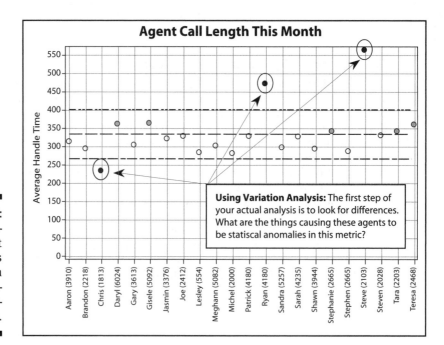

Figure 5-3: The control chart illustrates variation in individual's performance.

Agent Call Length This Month

Using Variation Analysis: The first step of your actual analysis is to look for differences. What are the things causing these agents to be statiscal anomalies in this metric?

If you feel it's necessary to have a specific target for call length, I'd suggest using the upper or lower control limit; whichever is easier to achieve — upper for call length, lower for conversion rate, for example. You'll need to make sure that these limits have been established for a reasonably long period; say, 90 days.

If something of consequence changes in your call center, impacting call length, the control limits will change and so should the target. The upper or lower control limit is the level of performance that most people — approximately 84 percent of the staff — are achieving. Many of those who are not achieving the lower limit will be just below it. Because the upper or lower limit is based on performance that the staff is actually achieving, it's a reasonable minimum target. Those who are just shy of it will be motivated to improve performance to the minimum.

Operationally, you should track the daily average call length on a run chart, along with the upper and lower limits at plus and minus one standard deviation, as Figure 5-4 illustrates. You're seeking understanding and control of the metric, so dive in to the exceptions — where the metric is exceptionally high or low, or where variation is greatest — to understand what happened and why.

For example, if you noticed that during a particular week call lengths increased significantly compared to previous weeks, maybe it was a week when you had a bunch of new hires on the phones, or the computer systems were slow, or you had a complicated billing problem that affected a lot of customers.

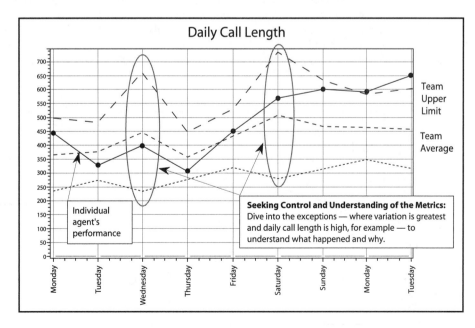

Figure 5-4: The run chart illustrates trends in variation.

Whatever the case, this analysis will help you to understand and quantify the impact of a lot of events — possibly using that understanding to justify changes to how your company works. This type of analysis and target-setting is useful with other metrics, including conversion, first-call resolution, and so on.

Occupancy

Occupancy is a tougher performance measure to get a handle on, but it's important to consider. Much debate exists among call center professionals on how to target and manage occupancy. Some believe that a good service-level target is sufficient — by achieving your service-level target, you've maximized opportunity. I would add that if your service-level target is well thought out — with a solid cost–benefit analysis — then achieving a consistent service level, as close to the objective as possible, is an effective and efficient way to run your operation.

When your actual service level is too high above the target, it's costing you too much in labor. If it's too far below the target it's costing you customer satisfaction, revenue, and other expenses. Cost control is balanced when service level is right on the target.

Maximizing occupancy and service level

Your goal is to maximize the occupancy you achieve while also reaching your target service level. The primary way you do that is through better scheduling. The more closely you can match the number of agents scheduled to the actual call load requirements, the more you reduce periods of under- or overstaffing. Figures 5-5 and 5-6 illustrate two ways — one good, and one bad — to achieve an 80/20 service level.

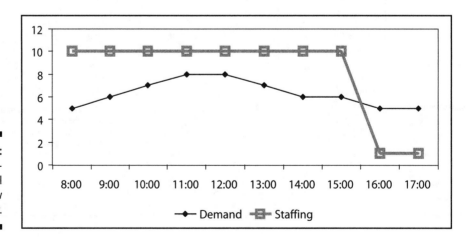

Figure 5-5:
Hitting service level with low occupancy.

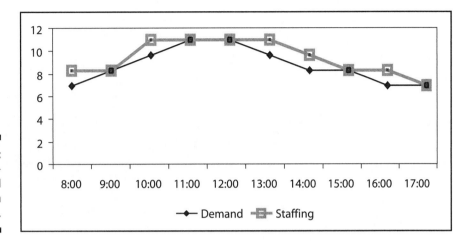

In each of the scenarios illustrated in these charts, at the end of the day the call center has achieved the target service level of 80/20 (80 percent of calls answered or abandoned in 20 seconds or less). In the first scenario — Figure 5-5 — they did this by achieving a very high service level (approaching 100 percent) for 80 percent of the day, while having a dreadful service level for the remainder of the day. In this case, occupancy would have been in the tank for that first 80 percent of the day, as the call center was way overstaffed during that time.

In Figure 5-6, on the other hand, the call center has met the service-level target by having an appropriate number of agents on the phones throughout the day, thereby maintaining a much higher occupancy.

Chapter 6

Right People, Right Place, Right Time: Resource Management

. . . .

. . . .

*I*f you're in the resource or scheduling department, your job is to ensure your call center has the right people, tools, and equipment in the right place and at the right time to support the service, revenue, and efficiency objectives of the call center as directed by the organization — via senior management (*les grands fromages*). A basic understanding of simple math will surely help you get the job done, but with the knowledge of just a few key concepts and processes you can become a call center resource management genius.

Understanding Resource Management Tasks and Concepts

Okay, relax. This won't hurt a bit. You need this stuff and it's easy. This is an overview of the key concepts and tools used in call center resource management — important for scheduling.

Forecasting

Similar to forecasting the weather (but with, one hopes, greater accuracy), forecasting in call centers refers to predicting the future — specifically, how much work your center is going to have.

The key is to accurately determine your workload and when you'll have it, so you can match available resources to demand. You've also got to forecast how much of different types of work you'll get and how long the work will take, because different types of work take different amounts of time.

Don't assume that the time it takes to process calls (or e-mails) is always the same. It makes sense that a very simple customer inquiry is likely to take much less time to process, on average, than a complicated, high-level technical support call. Contact length will fluctuate over time, as will call volume.

Scheduling

Scheduling is the process of assigning resources to meet your demand. Where forecasting provides the *how much* of resource management, scheduling answers the *who, what, where,* and *when.* I talk about scheduling in Chapter 7.

Full-time equivalent

Usually referred to by the short form FTE, *full-time equivalent* is a way to express how many people you'll need to schedule. Staffing requirements are expressed in terms of the number of people working full-time hours. In my company, in one day, one FTE equals 7.5 paid hours. (It might be slightly different in your company, say 7.0 or 8.0, but it is always equal to what a full-time employee works in one day.) Using my company as an example, if call demand required 750 total paid hours to get the work done for a day, this would equate to 100 FTEs.

Since not all your agents work full time, the actual number of staff scheduled is usually more than the number of full-time equivalents that are planned for.

Real-time management of resources

As the name suggests, real-time resource management refers to the process of managing call center resources *right now.* I provide a more detailed explanation later in this chapter and in Chapter 7, but, in essence, this refers to making the necessary ongoing changes from your original schedule based on real-life, up-to-the-minute changes in call volume and staff availability so that your call center achieves the best possible results each day.

Forecasting: Timing Is Everything

Resource management is a lot easier than people make it out to be. The math is straightforward, and projections for items like department budgets and staffing requirements can be done without complicated scheduling systems.

Determining how many resources are needed depends a great deal on the time frame in question. I recommend looking at four separate time frames when forecasting.

Long term: Budget and capital projections

Long-term planning is for requirements expanding beyond three months and up to a couple of years. In this phase, you forecast the demand on your call center and project the overall resources that you'll require: how many people, how many desks, how large the phone system needs to be, how much data access you'll need, and so on.

You'll use this forecasted information to develop operating budgets (how much money you'll need to spend *running* this pig) and capital budgets (how much money you'll need to spend *building* this pig).

Mid term: Creating the schedules

The long-term projection is where you determine how many people and desks you'll need, and the mid-term scheduling projection tells you when you'll need to use the people and equipment.

Typically, you should do this over a period that ranges from three months to one year — however long you think your schedules can reliably last. Some operations have schedules that last a few weeks at most, while others can keep a schedule together for a year or more.

During the mid-term scheduling phase, names get attached to schedules so you know (generally) who is going to work when.

Short term: Making adjustments

From the time you plan a schedule to the actual day of handling the calls, a lot of changes can happen. Changes to caller demand and changes to the availability of staffing are common. In the short-term projections, generally done approximately one week out, you adjust your schedules to accommodate any recent changes in demand or staffing availability.

Real time: Ch-ch-changes!

The easiest way to understand what the real-time resource is all about is to hear it from someone in the resource department in one of my call centers. Take it away, Suzie Queue:

"Okay, so the day begins and you start taking calls and, well, you might as well forget about all your great forecasting and scheduling work — things are a mess. It happens a lot, because forecasts are, like, never right.

"For example, this one day? There was a great party and a bunch of the staff still hadn't recovered from it so they called in sick. Totally rude! To make things worse, John in marketing had, like, put the world on sale and didn't tell anyone — what a loser. The phones were going berserk. So, tons of callers were waiting to get through and were, like, totally ticked off when they finally did. They were peaking, y'know? So, of course, they took a bunch of time telling the reps how ticked they were, and it was WAY too stressful, so everyone started taking extra breaks. Adam went home early, and everybody knew he was totally faking. Days like that are a total disaster. What are you supposed to do? I mean, you can't just leave. So instead, you do the forecasting thing all over.

"You just have to relax, take a look at the big picture, and ask yourself 'What's the rest of the day looking like? How bad's it gonna be?' After you know that, you can make changes that'll help with all the calls. You can cancel any meetings or training that's going on. You can ask the supervisors to go on the phones — as if they would, but you can ask. You can ask people already on the phones to work overtime. You can totally make a difference. It's way cool, ya know?"

Necessary and Useful Tools

In Chapter 7, I focus on the guts of doing the scheduling job — a job that can involve a lot of work, especially in larger call centers. Fortunately, many tools exist (some of which I outline here) that automate the scheduling function. Before you say, "Why didn't you tell me this before I read all this stuff?" I believe that good schedulers should understand how basic scheduling works, and know how to do it the old fashioned way — with paper, pencil, a calculator, and maybe an Erlang table or calculator. Armed with the core knowledge I provide in this chapter and the next, and the tools of the trade, great scheduling can happen.

Understanding Erlang C

Erlang C is a mathematical formula that helps to determine how many call center agents will be needed to meet forecasted demand. I'll spare you the actual formula, but it takes into consideration the expected call volume, call length, and desired service level to calculate the number of people required on the phones. What it really does for you is to calculate the occupancy of your agents so you don't have to estimate the level of occupancy in any half hour period.

I don't provide the Erlang C formula in this book; however, you can find Erlang C calculators and tables on the Internet.

A Great Dane started it all

Agner Karup Erlang was a scientist/statistical mathematician who was hired by the Copenhagen Telephone Company in 1908 to figure out, essentially, how many telephone lines (called *trunks* in telecom lingo) it would take to service a village full of folks with telephones.

Erlang realized there was no perfectly correct answer. At the extreme ends of the spectrum were two possibilities:

✔ Install just one line (trunk) and callers would just have to wait until it's available. This would be cheap to install, but the service provided would be dreadful.

✔ Install one trunk for each person who has a phone, so no one ever has to wait. In this case, service is awesome, but it would be incredibly expensive ... and nuts!

So, Erlang did detailed studies of telephone traffic and came up with a mathematical formula to evaluate the best possible scenario to balance cost and service. (He must have been a co-op student at some point.)

Since 1946, one basic unit (one hour) of telephone traffic has been known as an Erlang in honor of his work.

Planning with spreadsheets

Spreadsheets may just be the best tool ever created for the call center, and they're probably the most frequently used. Lots of scheduling systems are either professionally or home built in spreadsheet programs; Erlang C add-in utilities are also common.

The data reported in all the tables and illustrated on the respective graphs and charts throughout Chapter 7 are all easily managed using a simple spreadsheet program.

Using workforce-management software

If you have a very large call center, making manual scheduling a significant challenge, or if you'd just rather avoid doing any extra work, then you're in luck. The workforce management software business for call centers is alive and well. A large number of workforce management systems and providers exist and many of them are very good, even excellent. Many of these systems will do everything I describe in this chapter and the next — and more — including tracking of historical volumes and performance, forecasting, calculating staffing requirements (and doing what-if scenarios), creating work schedules, conducting a shift-bid, assigning agents to schedules, scheduling breaks, managing vacation and shift trades, identifying missing agents, and so on.

Forecasting is a valuable exercise and, done well, can save your company vast sums. So don't be surprised when you see the cost of some of these workforce management systems. The manufacturers know the value of their tools and the scheduling process. However, remember that the value is in the process of forecasting and not the tool. A great tool with a lousy forecaster won't do much good, but a good forecaster can make a great tool sing.

Forecasting the Amount of Work to Be Done

Long before you create staff schedules, you need to start by figuring out how much work needs to get done. The first step of the scheduling process (I talk about scheduling in Chapter 7) is to forecast the number of contacts expected, and the time required to handle those contacts for a given period of time. This is your workload demand.

Different call centers use lots of different ways to forecast. Some are simple and some are painfully complex. (Since this book isn't called *Call Centers For Mathematical Geniuses*, I won't be diving into tons of complex forecasting formulae. If that's what you're interested in, go get a book on quantitative methods and find a friend.)

The one thing I know for sure is that, whatever method you choose, your forecast will probably be wrong. How wrong it is will determine your success at planning resources effectively.

When forecasting, you have to forecast both the volume of calls (and e-mails, etc.), and their length, or processing time. When considered together, you'll arrive at a forecasted demand of workload, using the following formula.

Workload (or call load) = Call volume × Average call length

Understanding the difference between call volume and call load

It's a common mistake for newcomers to call center resource management concepts to equate the amount of work to be done with call volume. Here's an analogy to explain the difference.

Imagine you work for a company that distributes bricks. Basically, big trucks drop off lots of bricks that you then sort and load onto smaller trucks to be shipped out to construction sites for building homes, schools, hospitals, and so on. (Stay with me here … I'll get to the point, I promise.) Assume that you are the supervisor in charge. You know that on a particular day you and your team are going to have to handle a total *volume* of 10,000 bricks. Being a good supervisor, you also know that your brick distribution agents (your staff) can carry 1,000 pounds of bricks per day on average. So, how many agents do you need to schedule for the day?

If you said 10 agents, guess again. You can't know, because you haven't been given enough information! To determine how many staff you'll need, you have to account for the weight of the bricks. Think about it: if each brick weighs one pound each, then you'll have 10,000 pounds of *load* (volume = 10,000 bricks, average brick weight = 1 lb), meaning you will indeed require 10 staff (carrying 1,000 lbs each).

However, what if the bricks are 15 pounds each? That means your load is 150,000 pounds. You're gonna need to call some folks in for overtime!

Determining workload in the call center is essentially the same. It's not enough simply to forecast how many calls you'll be receiving. You also need to know the weight of each call, or, more accurately, the *load* of each individual call. The load of the individual call is just the average time it takes to complete a call.

So, overall workload in the call center is equal to call volume multiplied by average call length. And that's the information you need to really begin the process of forecasting staff.

A 5-percent increase in call length has the same impact on staffing demand as a 5-percent increase in call volume!

Before you're done your forecasting activity, you'll forecast the entire planning range — from long-term budgeting right down to the half-hour interval level (next Tuesday from 2:30 to 3:00 p.m., for example.)

Starting long: The first step in forecasting call volume

One approach for forecasting is to start with the long-term forecast and work down to the interval level.

A starting point is to consider the demand that you had last year. If last year your call center took 1,638,000 calls and you have no reason to believe that business level will change, then last year's volume is a good starting place.

You add a little insight into this forecast if you consider the trend year-over-year. If volume of work has increased by 10 percent every year for the last 10 years, then it would seem logical to assume that volume will increase this year by 10 percent.

A variation of this is to calculate the volume of calls you receive per customer. If you've consistently received 2.0 calls per customer over the last several years and you know that your customer base is increasing, then increase your demand forecast by the expected customer base increase.

Forecasted demand = contacts per customer × customer base expected

Of course, if you know of something that will materially change your volume of work, like a new product line or a bankruptcy, then you'd be wise to make an allowance for those factors in your forecast.

Breaking it down to the intervals

You can consider a long-term forecast to be annual or monthly; it's up to you and the specific dynamics of your situation. Wherever you choose to start, once you've made a long-term forecast you'll need to break it down into months, weeks, days, and half-hour intervals. To do these breakdown forecasts, which are simply the volume of calls for any period of time expressed as a percentage, you can use historical calling patterns.

Typical breakdown intervals include

- Monthly percentage of a year
- Daily percentage of a week
- Half-hourly (or hourly) percentage of a day

Table 6-1 shows the monthly percentage breakdown of call distribution, based on the actual call volumes from the previous year. These percentages are what you'll base the current year's call volume forecast on.

Table 6-1	Monthly Percentage Distributions from Previous Year	
Month	*Last Year's Call Volume*	*Percentage of Year*
January	150,000	9.16
February	145,000	8.85
March	148,000	9.04
April	135,000	8.24
May	130,000	7.94
June	120,000	7.33
July	110,000	6.72
August	105,000	6.41
September	150,000	9.16
October	135,000	8.24
November	140,000	8.55
December	170,000	10.38
Total	1,638,000	100

The data in Table 6-1 contain the total call volume by month for the entire year. The far right column is a calculation of each month's percentage of total annual call volume. Notice how the call volume — and the corresponding monthly percentage — decreased from June to August. In the retail industry this type of call pattern is common, as fewer customers tend to call for sales or customer service inquiries during the summer months. The call volume increases in September (9.16 percent of the total year's volume) as customers get back to school and business, and again in December (10.38 percent), due to people calling to do their Christmas shopping.

Ideally, the monthly percentage is calculated with several years of monthly call volume. These percentages are very useful in forecasting future volume. For example, if you know that next year your business is going to increase by 10 percent and call volume will increase with the business, then your forecast is as simple as increasing last year's call volume by 10 percent and then multiplying the new total call volume by the monthly percentages.

After calculating the percentage of volume by period (month, week, day) it's useful to graph the pattern, as shown in Figure 6-1, and look at any trends. Frequently, you'll find that the trends make sense.

You can easily see from Figure 6-1 that the call center in this example is fairly busy in the winter months, gets slower in the summer, has a busy spike in September, and reaches its highest peak in December. These trends make sense, particularly if this center is in the retail or travel industry; considering winter is a working time for most people, vacations and breaks from school happen in the summer, September is a return to work or school for many people, and December is the busiest retail period of the year.

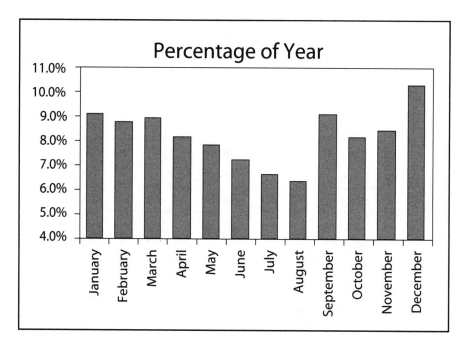

Figure 6-1:
Monthly call distribution chart, based on previous year's forecast.

To make a forecast based on last year's results, and still assuming that next year's call volume will increase by 10 percent, you start by multiplying last year's volume, 1,638,000, by 10 percent and adding the result to last year's volume.

$1,638,000 \times 10\% = 16,380$

$1,638,000 + 16380 = 1,801,800$

This gives you a forecast for next year of 1,801,800. If you want a forecast for the upcoming January's call volume, you'll multiply your forecasted annual call volume by January's historical percentage of 9.16 percent.

$1,801,800 \times 9.16\% = 165,045$

So, the forecasted total call volume for the upcoming January is 165,045 calls. Not complicated, but a forecast — and maybe a good one.

Next, you need to determine the distribution of work over days of the week and hours of the day, following the same process of reviewing historical patterns.

You'll need to constantly update these relationships. Generally, the more data you use, — that is, the larger the time frames you consider — the better.

With this information you can take a long-term forecast and calculate what it means in terms of any specific half-hour period of the year. For example, assume you've determined the following from your historical data:

✔ This year's annual forecast = 1,801,800

✔ March proportion of year = 9.04%

✔ Wednesday proportion of week = 16%

✔ 14:00 to 14:30 proportion of day = 5.1%

How many calls should you expect from 14:00 to 14:30 on Wednesdays in March if you are forecasting 1,801,800 calls for the year? The simple calculation is shown below.

Calculating forecasted interval call volume

Forecast / Distribution		Call Volume / Percentage
A	Year's forecast	1,801,800
B	March	9.04%
C	Wednesday	16%
D	14:00 – 14:30 interval	5.10%
E	$= A \times B / 31^* \times 7^{**} \times C \times D$	30

* 31 = days in March; **7 = active call center days in a week

To express the monthly volume in terms of one week of the month, you need to divide by the number of days in the month and multiply by the number of active workdays in a week.

With this information, you can now express your forecast in terms of each interval of the year.

Forecasting call length

You can choose from a variety of methods to forecast call length — from simple to very complex. I like to track the historical call length on a half-hourly basis and use the average — over, for example, a rotating four-week period, as shown in Table 6-2.

Table 6-2	Tracking Average Call Length by Half-hour Interval by Week				
Interval	*Week 1*	*Week 2*	*Week 3*	*Week 4*	*Average*
10:30	351	375	366	345	**359**
11:00	344	365	378	324	**353**
11:30	356	378	398	345	**369**
12:00	365	376	367	387	**374**
12:30	324	334	342	345	**336**
13:00	345	323	332	354	**339**

Accounting for unique situations

Forecasting future call volume isn't always nice and predictable. Sometimes things happen that disrupt historical patterns. And while these "special situations" tend to make forecasters crazy, they too can be planned for. The trick is to track their impact on historical calling patterns.

For example, holidays, like Christmas, disrupt historical calling patterns for most call centers; even if your call center is open on Christmas Day, it's unlikely that you'll get the same type of caller demand that you'd have on a normal workday.

A good forecaster will track the historical impact a day like Christmas has on normal calling patterns, and will adjust his or her forecast by the historical impact.

For example, assume that Christmas falls on a Wednesday this year. Looking at your forecasting data, you find

- ✔ Forecast for the year   1,800,801 calls
- ✔ December percentage   10.38%
- ✔ Wednesday percentage   16%
- ✔ Impact of Christmas   30%

In the first three lines, nothing's changed. You've assembled your normal forecasting data. Your forecaster knows from experience that Christmas Day has a lower call volume than a regular day — in fact, Christmas Day is only 30 percent of a normal day. So, your calculation of call volume forecast for next Christmas day is as follows:

$$1,800,801 \times 10.38\% \div 31^* \times 7^{**} \times 16\% \times 30\% = 2,026$$

*Number of days in December

**Number of days in a workweek

So, now you have a forecast for Christmas Day. The forecaster may also know that call volume is not distributed over Christmas Day as it is on other days. He or she would also have the historical call times for Christmas Day and will use this pattern when forecasting half-hourly call volume.

The same approach can be used for other special events that disrupt normal call volume, such as holidays, storms, promotions — anything that impacts call volume. Your forecaster merely tracks and applies these historical impacts.

Tracking Forecast Accuracy

A good forecaster will experiment and research new and different forecasting techniques. Whatever the method, it's important to know how successful or unsuccessful your forecast is.

A simple process for tracking forecast accuracy is what I call the "absolute forecast variance." The word "absolute" refers to "no negative numbers"; so when calculating how wrong your forecast was you always express the error in positive numbers, because over time tracking both positive and negative errors results in one canceling the other out, making your overall forecast appear more accurate than it really is.

Several years ago, I was helping a friend who was a call center forecaster improve his forecasting. I pointed out that he was tracking the accuracy of this forecast using positive and negative numbers and that a more realistic way to track his accuracy was to use absolute numbers. He immediately agreed that using absolute numbers was a better way to go, but said his company would not be doing this. What I asked him why, he said, "Oh, that's simple — my bonus is based on how accurate my forecasts are."

If you're using positive and negative numbers, your forecast variance may look like this:

Tracking forecast variance using positive and negative numbers

	Forecast	Actual	Variance
Forecast day one	10,000	20,000	10,000
Forecast day two	20,000	10,000	(10,000)
Summary	30,000	30,000	0
Percentage error			0%

Because positives and negatives cancel each other out, the total forecast above looked perfect, even though the forecast was very wrong on both days.

Using only positive numbers, variance tracking will look more like this:

Tracking forecast accuracy with "absolute forecast variance"

	Forecast	Actual	Variance
Forecast day one	10,000	20,000	10,000
Forecast day two	20,000	10,000	10,000
Summary	30,000	30,000	20,000
Percentage error			67%

This revised table does away with negative numbers to show the total error in daily forecast. It doesn't look as good, but does a better job of showing how good your forecast is.

Your forecaster should do this type of analysis for monthly, daily, and half-hourly calls and forecasts. The goal is to reduce error to the smallest possible margin. Some forecasters will use two or three different forecasting methods before settling on the most accurate method to do their call-volume forecasting.

A Final Word on Forecasting

Early in this chapter, I say that the one thing you know for sure about a forecast is that it will be wrong. While this is true, it merely serves to point out that the act of forecasting is a process. The closer you can get to predicting the future, the better your scheduling will ultimately be and the more effectively and efficiently your call center will run.

It's the *process* of forecasting that is so important to call center success. And — while I hesitate to say this — forecasting is both art and science. The good forecaster is artful in his or her feel for and understanding of the business and how unexpected events might impact the call volume forecast, but he or she is scientific in the use of mathematical techniques for forecasting.

The techniques I demonstrate in this chapter are not overly complex. However, what you learn here will provide the basis for sound, effective call center forecasting. The foundation this chapter provides can certainly be supplemented with more sophisticated statistical techniques; and while looking for better forecasting techniques, it's important to remember that the ultimate goal is to produce as accurate a forecast as possible — whatever works best.

Chapter 7

Call Center Scheduling: As Simple as 1, 2, 3...

....

In This Chapter

▶ Determining what resources are required

▶ Creating schedules to get the work done

▶ Understanding how to handle unique scheduling situations

....

Contrary to what the chapter title might suggest, creating a call center schedule is not a simple thing. It's more difficult than trying to hit a moving target. In fact, it's a little like trying to hit that moving target while you're moving too. Having said that, the mechanics don't have to be particularly complicated, as long as you follow a relatively specific process in your effort to ensure you've got the right people in the right place at the right time to answer all those calls.

In this chapter I provide an outline of the typical steps of the scheduling process.

Calculating the Resources Required to Do the Job

Once you forecast your call volume and average call length for each half-hour interval of the year (as I discuss in Chapter 6), the next step is to determine the staffing resources you'll need to handle the forecasted demand over the selected period of time to develop your schedules.

Considering occupancy

The most important relationship to understand in resource management is the one between call workload (call volume × average call length) and total staffing requirements. Not to worry; you only have to use a simple formula to determine the number of staff you require. (I talk more about occupancy in Chapter 5.)

This is important stuff! Seriously, fold down the corner of this page, put a star in the margin, and get out your favorite highlighter if you think it'll help!

Staffing required = Forecasted call volume × Forecasted call length ÷ Expected occupancy

The importance of accounting for expected occupancy

As much as you might wish (from a pure production standpoint, at least) that your agents were occupied — that is, dealing with customer contacts — 100 percent of the time, it's just not possible (nor is it wise). When determining your staffing requirements, you have to account for the fact that sometimes your agents will be idle.

So, once you've forecasted the workload — the total amount of time it's going to take to handle all the calls — you simply divide that number by the expected occupancy to determine the amount of staff time you need to schedule for.

For example, assume you've forecasted 150 hours of workload for the day — meaning you're expecting 150 hours of calls. Assume also that your expected occupancy is 75 percent — meaning your agents, on average, will be idle 25 percent of the time they're on the phones. The number of staff hours required to handle this load is 150 hours of load divided by 75-percent occupancy, which equals 200 hours.

Confused? Look at the equation the other way around. If you had 200 hours of agents staffing the phones, and they were occupied 75 percent of the time, for how many hours were they occupied?

75 percent of 200 on-the-phone hours = 150 hours of occupied time.

In other words, they were busy working (handling the load) for 150 hours.

I provide a more detailed explanation of occupancy in Chapter 5.

Calculating expected occupancy

So, in order to calculate your staffing requirements, you first have to know your expected occupancy.

You have a choice of a couple of ways to arrive at expected occupancy. For established call centers, the easiest way is to look at the occupancy that your operation typically achieves at any time when hitting the accessibility/service-level target. So, if your call center typically achieves a monthly occupancy of 74 percent when making its service-level targets, then 74 percent is a fair expected occupancy for the month.

Be a bit careful with this one, because in busier months expected occupancy will be higher, and in slower months it will be lower. The difference is not going to be dramatic, so don't get too worked up about it — just keep an eye on it.

You'll also need to be a bit careful about the time frames you are using when working with expected occupancy. Occupancy fluctuates throughout the day. As I explain in Chapter 5, occupancy varies with demand, and because call volume fluctuates throughout the day occupancy will also fluctuate. This will create a range of expected occupancies. The good news is that monthly and daily occupancies won't fluctuate a great deal at any given service level.

Don't forget that improved scheduling will increase the expected occupancy; so, over time, plan for and capture the small improvements in occupancy in your expected occupancy calculations. Even a 1-percent improvement in expected occupancy could justify your job for months or years.

Another way to calculate expected occupancy is to use an Erlang C table, which I describe in Chapter 6, to calculate the optimal occupancy for every hour or half-hour of the day. You then multiply the optimal occupancy achieved using Erlang C by your historical scheduling efficiency.

Or, you could just buy a good workforce management system and let it work out expected occupancy for you. Many will go this route; however, while you're allowing these great tools to do their job, I encourage you to constantly monitor and make sure you understand the difference between your actual occupancy and your optimal occupancy. Small improvements therein make a big difference in call center efficiency and cost control.

Expected occupancy versus optimal occupancy

As I discuss in Chapter 5, occupancy is defined as the time agents are actively busy doing something (they're occupied, not idle), expressed as a percentage of the time they're logged in to the phones. Some terms need to be defined when speaking about occupancy. The first is *optimal occupancy*. Optimal occupancy is the occupancy a call center would achieve if it staffed perfectly for every hour of the day. This would mean having just the right number of people idle and just the right number of people working, so that calls are answered within the service-level objective — no faster and no slower. One way to approximate optimal occupancy is to use an Erlang C calculator and calculate the number of staff required for each hour of the day. If you staffed exactly to this requirement, you would achieve the optimal occupancy for the day.

Call centers rarely achieve optimal occupancy while also meeting their service-level targets. More likely, they achieve a lower occupancy. This happens for a number of reasons. First, call volume doesn't always arrive exactly as expected. Even when your forecasts are very accurate, calls will not arrive exactly as you planned, creating an imbalance between actual staff scheduled and what you really need for optimal occupancy. Also, your staffing doesn't always work out exactly as you planned it, either. People often are late or absent, or last-minute demands, like training, come up that take people away from their primary call-handling duties. These unexpected changes detract from your staffing plan, making it difficult to achieve optimal occupancy.

Finally, the biggest challenge in achieving optimal occupancy is having a perfectly flexible workforce. In a perfect world your staff would come and go just as your callers came and went. This would allow the call center to precisely meet caller demand. In this wonderful world, your agents would work only when you needed them — a few minutes here, a few minutes there.

While you *can* increase flexibility, this perfect world doesn't exist. Typically, the best you can do is to come close to your demand curve — staffing a little over here, a little under there, but being approximately right overall. This approach reduces the efficiency of your schedule, hence reducing actual occupancy achieved further from your optimal occupancy. The first graph in Figure 7-1 shows a schedule in the perfect world, while the second illustrates a more realistic, imperfect schedule — "a little over here, and a little under there."

Determining your scheduling efficiency

I like to refer to the term "scheduling efficiency." This refers to how close the call center gets to achieving optimal occupancy. For example, if a center's optimal occupancy is 90 percent and the call center produces an actual occupancy of 80 percent, then the scheduling efficiency is 88.8 percent (80 percent divided by 90 percent equals 88.8 percent). About the best I see in scheduling efficiency is 92 percent.

In this example, the call center's expected occupancy is 80 percent. You know that the optimal occupancy is 90 percent, but you expect to achieve 80 percent. This doesn't mean you don't want to improve and get closer to their optimal occupancy, just that you know for the time being you're running at 80 percent. As scheduling efficiency improves, you'll adjust your scheduling efficiency forecast.

So, expected occupancy is the occupancy level that your call center expects to hit given its existing demand and scheduling.

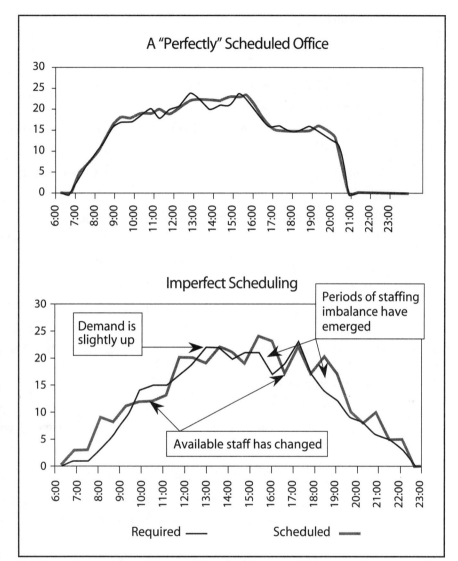

Figure 7-1:
Imperfect
scheduling
accounts for
the differ-
ence
between
optimal and
expected
occupancy.

When you do this type of analysis — calculating monthly staffing requirements — you're getting a big-picture view of how many staff will be needed,
which is something you might use for budgeting purposes. To do this calculation, you need a forecasted call volume, a forecasted call length, and
expected occupancy, which is based on your target service-level objective.

Here's an example:

- ✔ For the upcoming year, you've forecasted a 10-percent increase over last year's volume of 1,638,000 calls
- ✔ Calls in March represent 9.04 percent of the year
- ✔ Calls will average 350 seconds in length
- ✔ Your expected occupancy is 74 percent for the month at a service level of 80 percent in 20 seconds.

The following table illustrates the calculations of staffing requirement for one month.

Calculating staffing hours required for a given month

A	Last year's call volume	1,638,000
B	Forecasted increase	10%
C	March percentage	9.04%
D	Forecasted call length	350 seconds
E	Expected occupancy	74%
$F = A \times (1 + B) \times C \times D / 3{,}600^* / E$	Staffing requirement for March	21,400 hours

3,600 seconds in one hour

To handle the forecasted call volume at the forecasted call length, you'll need 21,400 agent hours on the phones.

Here's a little breakdown of the calculation of F, above:

1. $A \times (1 + B)$ — this part of the calculation creates the new annual forecast
2. $\times C$ — multiplying by March's percentage gives us the March forecast for next year
3. $\times D$ — multiplying by the forecasted call length determines the "workload" for March
4. $\div 3{,}600$ — dividing by the number of seconds in one hour expresses the workload in hours
5. $\div E$ — dividing by your expected occupancy turns the workload into total staffing requirements, in hours, for March

Remember to divide by 3,600 to turn the result into hours — otherwise, your forecasted staff requirements will be in seconds (and you don't want to risk giving your schedulers heart failure when they see that number!).

Making an impact on occupancy

According to the "immutable laws" of the call center, there are three primary ways to affect occupancy:

1. **Change how fast you answer the phone.** How fast you answer the phone in your call center has an impact on occupancy. Answering the phone faster means that your agents spend more time waiting for calls (occupancy goes down). Answering the phone slower means that your agents will spend less time waiting for calls — in fact, the calls may be waiting for them! Answering the phone slower *increases* occupancy.

2. **Pool your resources: bigger is better.** When you increase the size of your call center (by merging sites or pooling calls from different campaigns, for example), the overall randomness of call arrivals is reduced — because callers' decisions to contact you begin to merge and the call-arrival pattern begins to smooth out. (Figure 7-2 provides a comparison of call arrival between a small center and a larger one.) Because the difference between the peaks in call volume and the average call volume is less than in our lower-call-volume example, fewer staffing resources, as a percentage of total staff, will be needed to answer the phone quickly.

   The result is that the incremental staff needed for a bigger call center is not directly proportional to the increase in workload/call volume. As the operation gets bigger, you begin to realize economies of scale.

   To take advantage of these economies of scale, you have to make sure that you minimize the number of distinct answering groups in the call center by cross-training agents so they can excel on several different campaigns, and by merging groups wherever it's possible and practical.

3. **Get better at scheduling.** The third way to impact occupancy is through improved scheduling. If your staff schedule results in massive overstaffing for 80 percent of your operating hours and massive understaffing for the remaining 20 percent, then overall you'll have an 80 percent level of accessibility (a common target in call centers). However, your overall occupancy will be low, and 20 percent of our customers (the ones who called while you were understaffed) will be very unhappy.

Be careful what you ask for!

It costs money to deliver good service. Before you decide to save some costs by reducing staff and taking more time to answer the phone, check with your customers. They might have an issue with waiting an hour or two to receive the service they're seeking.

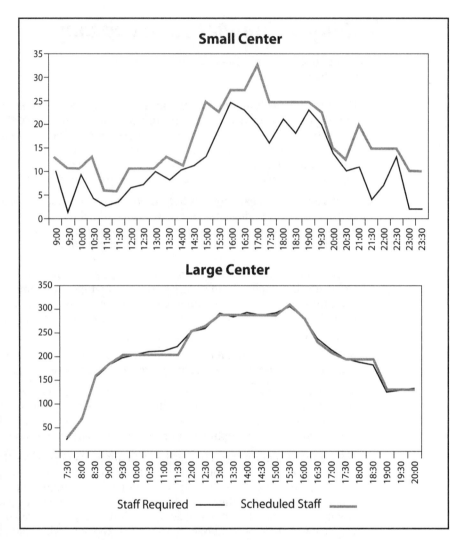

Figure 7-2:
Taking
advantage
of
economies
of scale.

Scheduling *close to the curve*, meaning that you match your staff schedule closely to caller demand, is a better way to achieve your accessibility target. During some times of the day you'll be slightly overstaffed, and at other times you'll be slightly understaffed. Overall, you'll still achieve the 80 percent accessibility, but your occupancy will be much higher — and the other 20 percent of callers will probably be less disgruntled because their calls will be answered only slightly less quickly.

I illustrate these scenarios in the graphs in Figure 7-3. Notice that the call arrival is exactly the same, and 80-percent accessibility is achieved in both cases, but the scheduled staff is much more in line with demand in the second chart and overall occupancy is increased.

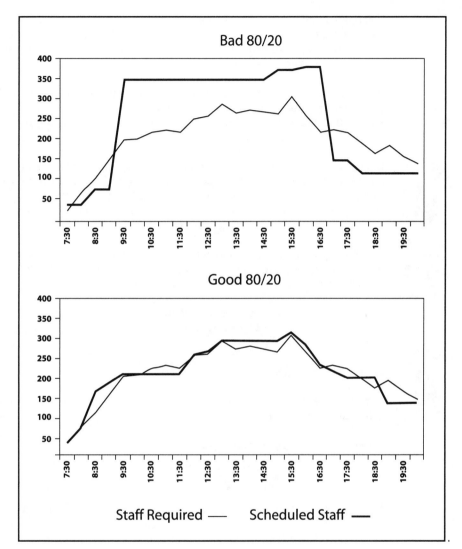

Figure 7-3:
Matching staff schedules more closely to demand improves occupancy.

Give 'em a break: Accounting for off-phone time

Calculating the on-phone staffing requirements isn't the whole story. When people work for your company, you pay them for more than just the time they're on the phones. Your staff also get paid for training, meetings, breaks, and so on. So, before you get all excited thinking you're done, I've got to say it — you're not.

You need to take *agent utilization* into consideration. Of the total hours that you pay your agents, what percentage of this time do they end up doing actual work — on the phones taking calls, or on the computer handling customer e-mails, for example?

After you've determined how much staffing you need just to handle the work, you need to think about giving those people time away for meetings, breaks, vacation, training, and so on. You need to apply your expected or targeted agent utilization rate to account for this.

In Chapter 5, I defined agent utilization as a measure that tracks how much of an agent's paid time is spent processing the work. I also refer to this as L/P — "logged over paid." If you pay an agent for 10 hours, and they spend 7 of those hours logged in working on telephone calls and three hours off-phone on breaks and in meetings, then utilization is 70 percent.

Tracking, planning, and understanding historical utilization rates is an important scheduling function. With a little time, most operations can forecast agent utilization rates with a fair degree of accuracy.

Similar to the calculation used to account for occupancy, you simply divide the forecasted hours of work by the agent utilization and you'll get the total paid hours required.

Paid hours requirement = Forecasted staff work hours ÷ agent utilization

Continuing with the previous example, assume that your forecasted agent utilization is 70 percent.

Calculating paid time requirements for a given month

F	Staffing required for March	21,400 hours
G	Agent utilization	70%
$H = F \div G$	Paid time requirement for March	**30,751 hours**

So, you need 30,571 hours of paid staff time to handle the forecasted calls.

Now, assume a typical full-time agent in your center receives 155 paid hours per month.

Using paid hours to calculate monthly FTEs required

H	Paid time required in March	30,751 hours
I	Hours per month per FTE	155
$J = H \div I$	FTE's required for March	**198**[*]

[*] Rounded up

TIP

Calculating the financial impact of changes in agent utilization

Calculating the additional cost of every percentage point decrease in your agent utilization is a good idea. Just run your staffing calculations for different agent utilization levels and multiply each by your cost of labor (including benefits).

In addition to shocking the life out of you, this information is very powerful in helping you to control your budget or make cost–benefit calculations.

Not long ago, I showed a call center director the impact of a 1-percent change in their agent utilization ratio. A 1-percent change in agent utilization was worth more than $30,000 per month to the call center. Up until this point the center had not paid a great deal of attention to agent utilization. After I went over this number with the director, agent utilization became a hot topic in the call center and improved dramatically the very next month.

So, you'll need 198 full-time equivalent agents in your office during March. (Usually called an FTE, a "full-time equivalent" is the number of hours the typical full-time person works in a given period — it's used to express staffing requirements, as I explain in Chapter 6.) Note that you need to round up the FTEs to the nearest whole number; basically, an FTE represents a whole person, and you don't generally schedule partial people. (Although you may occasionally schedule some who aren't quite all there.)

Determining When the Resources Are Required

So, you've determined you need 198 people in March. That tells you how much you're going to spend on staffing, but it doesn't tell you *when* those people are going to work.

You have to take the forecast down to a lower level of detail to determine when the resources are required — right down to the daily and half-hourly (interval) basis. To do this, you continue to apply your historical percentages and use your staffing formula to determine requirements.

Calculating base staff requirements by half-hour interval

Carrying on with the example from above, you need to calculate the staffing requirements for each interval in March to build the schedule requirement.

Using one interval as an example — 14:00 to 14:30 on Wednesdays — and the historical data provided below, I'll give you a sample of the calculation.

Additional historical data:

✔ Wednesday proportion of week = 16%

✔ 14:00 to 14:30 interval proportion of day = 5.1%

Calculating staff required for a half-hour interval

A	March forecasted call volume	162,883
B	Wednesday percentage of week	16%
C	Interval percentage of day	5.1%
D	Forecasted call length (seconds)	350
E	Expected occupancy	77%
$F = A \div 31 \times 7 \times B$ $\times C \times D \div E \div 1,800^{*}$	Staff required for 14:00–14:30 interval on Wednesday	**76**[**]

*1,800 seconds per half-hour interval

**Rounded up

So, you need 76 agents on the phones from 14:00 to 14:30 on Wednesdays in March.

You'll notice a few things while going through this calculation:

✔ You arrive at March's forecasted call volume by taking last year's volume, increasing it by 10 percent, and multiplying by March's historical proportion of the year (9.04 percent), as I show in the calculation of staffing hours required for a given month earlier in this chapter.

✔ At the beginning of the calculation, you divide the monthly call volume forecast by the number of days in the month, giving the average daily call volume; then multiply by the number of working days in the week to get the call volume for the average week of the month.

In the example, I divide March's forecasted call volume by 31 (because there are 31 days in March) and then multiply by 7 (the number of working days per week for this call center). This expresses the monthly volume in terms of one week of the month, making it easy to calculate Wednesday's forecast by simply multiplying the weekly forecast by 16 percent (Wednesday's proportion of the week) — giving you 5,885 calls.

✔ Multiply this by the 14:00 to 14:30 interval percentage (5.1 percent) to arrive at the forecasted interval call volume — 300 calls. Then, multiply that by the average call length of 350 seconds to get an overall staffing workload requirement of 105,000 seconds.

Occupancy changes throughout the day

A call center is really many different call centers throughout the course of a day. When you open in the morning, you're basically running a smaller operation, receiving a lighter call volume than you will later in the day. One of the things that affects occupancy is call volume — higher volumes lead to higher occupancy.

In the calculation of staffing hours for a given month, divide the staffing calculation (stated in seconds) by 3,600 (seconds per hour) to express the requirement in terms of hours of work. However, to determine how many staff you need to handle the work in a half-hour interval, divide by 1,800 (the number of seconds in a half hour) to determine staff required on the phones.

So, in the example, 105,000 seconds divided by 1,800 seconds per hour gives 58.33 occupied staff required during the half-hour interval of 14:00 to 14:30.

If you want to understand how many hours of work you need to do, divide by 3,600, then multiply the total work hours by two to determine how many people are needed to get this work done in half an hour. You'll end up with the same answer as by simply dividing by 1,800.

Next, notice that I used a forecasted occupancy of 77 percent, not the 74-percent average for March that I used in the calculation of staff hours for a month. This is done because occupancy changes throughout the day.

Based on the volume expected from 14:00 to 14:30, the call center will be near its peak, resulting in a higher occupancy than average — around 77 percent. Divide the occupied staff requirement by your 77-percent expected occupancy, and you see that you need 75.76 total staff required on the phones. Rounding this up — unless you have three-quarters of a person somewhere on staff — means you'll need to schedule for 76 agents during the interval of 14:00 to 14:30 on Wednesdays in March this year.

Is that cool, or what?

Now, just go back and do this calculation for every half-hour period of the month (and year) to determine your staffing pattern. I help to get you started with an example in Table 7-1, calculating staff requirements by interval for all of Wednesday. The result is charted in Figure 7-4.

Table 7-1		Calculating Base Staff Required by Half-Hour Interval		
Interval	Call Volume	Call Length	Expected Occupancy	Staffing Required
	A	B	C	$D = A \times B \div C \div 1800$
8:00	81	355	68%	24
8:30	115	357	72%	32
9:00	185	360	75%	49
9:30	265	357	76%	69
10:00	300	365	77%	79
10:30	323	367	77%	86
11:00	312	355	77%	80
11:30	300	352	77%	76
12:00	265	349	75%	68
12:30	277	376	77%	75
13:00	312	371	77%	84
13:30	312	368	77%	82
14:00	300	350	76%	76
14:30	277	354	76%	72
15:00	277	349	76%	71
15:30	265	343	75%	67
16:00	254	341	76%	64
16:30	242	338	76%	60
17:00	231	339	75%	58
17:30	196	343	74%	51
18:00	185	340	74%	47
18:30	173	335	74%	44
19:00	162	333	73%	41

Interval	Call Volume	Call Length	Expected Occupancy	Staffing Required
	A	B	C	$D = A \times B \div C \div 1800$
19:30	138	329	72%	35
20:00	81	331	66%	22
20:30	58	335	65%	16

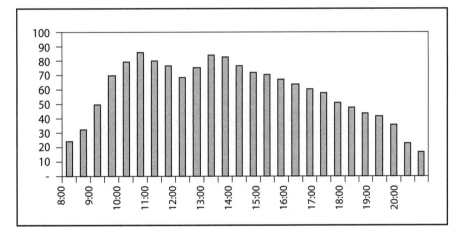

Figure 7-4:
Base staff required by half-hour interval.

Adding in the off-phone requirements

Now that you've determined the number of base staff required for each half-hour interval of the day, you need to layer in the staffing requirements for non-phone needs, such as breaks, training, meetings, sick leave, and vacation.

First, determine what percentage of your staffing will go to each of these activities. You can use historical averages or build a plan of what you expect to need. Some items, like sick leave, are just going to happen and you can't predict them exactly, so you'll need to allow for them as a percentage based on historical averages. Others, like meetings, can be planned around peak periods. Table 7-2 shows Wednesday's staffing requirements from the calculation of staff required for a half-hour interval, with off-phone allowances considered, providing actual total staffing requirements for each interval of the day. The resulting chart is illustrated in Figure 7-5.

| Table 7-2 | | | | | | | Calculating Total Staff Required by Half-Hour Interval | | |

Interval	Call Volume	Call Length	Expected Occupancy	Staff Required to Handle Calls	Sick	Breaks	Meetings	Total Staffing Requirement
	A	B	C	$D = A \times B \div C \div 1{,}800$	E	F	G	$H = D + E + F + G$
8:00	81	355	68%	24	2			26
8:30	115	357	72%	32	2			34
9:00	185	360	75%	49	3	30		82
9:30	265	357	76%	69	4	30		103
10:00	300	365	77%	79	5	5		88
10:30	323	367	77%	86	5	21		112
11:00	312	355	77%	80	5	20		105
11:30	300	352	77%	76	5	19		100
12:00	265	349	75%	68	5	17		90
12:30	277	376	77%	75	5	19		99
13:00	312	371	77%	84	5	21		110
13:30	312	368	77%	82	5	21		108
14:00	300	350	76%	76	5	19		100
14:30	277	354	76%	72	5	18	10	105
15:00	277	349	76%	71	5	18	10	104
15:30	265	343	75%	67	5	17	10	99
16:00	254	341	76%	64	4	16	10	94
16:30	242	338	76%	60	4	16		80
17:00	231	339	75%	58	4	16		78
17:30	196	343	74%	51	3	16		70
18:00	185	340	74%	47	3	17		67

Interval	Call Volume	Call Length	Expected Occupancy	Staff Required to Handle Calls	Sick	Breaks	Meetings	Total Staffing Requirement
	A	B	C	D = A × B ÷ C ÷ 1,800	E	F	G	H = D + E + F + G
18:30	173	335	74%	44	3	12		59
19:00	162	333	73%	41	2	12		55
19:30	138	329	72%	35	2	2		39
20:00	81	331	66%	22	2			24
20:30	58	335	65%	16	2			18

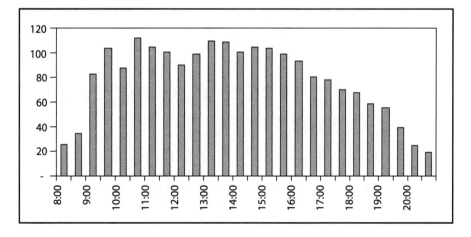

Figure 7-5:
Total staffing requirement by half-hour interval.

Continue this calculation for each half-hour interval of every day of every week of the month and you'll know how many actual "bums in seats" you need at any point during the month. You'll use these data for planning and building your call center work schedules.

Careful: Don't forget shrinkage!

Did you know that 2 percent of whiskey that is aging in kegs evaporates every year? It's frequently referred to as "The angels' share." Well, in call centers, some of your staff evaporate when they are working on the phones. Missing time comes from a lot of sources, including breaks that go too long, extra breaks, unplanned meetings and discussions, and so on. It happens and, to the best of my knowledge, can't be avoided. Don't ignore it. Try to minimize it, of course, but at the same time plan for it. If your lost time is 5 percent, then add it back into your scheduling. It's better to add in a little extra than to be short-staffed.

Using your forecast to determine call center size

If you're planning to build a call center of your own (as I discuss in Chapter 4), this "bums in seats" calculation is basically what you need to determine the size of your center. Simply follow the steps above to calculate the staffing requirement for each interval of the year, and then find the peak interval — the one requiring the highest number of staff. That number represents the maximum number of agents you'll need in your center at any given time to meet your service-level targets and projected occupancy, and it tells you how many seats you'll need. It's a simplified method, but it works.

Scheduling Available Resources to Meet Caller Demand

Once you've determined what the half-hourly staffing demand looks like, you need to plan schedules around that demand. At this point, don't worry about who, specifically, is going to work these schedules, just build schedules to match staffing as closely as possible to the demand.

Starting to build your schedules with full-time shifts

One very useful approach to matching available resources with caller demand is to create a graph to compare caller demand to total staff scheduled. In Figure 7-6, caller demand throughout the day is graphed using the demand calculated in Table 7-2.

Next, I've added scheduled shifts to this graph in an effort to match staffing with caller demand. As the first step in building a schedule, I've added one shift of 26 staff working from 8:00 until 16:00 The bars in the figure represent the total staff required to meet customer demand for every half-hour. The line represents the cumulative number of people that you've scheduled on the phones for every half hour.

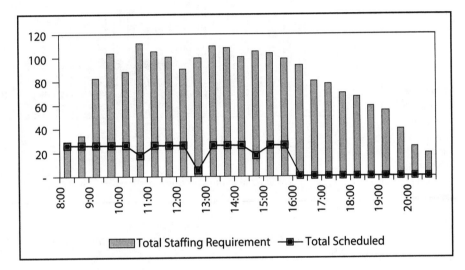

Figure 7-6:
Adding full-
time shifts
to meet the
staffing
requirement.

In this figure you'll notice that the staffing line is not consistent. The chart shows that total staffing scheduled dips at 11:00, 13:00, and 15:00. These dips in staffing represent breaks that scheduled staff will take during their day. Of course, not everyone will take their breaks at the same time, and you can stagger breaks if you choose. However, at this point in the scheduling process you'll leave the breaks as they are because you're still dealing with broad strokes. Later on, as you're fine-tuning the schedule you'll adjust the breaks.

Obviously, the graph shows that this one eight-hour shift of 26 staff is not enough to cover the entire day's caller demand. Next, you need to continue to add shifts toward completing your schedule.

In Figure 7-7, notice that in the middle of the day, from approximately 13:30 until 18:00, there is a "bump" of overlapping shifts. This bump occurs because the end of one full-time shift overlaps with the beginning of another full-time shift. This is one of the challenges of scheduling with a lot of full-time staff. As you can imagine, if you were to continue adding shifts in only full-time staff, you'd likely end up with a significant amount of overstaffing — a *big* bump — in the middle of the day.

These periods of overlapping shifts can be minimized through the use of part-time staff.

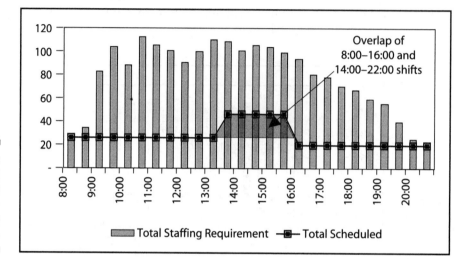

Figure 7-7:
Overlapping happens as more full-time shifts are added.

Continue adding shifts and before long a pattern emerges, as illustrated in Figure 7-8.

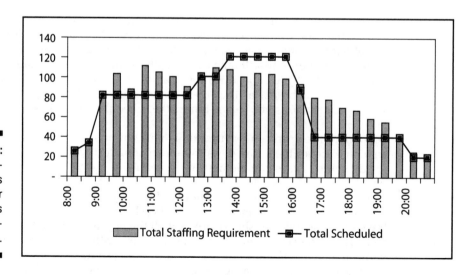

Figure 7-8:
Using full-time shifts only, your schedule is almost complete.

At this point scheduling starts to get fun. You will continue to add shifts with different start and stop times. The goal is to make the staffing-available line exactly equal the caller demand bars. But there's a wrinkle! You can use only as many shifts as there are people to work said shifts. One shift per employee — that's it.

Now, you're almost done; you just have to fill in the cracks. In this case, adding any more full-time shifts would create a great deal of overlap. You can either accept this overlap, continuing to use full-time shifts, in which case you'll likely be moderately overstaffed or understaffed at various times throughout the day, and the efficiency of your schedule will be decreased (your scheduling efficiency will decline resulting in occupancies below optimal). Or, you can attempt to schedule some part-time shifts into the mix, as I discuss next.

Filling in the gaps with part-time shifts

Part-time shifts are great, because they help fill the cracks in your schedule created by the overlap when using full-time shifts only. Figure 7-9 shows the final completed schedule for the Wednesday example.

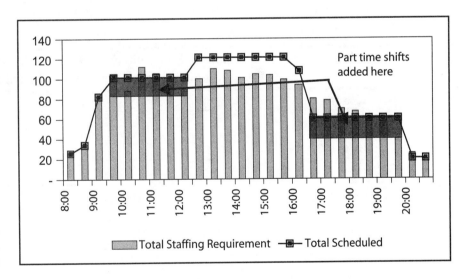

Figure 7-9: Completed schedule, using full-time and part-time shifts.

You won't make the schedule perfect — and that's okay. Ideally, you'll be as close to your requirement line as possible. Some overlap (appearing as overstaffing) during the middle of the day might be useful as a time to conduct training and meetings or to do essential non-phone work.

You can also help shore up the weak areas — where you've got some under-staffing — by adjusting breaks and lunch times. Certainly, your department scheduler should make everyone aware of the weak spots in your schedule so no one plans meetings during this time.

Part-time shifts do, however, present some problems. Managing is more difficult when you have a large number of agents staffed for short shifts, and it is often hard to attract good part-time agents. Attracting good part timers is even more difficult in operations that compensate part-time agents at a lower wage level than full-time agents.

My advice is to compensate part-time agents at least as well as full-time agents on an hour-by-hour basis. The payback in increased efficiency (occupancy) is immediate.

Creating a summary of schedules

When you're done, you'll end up with a bunch of different shift schedules, each requiring a certain number of positions. Table 7-3 shows what the total number of schedules for the Wednesday example might look like.

Table 7-3	Example of Shift Schedules and Number of People Required for an Entire Day's Schedule
Schedule	*Positions*
8:00 to 16:00	26
8:30 to 16:30	8
9:00 to 17:00	48
13:30 to 21:30	20
12:30 to 20:30	20
9:30 to 13:30	20
16:00 to 20:00	20

With Wednesday completed, you get to do this all over again, and again, and again — for each day of the week. When you're done, you'll end up with a summary of schedules, something that looks a lot like Table 7-4.

Table 7-4			Summary of Schedules for a Full Week			
Shift	Monday	Tuesday	Wednesday	Thursday	Friday	Saturday	Sunday
1	8:00 to 16:00	8:00 to 16:00	8:00 to 16:00	8:00 to 16:00	8:00 to 16:00	9:00 to 17:00	9:00 to 17:00
2	8:00 to 16:00	8:00 to 16:00	8:00 to 16:00	8:00 to 16:00	8:00 to 16:00	9:00 to 17:00	9:00 to 17:00
3	8:00 to 16:00	8:00 to 16:00	8:00 to 16:00	8:00 to 16:00	8:00 to 16:00	9:00 to 17:00	9:00 to 17:00
4	8:00 to 16:00	8:00 to 16:00	8:00 to 16:00	8:00 to 16:00	8:00 to 16:00	9:00 to 17:00	9:00 to 17:00
5	8:00 to 16:00	8:00 to 16:00	8:00 to 16:00	8:00 to 16:00	8:00 to 16:00	9:00 to 17:00	9:00 to 17:00
6	8:00 to 16:00	8:00 to 16:00	8:00 to 16:00	8:00 to 16:00	8:00 to 16:00	9:00 to 17:00	9:00 to 17:00
7	8:00 to 16:00	8:00 to 16:00	8:00 to 16:00	8:00 to 16:00	8:00 to 16:00	9:00 to 17:00	9:00 to 17:00
8	8:00 to 16:00	8:00 to 16:00	8:00 to 16:00	8:00 to 16:00	8:00 to 16:00	9:00 to 17:00	9:00 to 17:00
9	8:00 to 16:00	8:00 to 16:00	8:00 to 16:00	8:00 to 16:00	8:00 to 16:00	9:00 to 17:00	9:00 to 17:00
10	8:00 to 16:00	8:00 to 16:00	8:00 to 16:00	8:00 to 16:00	8:00 to 16:00	9:00 to 17:00	9:00 to 17:00
11	8:00 to 16:00	8:00 to 16:00	8:00 to 16:00	8:00 to 16:00	8:00 to 16:00	9:00 to 17:00	9:00 to 17:00
12	8:00 to 16:00	8:00 to 16:00	8:00 to 16:00	8:00 to 16:00	8:00 to 16:00	9:00 to 17:00	9:00 to 17:00
13	8:00 to 16:00	8:00 to 16:00	8:00 to 16:00	8:00 to 16:00	8:00 to 16:00	9:00 to 17:00	9:00 to 17:00
14	8:00 to 16:00	8:00 to 16:00	8:00 to 16:00	8:00 to 16:00	8:00 to 16:00	9:00 to 17:00	9:00 to 17:00
15	8:00 to 16:00	8:00 to 16:00	8:00 to 16:00	8:00 to 16:00	8:00 to 16:00	9:00 to 17:00	9:00 to 17:00

(Continued)

Table 7-4 *(Continued)*

Shift	Monday	Tuesday	Wednesday	Thursday	Friday	Saturday	Sunday
165	13:00 to 21:00	13:00 to 21:00	13:00 to 21:00	13:00 to 21:00	13:00 to 21:00		
166	13:00 to 21:00	13:00 to 21:00	13:00 to 21:00	13:00 to 21:00	13:00 to 21:00		
167	113:00 to 21:00	13:00 to 21:00	13:00 to 21:00	13:00 to 21:00	13:00 to 21:00		
168	13:00 to 21:00	13:00 to 21:00	13:00 to 21:00	13:00 to 21:00			
169	13:00 to 21:00	13:00 to 21:00					
170	13:00 to 21:00	13:00 to 21:00					
171	13:00 to 21:00	13:00 to 21:00					
172	13:00 to 21:00	13:00 to 21:00					
173	13:00 to 21:00	13:00 to 21:00					
174	13:00 to 21:00	13:00 to 21:00					
175	13:00 to 21:00	13:00 to 21:00					
176	13:00 to 21:00	13:00 to 21:00					
177	13:00 to 21:00	13:00 to 21:00					
178	13:00 to 21:00	13:00 to 21:00					

Creating weekly schedules

The summary of schedules lists every schedule that you created to meet the daily demand for agents. The next step is to select shifts from the summary and create weekly work schedules.

A weekly work schedule includes several days' worth of shifts and at least two consecutive days off.

The process of creating weekly work schedules is a simple matter of selecting shifts from the summary of schedules, placing them onto a weekly schedule template, and making sure that each shift has at least two consecutive days scheduled off.

There will be more rows in weekly work schedules than there are rows of shifts in the daily schedule. This happens because as you add days off to complete the schedules, you are essentially creating five-day workweeks over the seven days, creating more rows.

The important consideration is that you use all of the daily shifts created and assign each to a weekly schedule

Assigning Staff and Creating Schedules That Work

Your schedule is now ready for you to attach the names of the agents who will work the shifts. The easiest way to do that is for you to simply pick names and assign them to a schedule — if, that is, you really don't want people to like you.

Probably the safest (and fairest) way, especially in larger call centers, is to post the schedules and allow staff to bid on the available shifts.

An agent's bid priority is usually determined by seniority — the most senior agents get the highest priority. You could determine bid priority based on other criteria, such as performance — where agents who've performed the best over the previous period are given the highest bidding priority.

Allow the employee with the highest bid number to pick first — eliminating the shift he or she picks, so it's not available for others. The next highest bid number chooses next, and you continue that way until all the shifts are assigned.

Shift bids can be time-consuming. Here's how it works:

- ✔ Available shifts are communicated to all staff, and the staff will need time — frequently more than a week — to review those shifts.
- ✔ You then need to collect the shift bid responses indicating each agent's preference.

> ✔ Next, you sort the agent bid requests in order of bid priority, and then begin assigning shifts — starting with each employee's first choice, seeing if it's available, and, if it is, assigning that shift to the employee. If the agent's first choice is not available, you look to the employee's next preference, and so on.

Needless to say, when done manually this is a very complex and lengthy process.

Some call centers use alternatives to shift bids. These might include rotating staff through all shifts (essentially, sharing the pain), working around employees' personal preferences, assignment by employee performance, or fixed permanent shifts. All of these have been used in call centers.

However, many call centers gravitate toward a seniority-based shift bid as they get larger, because as a call center grows it becomes increasingly difficult to accommodate the individual needs of every staff member. Also, in larger call centers shifts can change a great deal. Rotating staff through all schedules is very effective and equitable, but not always preferred by the most senior staff. In my experience, the seniority-based shift bid is the most common (and agreeable) way to assign schedules in larger call centers.

If you choose to use performance or seniority to determine shift-bid priority, be careful when assigning schedules for newly hired staff. If a number of new staff start working at the same time, you might want to assign them a temporary post-training work schedule, rather than simply giving them the lowest shifts on the totem pole. Otherwise, you're likely to end up with a large percentage of new hires working at the same time (usually on night shifts), which puts a strain on the management team and creates an imbalance in staffing. Keep in mind that new people usually take longer to serve customers, and as a result skew average call length.

With a temporary post-training schedule, however, you can spread the *newbies* around on the shifts and thereby spread out the impact caused by their lack of experience.

Making schedules work for your staff

Let's face it — many call centers have less than desirable shifts. This can be somewhat demoralizing for staff, considering that the majority of folks would rather be working 9 to 5, Monday to Friday. Some things you can do to ease their angst include

> ✔ **Re-bidding:** Redoing the schedule from time to time is a good idea, since problems will gradually creep in. For example, as new staff members join, and other folks move on, seniority of those remaining improves. A

re-bid provides a light at the end of the tunnel for your staff, allowing them to move up the chain and get more desired shifts — it can really improve your team's motivation.

If your call center doesn't use a shift bid, you'll need to fill vacancies in your schedule with new staff in some manner that is seen as being equitable by your staff.

✔ **Shift-trading:** Ah, the time-honored tradition of trading shifts. It really is as simple as it sounds: give your employees a mechanism for trading their shifts — "You work my 9 to 5 and I'll work your 1 to 9." It's usually done on a one-day-at-a-time basis, but you can also allow employees to trade entire schedules.

✔ **Time bank/flex time:** In addition to regular vacation, you can allow employees the option to *bank* the extra hours they work and take them as time off at a future date. This approach works well if it's administered and tracked carefully. Some kind of mechanism to allow employees time off, one day at a time, in addition to their regular vacation process is essential.

Accounting for Unique Situations

In discussions about call center scheduling, the focus tends to be on a rather typical, generic, inbound operation: one type of call coming in to one site. If only life were that simple! Here are some special situations and circumstances you may need to consider.

Scheduling for different types of work

Non-inbound call work must be planned for and scheduled, but the question of what to do with it regularly challenges schedulers. How to schedule non-inbound work depends on the specific type of work.

Outbound calling is likely the most common type of other work you'll be scheduling, and it's actually easier to forecast than inbound calling. Outbound call volume is very predictable (even when using a *predictive dialer;* see Chapter 8), and so should be your occupancy and average call length.

As I explain in Chapter 8, a predictive dialer is a piece of technology used to increase efficiency when dialing outbound calls. The dialer places more outbound calls than the available number of agents, but sorts out answering machines, busy signals, and other non-human interactions before delivering live calls to the agents.

If you're conducting a standalone outbound project, scheduling is a simple matter of deciding how many calls you want to make by a certain time of day, calculating how many staff that equates to per hour, and staffing to fit. The math behind this is exactly the same as it is for inbound forecasting, as I describe in detail in Chapter 6.

Contingency plans: What to do when things don't turn out right

So, what happens when you do all the planning and you've still got more callers than you can handle — or you've got too many staff and too few callers (in which case, the boss is probably asking "Why is everyone just sitting around?"). And believe me, it happens!

A lot can change from the time you do your forecast and create your schedule until the time calls arrive. You can get an unexpected increase in call volume, a large percentage of staff can call in sick, and/or systems can get slow, causing call length to go up. As with anything, situations are going to arise. Success is determined by how you handle these situations. Here are some strategies.

Blending various work types

Blending refers to mixing inbound call handling with other work, preferably work that can be put aside or stopped when inbound traffic warrants it. Examples include outbound work (collections, customer service, telemarketing), e-mail, opening regular mail, and so on.

Implementing envelope scheduling

A technique I call *envelope scheduling* is a great strategy that takes advantage of call blending to greatly increase flexibility and maximize scheduling efficiencies.

The way envelope scheduling works is simple:

- First, you go through the normal scheduling process for your inbound calls — as I describe earlier in this chapter.

- Next, you simply add extra staff, over and above the number necessary to cover the inbound demand — basically creating an *envelope* of extra agents. Add enough extra agents to give you the additional hours needed to do any outbound or other work that you have.

- Then, during low inbound-call-volume periods, you can switch some agents to dialing outbound leads — which will generate sales, thereby maximizing cost control while also maximizing revenue generation.

Figure 7-10 shows how it works. Wherever the envelope staffing line is above the required staffing line on the chart is where you would be switching agents over to other work.

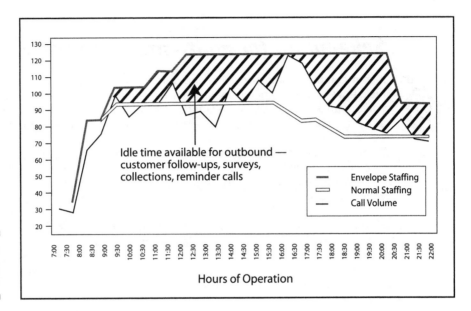

Idle time available for outbound — customer follow-ups, surveys, collections, reminder calls

Envelope Staffing
Normal Staffing
Call Volume

Hours of Operation

Figure 7-10:
Envelope
scheduling.

Using this combination of envelope scheduling and blending can reduce your overall cost per call by as much as 25 percent.

Extending overtime

Strategic use of overtime can help too, especially during the transition between shifts. You can either extend the shifts of those already on the phones, or ask agents who are scheduled for later in the day to come in early.

Allowing early leave, late start, or extended lunch

During times of lower-than-expected volume, if you provide your staff with the opportunity they'll frequently sign up to go home early or to come in late. A variation of this is to offer extended lunch breaks. All of these options reduce staff on the phones during slower periods, and thus increase occupancy of the remaining staff. The impact on cost per call can be significant.

Engaging an overflow partner

Having an overflow partner — another call center to which you can send calls when your call demand exceeds your staffing levels — is an effective way to handle peaks and valleys in call volume. The overflow partner can be a third-party outsourcer who specializes in this type of relationship, or another call center within your own organization. In addition to providing quick access to additional staffing, the overflow partner can provide a disaster-recovery capability.

Scheduling for multi-site call centers

If your company runs more than one call center, scheduling may be more complex; however, you can make your life (or your scheduler's life) much easier if you organize your call flow — what and how many of various groups of calls are sent to particular groups of agents or call center sites — appropriately.

If you treat each call center as an island — getting its own call volumes from its own customer base or a subset of the overall customer base — then you can schedule each center independently, as if it were the only call center in your operation.

Frequently multi-site call centers are on the same network, so they work together just like one larger center. Calls from your customer base are directed to the first available agent — wherever she's sitting. It doesn't matter if the centers are separated by a few hundred feet, several thousand miles, or even an ocean: you can treat them as one for scheduling purposes.

Part III
Making Life Better with Technology

The 5th Wave   By Rich Tennant

"For additional software support, dial "9", "pound", the extension number divided by your account number, hit "star", your dog, blow into the receiver twice, punch in your hat size, punch out your landlord, ..."

In this part . . .

Any sufficiently advanced technology is indistinguish- able from magic.
— *Arthur C. Clarke*

Part III helps to demystify the apparent magic that makes the call center machine hum. It reviews call center technologies — including basic requirements and valuable enhancements — in layperson's terms. A central argument in this part is that technology should not be implemented unless it can be shown to advance the business causes of the call center.

Chapter 8

Making It Go: An Introduction to Call Center Technology

In This Chapter

▶ Finding the right technology for your call center

▶ Using telecommunications technology

▶ Managing data and information

▶ Keeping score with technology

*B*roadly speaking, technology does three things for your call center:

✔ It gives your customers a way to communicate with your company.

✔ It allows the call center to more readily collect, access, and edit information about your customers.

✔ It provides a means for reporting on activity within your call center.

Call center technology is becoming increasingly integrated — making for improved processes and resulting in increases in customer satisfaction, efficiency, and revenue generation.

The Need for Appropriate Technology

Call centers are both a product of, and a requirement for, the information age. The advancement of the telephone and telecommunications made the call center possible, while advancements in data communications and the Internet have made it more sophisticated, efficient, and permanent.

Call centers are a response to the demand for convenience in a world that continues to move faster. Consumers don't have the time, or the desire, to go to the market square for every purchase or to receive services. Technology speeds things up, and is the foundation upon which call centers are built.

Running your call center, however, is still about people and processes, and since technology is so fundamental you have to be careful not to over-rely on it. Technology for technology's sake can be a problem — an expensive problem — if it's not providing adequate benefit to your company.

Good operations blend people, processes, and technology into effective solutions that maximize customer satisfaction, cost control, and revenue generation — they maximize the lifetime value of the relationship. When you apply proper technology to a well-thought-out call center plan, involving good people and well-designed processes, you'll build an effective business solution.

The call center network diagram

Figure 8-1 shows the basic layout of a typical call center network, illustrating many of the pieces of technology I speak about in this chapter.

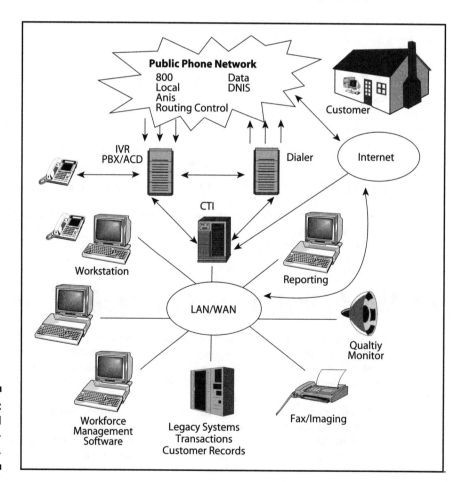

Figure 8-1:
The call center network.

Telecommunications: Getting the Customer's Call to the Call Center

The first piece of technology you need is a means of getting the customer's call to your call center. For the most part, this is done through the public telephone network, something that's such an integral part of the call center world that people don't give it much thought. Customers just pick up their phone and dial a number to be connected to your operation.

Like most call center operations, yours probably makes use of *toll-free* 800 numbers. Your customer dials a number that has an area code starting with an 8, and — even though the call center might be thousands of miles away — the customer doesn't pay long distance charges (hence the "toll-free"). Of course, somebody still has to pay the bill — it just goes to the call center instead of the customer.

On the other side of the coin are those call centers that use phone numbers starting with a 9 — usually 976. For these calls, the customer does pay ... sometimes a lot! I tried to get a job at one of those call centers once, but apparently I didn't have the right "tone" for the job.

Today's telephone networks provide your call center with a number of valuable services, including

- Automatic number identification (ANI)
- Dialed number identification service (DNIS)
- Dynamic network routing
- Automatic call distribution (ACD)
- Predictive dialer
- Interactive voice response (IVR)
- Voice recognition

Automatic number identification (ANI)

Automatic number identification (ANI) is a service that transmits the customer's telephone number and delivers it to your call center's telephone system. This can be very valuable, because the information can be used to identify the customer and look up their account information before an agent even says hello. You can use this information to give the caller special treatment—your very best customers might be routed to an elite group of agents, for example. Special routing is a great way to boost customer satisfaction and revenue per customer. I talk more about routing later in the chapter.

A popular use for ANI

On your home phone, you see automatic number identification in action if you subscribe to a *call display* service. The number of an incoming call is displayed for you — allowing you to decide, for example, if the caller is important enough to interrupt the 12-hour *Star Trek* marathon you're watching on TV. Who knows? Maybe it's the dry cleaner, calling to let you know your Klingon costume is ready for pickup. You wouldn't want to miss that call!

Alternatively, you might just use ANI to pull up a caller's account information so that your agents can be ready to handle the customer's inquiry. Having this information might shave only a few seconds off average call length, but the resulting savings compounded over thousands of calls is tremendous.

Dialed number identification service (DNIS)

Since your call center probably has several different 800 numbers — depending on the various services or products you offer — it's important for you to know which of those numbers the customer called. Through DNIS, the telephone network provides you with the number that the customer dialed. This information tells the telephone system how to route the caller.

Dynamic network routing

This service goes by a number of different names, but the basic concept remains the same. Some call centers have a computer terminal that is directly connected to the telephone company's switching office. This computer allows you to control the routing of your customer's calls at the network level — before they hit your telephone system.

For example, when call volumes peak beyond a level that can be serviced in your call center, you can redirect calls to other centers that you have overflow agreements with. (I talk about overflow agreements in Chapter 6.) Calls can be routed based on a number of different criteria, such as a predetermined percentage allocation to each office. And, because the routing occurs in the telephone network, your 800 expenses are not adversely affected and the routing appears seamless to the customer.

Dynamic network routing also gives you the ability to provide call-promoting (press 1 for English, 2 for French, for example) right in the telephone network.

Automatic call distribution (ACD)

Automatic call distribution (ACD) could be considered the heart of the call center. When customer calls arrive, they are delivered to the ACD — a phone system that routes a large volume of incoming calls to a pool of waiting agents. It's different from other phone systems in that it makes use of telephone queues instead of extensions.

Queues act as a sort of waiting room for callers. That's where your callers will likely hear a recording similar to, "All of our agents are currently getting coffee ... er ... assisting other customers. Please hold and we will be with you shortly."

Call center operators learned years ago that queuing incoming calls as they arrive and then distributing waiting callers to the first available agent could achieve large staffing efficiencies. (Imagine the alternative: thousands of customers calling individual agent extensions.) This queuing ability is a key part of call center efficiency. You can create a large number of different queues within your ACD — callers can then be routed to various queues depending on service required, language preferences, and so on.

The ACD has a number of other important capabilities:

- ✔ **Delay messaging:** This is the recording that says, "Thank you for calling; all of our operators are currently busy...." Delay messaging tells customers that they have reached the right place and it is very effective at getting callers to wait briefly. The ACD provides the center with multiple messages, which you can play at any time during a customer's wait.

- ✔ **Music on hold:** Music on hold plays between delay messages. Again, the main objective of music is to encourage customers to wait for the next agent. It's important to play appealing music or information. You have to be careful not to have your delay messages interrupt the music too frequently, or they can become a nuisance and possibly result in the customer actually hanging up *faster*.

- ✔ **Skills-based routing:** As a variation on routing to queues, most ACDs have the ability to route to skills instead. As the name suggests, skills-based routing is used to match each caller's needs with the agent who has the best skill set (of those available at the moment) to service those needs.

  The first step in skills-based routing is to establish a skill set for all agents. Next, you must attempt to identify the skill requirements of callers. This can be done in a number of ways, including looking at the number dialed by the customer (DNIS), collecting caller information through telephone prompts ("Press 1 for English..."), or looking up the caller's phone number using automatic number identification and searching your customer database to pick up some important information about the caller. For example, using ANI you might determine that a caller is a high-spending VIP. Knowing this, skills-based routing can be used to send the caller to one of your best agents.

Skills-based routing doesn't eliminate queues; what it does do, however, is to dynamically change the agent queue for each caller.

✔ **Reporting:** ACDs provide a great deal of reporting — both historical and real-time. Real-time ACD reporting tells you everything you need to know about your current call center performance. By looking at the real-time reports, you can see how many callers are waiting to be served, how many agents are staffing the phones, and how long it's taking the agents to process calls. They'll also tell you how many customers have hung up waiting for service, and how quickly they're hanging up.

ACD: Best friend to the telethon

Ah, the days of my youth — watching the Labor Day telethon with my family. Little did I realize then how well that TV time would serve me in years to come, if only to help explain ACD.

During the telethon, the national network would occasionally switch over to the local affiliate. Remember? Often, you'd see a group of volunteers at a bank of phones, waiting to take pledges. Usually they were sitting at tables in rows of three to five, with a phone in front of each volunteer, the next table behind slightly elevated so we could see all their smiling faces. Well, if you looked carefully, you might've observed that the person at the bottom left of your television screen seemed to always be on the phone taking a pledge. The person next to him or her was also almost always busy taking a call. The next person was slightly less busy, until finally, the person in the top right-hand corner of your screen seemed never to be on the phone. Why? They didn't use an automatic call distributor.

Without an ACD, the phone lines at the local TV affiliate would be set up much like they would be if you had multiple phone lines in your home or small business. So, when that first call comes in it goes to the first available agent — the person in the seat at the bottom left. When the next call arrives, the phone system sees that the first person is busy, so the call is routed to the next available agent — Agent 2. Similarly, when call 3 comes in it's routed to Agent 3, since 1 and 2 are busy. By this time, assume Agent 1 has completed his or her call. Guess what happens when call 4 comes in? Well, the phone system looks for the first available agent, right? Since the phone lines are, in essence, set up in series, it means that Agent 1 will again get the call as the first available agent. That's why agents at the end of the line are so bored. The only way that Agent 15 will take a call is if all 14 agents before him or her are all simultaneously busy taking calls. Doesn't seem fair, does it? It isn't. And in a call center environment, where you're likely to have hundreds of agents on the phone, all being paid to do the same work, it simply doesn't make sense to have some constantly busy and some almost constantly idle.

That's where ACD comes in. As calls come in to the call center, the ACD finds the caller who has been waiting the longest of those calls waiting in queue and looks for the agent who has been idle (that is, not on a call) the longest, and links them up.

Gathering reports from the ACD

The automatic call distribution component of your telephone system provides the basis of your reporting requirements. You can collect reports from the ACD on three general areas: agent performance, queue performance, and trunk performance. All activity effort starts with a customer call, and the phone system tracks volume, timing, and effort associated with accepting phone calls.

Agent performance

ACD agent performance reports, like the example shown in Figure 8-2, provide statistics on each individual agent: how long the agent took to service calls, how many calls were answered, the amount of time that the agent was logged in, and when they logged in. (I talk more about measuring agent performance in Chapters 5 and 11.)

Agent Report

QTD	(All)			
Month	(All)			
WeekEnding	(All)			
Date	(All)			
Supervisor	(All)			
TARGET			660	

AGENT	LOGGED HOURS	OCCUPANCY	CALLS ANSWERED	AVG HANDLE TIME	AVG TALK TIME	AVG WORK TIME	AVG HOLD TIME	OUTBOUND CALLS MADE	AVG OUTBOUND TIME	AVG AUX TIME
Agent 1	285.59	59.44%	1304	458.75	458.64	0.10	8.16	32	64.66	1.76
Agent 2	149.93	65.33%	684	489.58	487.59	1.99	18.21	57	77.23	7.76
Agent 3	432.24	60.08%	1652	510.11	476.92	33.18	50.65	89	59.57	5.17
Agent 4	263.42	66.52%	1099	534.89	486.51	48.38	37.26	42	15.38	1.81
Agent 5	407.09	56.96%	1454	493.16	471.45	21.71	78.22	21	127.76	274
Agent 6	355.24	60.28%	1322	538.10	533.41	4.68	36.70	85	97.68	8.34
Agent 7	501.58	63.24%	1896	522.27	481.85	40.42	73.83	96	105.39	6.22
Agent 8	382.66	59.41%	1338	570.05	539.89	30.16	32.71	54	108.48	8.93
Agent 9	358.05	63.78%	1335	549.35	546.76	2.59	57.76	95	95.41	8.67
Agent 10	265.29	62.04%	962	583.26	580.19	3.07	25.26	46	96.37	7.43
Agent 11	202.82	69.91%	826	576.75	565.89	10.86	28.57	77	108.09	12.62
Agent 12	2.05	75.92%	9	585.67	585.67	0.00	22.89	2	57.00	14.78
Agent 13	281.71	62.77%	1019	566.11	529.52	36.59	50.88	61	102.23	7.74
Agent 14	178.06	61.54%	631	575.58	533.70	41.88	38.97	32	93.16	10.64
Agent 15	275.95	65.53%	1034	562.20	535.80	26.39	57.32	61	125.46	9.27
Agent 16	374.19	62.21%	1331	573.09	554.89	18.20	50.14	61	105.00	6.35
Agent 17	468.34	62.55%	1671	568.13	539.58	28.56	55.70	66	108.24	7.28
Agent 18	422.08	63.26%	1512	593.81	522.93	70.88	36.07	32	143.53	5.88
Agent 19	274.35	57.04%	882	592.93	580.63	12.30	37.81	62	88.48	7.95
Agent 20	194.33	70.65%	767	601.89	579.76	22.13	26.20	95	92.76	16.36
Agent 21	405.56	62.80%	1413	555.83	521.47	34.36	86.66	84	91.99	6.38
Agent 22	175.06	71.00%	686	618.23	616.19	2.04	27.16	48	53.50	6.90
Agent 23	208.52	65.54%	750	630.16	608.21	21.95	1.13	36	143.00	24.65
Agent 24	314.00	63.26%	1808	600.44	577.38	23.06	43.23	107	120.27	13.77
Agent 25	451.88	62.37%	1537	630.96	619.42	11.54	21.04	79	80.28	8.18
TOTAL	7630.07	63.74%	195195	563.25	541.37	21.88	40.10	1520	94.44	8.70

Figure 8-2: An ACD agent performance report.

Queue performance

A queue is an answering group — it represents service provided and received by a universe of callers with similar needs. Different queues are usually set up for callers with different needs. Customers with different language requirements, for example, will be directed to queues staffed with agents who are capable of providing service in the needed language.

Queue reports will tell you how many people called, how fast you answered the phone, how many customers hung up, how long it took to service the average call, how many agents were logged in to the system, and so on.

Trunk performance

Telephone lines are frequently referred to as trunks. Trunk performance reports provide information on the telephone lines leading into the ACD, and can be used to ensure appropriate facility sizing, for example. They provide information on the utilization of each line and the amount of time that all lines were busy (raising the potential that callers received busy signals). They also provide information on the average time that each line was in use.

You can also tell how fully utilized your seating and phone lines are. Unlike your local bank branch, in a call center you can't physically see the customers being served or waiting for service, but you can still have a very clear picture of what they are experiencing. From the ACD reports you can determine if your customers are waiting too long, if your agents aren't busy enough, or if your office is operating perfectly. You can then take action to correct any imbalances — adding staff to help waiting customers, for example, or moving agents into other work when you're overstaffed.

The ACD's historical report provides a complete view of the level of service and productivity achieved in servicing customers over days, weeks, and months. The amount of data that is available is tremendous, and your analyst can give you even more details. In general, the information that you'll get from historical reports includes call volume, call length, information on how quickly customers were served (speed of answer), information on how busy your agents were, and information on how many of your staff were operating the phones. All of this information is summarized and presented in a variety of time frames, including by interval (time of day), by day, by week, or by month.

 While all the data that comes from the ACD is very important, what is most important is that you have the ability to download this information into your reporting warehouse. The ACD manufacturers have made it very easy to transfer historical data across the LAN (local area network) and into a warehouse. (A LAN is an internal network that delivers online services across an organization; I provide a complete definition later in this chapter.) By doing this, ACD data can be mixed with information from other systems to generate some very powerful information for your management team, as I describe in Chapter 5.

Predictive dialer

A predictive dialer is a device used by collections departments and telemarketers, for example, to manage large volumes of *outbound* calls — calls originating from your call center. The dialer increases agent productivity by placing more outbound calls than the available number of agents. The dialer then sorts out answering machines, busy signals, and other non-human interactions before delivering live calls to the agents.

This technology can increase agent productivity by 300 percent or more over manual dialing, by removing list administration from the agent and reducing agent wait time between live calls. It can also increase customer irritation by 500 percent when it is used irresponsibly.

In addition to filtering out answering machines, busy signals, fax machines, and so on, the call center can control how aggressive the predictive dialer is in dialing customers. If you want to keep your agents very busy, you make the dialer dial faster. This comes at a cost, however.

In some cases, the dialer can be programmed to be so fast that it no longer filters out just unwanted calls, but also makes live customers wait for available agents. That's why you sometimes hear a long delay before an agent speaks on some telemarketing calls. (Ring, ring ... "Hello" ...long pause... <click> "Hi, may I speak with...er...um...Ray Alburgiven, please?)

I agree that this is an inconsiderate and overly aggressive practice. Fortunately, a number of countries are placing laws on how aggressively companies may use their predictive dialers.

The list of customer names being dialed will be key to your level of success when using a predictive dialer. Lists generally include the customer's name, some pertinent customer information, and their phone number.

Managing your customer list effectively is an important part of outbound dialing. To maximize the effectiveness of each list, you must check the list for incomplete or incorrect information. Scrubbing refers to the process of removing from the list names that you don't want to dial.

It's best to also scrub lists based on other information you might have about a customer's interest in the product or service being offered. For example, customers who live in low-income areas could be removed from lists designed to promote a premium, high-end product. By scrubbing out customers who are less likely to want a product that you are promoting, you will increase the quality or effectiveness of your list and make more sales over the life of the list. As a result, dialing will be more effective.

Most countries have tabled or enacted legislation targeted at call center practices. These laws are generally directed toward telephone sales, the use of predictive dialers, and privacy. For example, the United States has implemented "do not call" legislation; this law requires call centers to scrub their telemarketing lists against government-provided do not call lists. By checking every list against both government lists and your own internal do not call list, you can be sure that you aren't calling customers who prefer not to be called for any offer. I talk more about legislation that affects call centers in Chapter 12.

Take this seriously! It's a really, really good idea to scrub against a do not call list. Your dialer makes lots and lots of calls per agent hour. Staffing with even only ten agents means you'll be making thousands of calls per day. If you've forgotten to scrub against the do not call list, you could be violating the law thousands of times per day! The fines are as much as $11,000 per violation, so it doesn't take long to add up to lots of money. Oh, and the legislative governing bodies mean business — violate and you'll be paying.

The do not call list is a positive for the call center in that it provides more information about the customer along with a quick and cost-effective way of improving lists and, ultimately, dialing effectiveness.

Predictive dialer reports

Like the ACD, the predictive dialer reports on agent productivity, office productivity, and trunk performance. The dialer reports on the results of each call, including sales per hour, refusals, reasons for refusals, and how many answering machines were encountered. Because the dialer dials more customers than it has agents to handle, you'll occasionally run into situations where agents are not available when the customer answers the phone. The dialer needs to be able to report on how many customers had to wait for an agent and how many customers hung up while waiting.

Interactive voice response (IVR)

Interactive voice response (IVR) is the use of automation — automated voice prompts and, sometimes, synthesized speech — to provide service to customers. Think of IVR as a robotic agent. Whenever you've called your bank to determine your credit balance and used the automated account lookup, which reads your account balance in a computerized voice, you've used IVR.

IVR is very cost-effective. The cost of a service provided by IVR can be less than 1/5th the cost of providing the same service using a live agent. What's more, IVRs generally provide faster and more convenient service. Rarely will your customer have to wait for the "next available IVR agent" — and, since IVR is virtually always available, it's there whenever the customer is: 24 hours per day.

The payback on investing in IVR should be very fast for you — well under a year. You can measure the benefit in terms of call avoidance. Calls that don't make it to call center agents reduce the total calls offered per customer.

Here are some simple keys to greater IVR success:

- ✔ **Provide a quick "out."** Give callers who don't want to use the IVR a quick way out by pressing 0 at any time to get an agent.

- ✔ **Keep it short and sweet!** The IVR script should be up-tempo, clear, and to the point. Humans can interpret speech much faster than 100 words per minute, yet most IVRs are paced slower than this. The result is that callers get bored and opt for the quick out. Formalities are not necessary. Callers know that they are listening to a machine, so keep it polite but don't bother with a lot of extra pleasantries.

✔ **Follow the "3 by 3" rule.** Try to avoid offering more than three options at a time and don't drill down more than three options deep into the IVR script. If you break this rule, you may find that customers begin to drop out of your IVR service, opting for a live agent.

Voice recognition

Traditional IVRs accept input through touch-tones. With voice recognition (or speech recognition) software, however, the IVR can accept human language commands. Voice recognition can range from the simple, "If you'd like to reach sales, say 'sales,'" through to the more sophisticated, "Please state the name of the party you are looking for," to which you might answer, "Joe's Pizza and Spam Emporium." The IVR would look Joe up and provide you with a phone number. Neat stuff!

"Robotic agents" don't take coffee breaks!

IVR reports

The IVR unit provides reports on calls received, options customers selected, the length of time customers spent using IVR services, and when they used IVR services. Figure 8-3 shows an IVR report for a customer opinion survey application. The report shows how many calls were taken and the average call length during each half-hour interval of the day, and the IVR selections made by the customers who completed the survey. The detail in the IVR report will tell you about the success of the applications that the IVR is running.

Figure 8-3:
An IVR
Report.

IVR Report

Responses Results

How satisfied were you with the amount of time our representative took to process your request?

Interval	Calls Recieved	Avg C.S.T. (Customer Service Time)	1 — Very Dissatisfied	2 — Dissatisfied	3 — Neutral	4 — Satisfied	5 — Very Satisfied	Grand Total
10:00	11	153.14				1	10	11
10:30	14	142.01					14	14
11:00	10	100.90			1		5	6
11:30	17	105.79	3			2	12	17
12:00	11	142.53			1		17	18
12:30	15	162.77		1	1	3	13	18
13:00	14	124.01	2			1	23	26
13:30	15	151.68	1				17	18
14:00	11	147.48					7	7

Getting Information to the Agent

The two most important devices for your call center agents (or managers) are the phone and the computer. The phone routes a call from the customer's house, cell phone, or office to one of your skilled agents. Without the phone, you obviously wouldn't have much of a call center.

After the call is routed to an agent, that agent needs the best possible tools and resources to provide the customer with quick and accurate service. Today's networked computer systems are the means by which your agents access these capabilities, which include

- ✔ Customer accounts
- ✔ Product and service information and pricing

This is the minimum and pretty much what every call center provides to its agents. More sophisticated environments also include access to

- ✔ Company knowledge bases including problem-solving guidelines and policies and procedures
- ✔ Call guides and scripts, sometimes including dynamic scripts that customize call-handling recommendations based on individual customer characteristics and preferences
- ✔ A personal performance "dashboard," which provides agents with critical information pertaining to their job performance
- ✔ Communication tools for communicating with other departments, peers, and management
- ✔ The Internet
- ✔ Other tools such as software for e-mail, chat, collaboration, faxes, and letters

The key is to provide at the agent's fingertips everything they'll need to perform their job. If this can be done with as few applications as possible, all the better.

The more easily your agents can access anything needed to serve callers — including account information, knowledge, troubleshooting tips, call strategies, and phone services — the more successful they will be on every call.

There's no tool like an old tool...

Not that long ago, I was working with a call center for a travel agency. Call length had always been long, but was getting longer. Management was understandably becoming very concerned. As a result of the increasing call length, costs were of out of control and customers were becoming dissatisfied. I quickly determined that the number-one reason for the long calls was that the agents needed to call other travel companies to book travel packages. In some cases, my client's agents were waiting 40 minutes or more to get through to the other company's agents. We calculated that this delay was 100-percent the cause of my client's call-length woes.

We immediately set about to find an online travel reservations system that would allow agents to bypass the other company's call center. After more than a week of research, I was having lunch with one of my client's agents when I described what I was trying to find. This agent knew what I was talking about immediately. "Something like vacations online," the agent said. "Yeah, something like vacations online," I said. "We really could use vacations online," the agent said. "Yup, we really could

use something like vacations online," I said. This went on for several minutes until I realized that the agent was telling me there really was an application called Vacations Online. "What does Vacations Online do?" I asked. "It allows you to deal directly with all of our suppliers' data," the agent said. "Where do you suppose we could get Vacations Online?" I asked. "We have it," said the agent. "Come again?" I said. "We have it. We've had it for a long time," the agent said. "Is it any good?" I asked. "It's fantastic!" said the agent. "So why don't you use it," I asked, getting ready to jump out a window. "It's not approved yet, it's still in testing," the agent said.

Needless to say, everyone was surprised. Seems that the person who purchased the software had left the company some time ago. To make a long story not so long, they immediately began using the software and chopped more than 100 seconds out of average call length. I don't need to tell you the financial impact that this had. (In case I do, see Chapter 5.)

The moral of the story is the power of fingertip access to call center tools.

Recruiters and trainers can put a very skilled and motivated person on the phone. The capability of that agent is magnified by what is delivered to the agent through the workstation, resulting in improved performance in performance drivers and, as a result, in your larger business objectives.

The workstation itself should be very neat and relatively spacious. The terminal can make use of industry-standard operating systems, which use a graphical interface and can be navigated with a mouse or keyboard.

The pain of processing paper

Several years ago, in my own call centers we had two processes: a paper process with lots of binders and forms, and network access to our customer billing system. While our billing system was very reliable in terms of up time, it wasn't very flexible. It was almost impossible to automate agent processes. Anything we were able to automate usually took months to implement. As a result, we created more paper and additional back-end work to process this paper. The system worked, but it wasn't very efficient and was prone to lots of errors. At the end of the day, this type of system isn't very user-friendly for a call center agent.

Creating the "everything at your fingertips" workstation is important, but it's even more important to have the ability to make quick changes and enhancements to the workstation. New policies, products, and services will continue to be created and your team should always be finding better ways to do their jobs and service the customer.

This continuous improvement will be very difficult if you don't have the ability to quickly modify your tools. For this reason, it's wise to maintain at least one "application master" who maintains control over the content of the application.

The benefit of being able to make constant improvements in the process of handling tens of thousands of calls per month can greatly outweigh the cost of maintaining a dedicated application master. (I talk about ways to measure improvements in Chapter 5.)

The call center world is full of packaged workstation tools and applications, many of which have been specially built for the call center industry — even specialties *within* the call center industry. Others are classic customer billing and information systems that exist inside and outside of the call center.

Some examples of call center applications include

- ✓ **Contact management software:** software that tracks customer contacts, reasons, resolutions, and follow-up

- ✓ **Help desk software:** software that records, tracks, and allows for the analysis of support requests within an organization

- ✓ **Knowledge-management software:** software that provides call center agents with a path of questioning and diagnosis that leads to a solution/resolution for a customer request

- ✓ **Sales and marketing software:** software that helps call center agents maximize their sales and marketing efforts by providing product information details, pricing, cross-sell and upsell opportunities, as well as scheduling follow-up activities for agents

- ✔ Telemarketing software
- ✔ Billing systems
- ✔ Reservations systems

Connecting to the local area network (LAN)

The local area network (LAN) is an internal network that delivers online services across the organization to anyone who has some kind of intelligent terminal, such as a personal computer. With the development of a LAN and an intelligent terminal at the agent's workstation, you'll create a number of possibilities. Services, for example customer billing systems, can be connected to the LAN, making them more easily available to anyone on the LAN without drastically changing the look and feel of the billing system for the user.

Examples of other services that can be connected to a LAN include

- ✔ Fax and imaging server
- ✔ E-mail and chat server
- ✔ Customer relationship management (CRM) technology
- ✔ Data management tools
- ✔ The Internet
- ✔ Workstations

Fax and imaging server

In the past, whenever a customer needed to fax information to the call center, it would have to be printed on a local machine and put into an agent's in-basket. The agent would then process the fax and file it — creating lots of potential problems. Faxes can easily be misplaced or misfiled, resulting in the customer having to resend. The resources wasted could be tremendous.

By installing a fax server to the LAN, these problems are avoided. When customers need to fax you, the faxes are stored electronically on your fax server; agents can easily retrieve faxes from their workstations with no worries about filing. The time saved and reduction in errors is significant.

This same server is capable of storing images (that's the *imaging* server part), giving you the ability to scan any document and store it electronically. Your agents then have network access to the stored documents through their workstation. So, should a customer write a letter or send documentation regarding warranty claims, for example, the documents can be permanently scanned, stored, and quickly retrieved when needed.

Faxing and imaging help a great deal in the mission to eliminate paper. Call length is reduced, as agents are provided with easier and quicker access to information, and there is a reduction in errors and rework, as you'll have fewer (or zero) misfiled documents.

E-mail and chat server

Increasingly, customers want to contact call centers electronically, such as by e-mail and chat. The e-mail and chat server delivers these capabilities to the agent workstation.

This server is a little more complex than the e-mail or chat services that you may have in your home. In a call center, the e-mail and chat server routes customer contacts to agent workstations and manages the large volume of contacts in an organized fashion, much like how the ACD manages large volumes of calls (see the section on ACD in this chapter).

The system coordinates which agent receives the next contact — from a large pool of customer contacts — while also collecting statistics on the level of service and productivity that the call center brought to these contacts. It also allows you to build and reuse templates to answer common customer questions.

Scheduling software

Y'know the scheduling I discuss in Chapter 7? I have great news — there is software that does all that work for you! Workforce-management software is a system that forecasts call volume and length, determines staffing requirements, creates and organizes work schedules, conducts an automatic shift bid, tracks where your employees should be, gets your whites whiter, and gets those really tough stains out. Today's systems are integrated into the call center's computer network, making it possible for the system to share data with other systems and also for users anywhere in the center to take advantage of its capabilities. The systems have been evolving beyond mere scheduling and now provide other services, such as quality control, agent performance management, payroll, and reporting.

Remarkably, many of these systems start out quite simple. Much of what you learn from the chapters on scheduling is very close to what the systems are doing. They store historical data, forecast call volume data at the half-hourly level, do Erlang C calculations, and match available agents to staffing requirements. Probably the biggest benefit of workforce management software is its ability to keep track of all the thousands of bits of information required in preparing a call center schedule. Don't leave home without it.

Workforce-management reports

The workforce-management system provides a great deal of data and reporting relating to the use of call center labor power. Current systems will track and report on agent performance, uses of labor resources, and the efficiency of your call center staffing.

Reporting and Data: Using Various Technology Sources to Keep Score

Routing calls to your center starts the process of providing service to your customers. Keeping a well-designed set of tools and information at the agents' fingertips helps to make sure that you're providing that service with a decent level of efficiency and accuracy. However, without reporting you have no way of knowing how good you are, if you're improving, or if you're actually getting worse.

To be effective, reporting must be timely, complete, and accurate — all a lot easier said than done. It's worth the great deal of time and diligence needed to build good reporting systems. Few decisions should be made without reference to your management reports.

Call center systems tend to put out a lot of different reports. Your call center managers will tell you that reports provide the vital feedback on the drivers and business measures that make continuous improvement possible, and most managers and supervisors alike find that the reports available to them are very useful tools — they certainly wouldn't want to be without them.

As I describe throughout this chapter, your call center can get reports from the following systems:

✔ Automatic call distributor (ACD)

✔ Predictive dialer

✔ Interactive voice response system (IVR)

✔ Scheduling system

✔ Workstation applications

Not enough data for you? You can also conduct surveys.

Other systems, such as the department payroll system, can also provide reporting data, which is useful to the call center.

The payroll system can provide important reporting information on the number of hours your agents were paid for and the cost of paying these agents for their time.

These systems provide a lot of reports and a huge volume of data. By themselves, they tell us bits of information, but they don't paint the complete picture. In fact, looking at one piece of information without the benefit of other data can be very misleading. For example, an agent with very high call length might appear unproductive until it's learned that the same agent has the highest level of sales and customer satisfaction in the company.

Avoid getting caught up in the maze of call center reports and reporting. The best solution is to combine data from the various systems to create meaningful information about your drivers and business performance.

You can imagine how difficult and painful a process it is to combine data manually. It's labor-intensive, slow, and not very sophisticated. In some call centers, pulling reports together amounts to printing out daily results from a variety of systems, then keying those results into a formatted spreadsheet. With a process this cumbersome, creating detailed reports that drill down into processes is almost impossible. Supervisors have to create their own agent performance reports, and these reports will frequently be filled with errors. You'll spend a lot more time building reports than analyzing and acting on them.

Other call centers (mine included) have made dramatic strides in their reporting capability by automating the collection of reporting data through the creation of a data warehouse attached to the LAN. Routines are created that populate report data into prepared reporting templates. Then, the reporting team creates templates and checks to ensure that the reporting data have populated correctly. This greatly increases productivity. More important, it makes it possible to create a much larger number of reports, which drill down into processes with great detail.

Supervisors no longer need to prepare their own agent performance reports; instead, they use the reports that are automatically generated to provide targeted coaching to their agents.

Being able to report with this level of detail, speed, and accuracy is very important in a call center's efforts to manage processes and the key performance drivers. The old adage "if you can't measure it, you can't manage it" proves very true in the call center industry.

With all the data available to you and an automated method of pulling these data into meaningful information as it relates to your performance drivers and business objectives, you should have a very good understanding of your operation's performance. You'll understand how you're performing, why you're getting these results, and how you might improve performance, all giving you very strong control. And, it won't have been a tremendously expensive exercise. The payback of being able to read performance and manipulate it as you need to is practically immediate.

Chapter 9

Technological Enhancements: Getting the Newest and Coolest Stuff

. . . .

In This Chapter

▶ Using enhancements in technology to ensure continuous improvement

▶ Knowing how to recommend appropriate technology

. . . .

*A*s part of a strategy of continuous improvement, call centers are always looking at cool new technologies that may provide improvements in their business practices. Okay — maybe they're not all that "cool," but they definitely make things work better!

Driving Improvement with Technology

Your call center's analyst is primarily responsible for identifying opportunities for improvement, but everyone contributes ideas and recommendations. The manager of technology, for example, is likely to read trade journals and visit with vendors to keep abreast of new developments. He or she may come across something that will have a net improvement, and so should generally have an answer when someone asks if there's a technological solution to affect a driver in a particular way.

In this chapter, I give some examples of technological enhancements.

Computer–telephone integration (CTI)

Computer–telephone integration (CTI) refers to a system of hardware and software that allows for communication between the telephone system and the computer system. With this communication, you're able to instruct both systems to work together to produce some interesting and powerful applications. CTI is like call center superglue, only better.

A common and popular CTI application is the "screen pop," in which the phone system collects the caller's telephone number, either through automatic number identification or interactive voice response (I discuss ANI and IVR in Chapter 8), and passes this information over to the computer–telephone integration system. The CTI system then looks up the customer's information in the database. When a customer account is found, the CTI system coordinates with the telephone system to send the call and the customer information simultaneously to an agent's telephone and workstation. The agent doesn't have to look up the account — it arrives on her computer screen at the same time the call arrives on her telephone. Estimates suggest that the screen pop saves 10 to 15 seconds in average call length. As you know, this timesaving directly reduces the costs of running a call center.

This is just one example of a computer–telephone integration application. Some other neat examples that are made possible by this technology include

- **Mandatory data entry:** CTI can be used to make the entry of critical data mandatory before agents can take the next call. For example, frustrated that some agents forget to ask the customer what prompted them to call? Make completing the "reason for calling" field a mandatory task before the agent can move on to another call.

- **Soft phone functionality:** "Soft" phone is a techno-whiz way of saying that the agent's telephone acts as an application linking the agent and his computer. Using a software-based telephone increases the amount of information that can be collected about how agents use their time. For example, whenever the agent leaves his desk the soft phone application can prompt the agent to account for his time. "Lunch break" might be an entry that agents input into the soft phone when they're away from their desk for 30 minutes.

- **Enhanced reporting:** The CTI system tracks a customer call from cradle to grave. This means that the moment the telephone system recognizes a customer call, it's tracking that call through its entire life cycle in the call center. CTI knows how long the customer waited for service, what they selected in the IVR, their phone number, which agent they were routed to, what actions the agent took using company applications, whether the customer was transferred, and to whom. This incredibly rich source of information makes for very detailed reporting and analysis. For example, you can report not only on call length, but also on how long an agent spent in each part of the company's applications.

✔ **Idle-time training:** This one's really cool. CTI can monitor how busy the call center phones are at any point in time. When it identifies a lull in caller demand, it can route training information to idle agents. Better still, it can identify individual agent weaknesses and route the most appropriate training to each agent. What a great application! You get customized agent training with no loss in agent utilization. That's what the propellerheads call a "killer app."

✔ **Coordinated screen transfer:** This function enables agents to transfer what's on the customer screen as they transfer calls to another agent or supervisor. This way, the customer does not have to repeat their name and account information after they've been transferred. Not only does this save time, it also represents good customer service.

✔ **Call routing:** CTI can be used to control the routing of calls to agents, essentially taking this function away from the automatic call distributor (ACD). The benefit of using CTI to control call routing is the ability to add sophisticated logic to routing decisions. For example, using CTI a variety of information can be used to make dynamic routing decisions. When a customer calls, CTI may look up the customer's account history, refer to the analytics prediction on this customer's preferences and likely behavior, and then refer to the customer's selections in the IVR before deciding which agent to route the call to.

✔ **Dynamic scripting:** Once the caller has been routed to an agent, CTI may prompt the agent with a customized script or call-handling approach to serve the specific customer. In doing so, CTI refers to a customer's analytics database, which predicts the customer's preferences and suggests the most appropriate call-handling strategy.

✔ **Call blending:** Call blending occurs when agents can be switched among different types of work at any time. For example, an agent might be blended between inbound customer service calls and outbound collections. CTI can control this process by monitoring inbound caller demand and dynamically moving agents between inbound and outbound calling. This greatly increases the efficiency of inbound call handling. In Chapter 7, I discuss optimal occupancy; CTI-assisted call blending is an effective way to move occupancy closer to optimal.

✔ **Web-enabled call center:** As I discuss in Chapter 1, call centers are increasingly being called *contact centers* because multimedia contact methods have been added to inbound and outbound telephone calls. One way that other methods of contact are weaved into the call center is through CTI integration and blending. In these cases, other forms of contact, such as e-mail, chat, collaboration, or scanned letters, are routed to call center agents who possess the skills needed to handle these methods of contact.

Again, the CTI system is controlling the routing of these contacts. CTI can also blend these other forms of contact with inbound calls, creating more call-blending efficiencies. Presto! Your call center just became a contact center.

Lots and lots of other CTI applications exist. After years of using CTI, I'm still amazed at the magic this technology can perform in a call center. It's one tool that's ideally suited for creativity and continuous improvement. With a good CTI team, management is limited in what they can do only by their imagination.

Agent reporting warehouse

An agent reporting warehouse is something that may be difficult to find in the market. In fact, my team and I developed it for our own call centers. Our employee-performance supervisors wanted a quick method of summarizing all the agent performance reports that came out of our various systems, including payroll, scheduling, automatic call distribution, and customer relationship management applications. Some supervisors were building their own reports by keying data from the various systems into spreadsheets. This took a lot of time and was prone to errors, so we developed our own agent performance warehouse.

In our case, my programmers developed a data warehouse that captures all the necessary agent data, uses statistical tools to analyze the data, and provides summarized reports detailing agent performance on each driver and on a composite of all the drivers combined. We call this system our "continuous improvement module," or CIM.

This system collects data from all agent systems, combines the data into meaningful information, and presents this information in a consistent manner. It does all of this at the agent level and is available when the supervisors get to work in the morning.

The objective is to collect data on performance drivers and report on individual agent performance relative to these drivers. It's a very powerful means of targeting improvements in operational effectiveness to meet the business goals and mission. However, without a tool to summarize all of the reporting information and report on individual agent performance, it's virtually impossible to produce consistent, timely, and reliable reports.

A tool such as CIM helps to identify which agents truly are the star performers on an overall basis, aiding the cause of continuous improvement and competitive learning tremendously.

Quality monitoring

Most call centers do a great deal of quality monitoring. In many cases, they do this by randomly listening to and grading agent telephone calls, often recording them using a cassette recorder. Occasionally, the supervisor (or a member of a quality team) will sit beside the agent and review the call immediately upon its conclusion.

Other times, the supervisor will record the call remotely and review it with the agent at a later date. This method can be effective, but it has its drawbacks. Most significant is that it is very time consuming for the supervisor. Idle time between calls and the administration of storing, recording, and grading calls make the process very inefficient. Some supervisors have claimed that they can do about one call per hour when they included feedback. (I talk more about feedback in Chapter 11.)

Because the process is so labor intensive, it's difficult and impractical to target specific agent needs — such as high call length, low customer opinion, poor sales, or high returns.

For most call centers it's beneficial to purchase an automated quality monitoring system and integrate it into your LAN. Doing this will dramatically increase your supervisors' productivity and enable them to provide to the agents a greater volume of feedback with more specific detail.

The system automatically captures complete agent phone calls — recording both the voice conversation and a video picture of the agents' navigation of the systems. When supervisors are ready to review agent calls, they simply log in to the system from their workstation, retrieve sample calls from the agent they wish to review, and begin scoring.

Scoring is also done through the system. After they're done scoring, the supervisor can e-mail the results to the agent, with comments. The agent can also retrieve and review the call. The supervisor is relieved of the administration and wait time associated with manual quality monitoring. As a result, in some call centers using this technology supervisor productivity has more than tripled. Because they can retrieve calls from any agent without waiting, supervisors can target individual agents and try to understand performance deficiencies that are evident from the statistical analysis.

This more targeted and frequent feedback will help to drive the performance of the key metrics. Because of this, your individual agents will improve their performance and your overall business performance will improve as well.

CRM technology

Customer relationship management (CRM) is a business term that refers to the process of relating to your customers to maximize the length and value of that customer relationship. It involves data collection and analysis to better understand your customers' needs and wants. It also includes customized strategies for addressing unique customer needs. The whole point of CRM is to get new customers, to keep the customers you've got, and to maximize the value of the relationships you have with those customers.

The technology of CRM is diverse. However, it doesn't have to be overly complex or uncommon — especially in the beginning. I think of CRM technology in terms of four components: data collection, data management and analysis, the creation of business rules, and customer contact applications.

Companies collect data on their customers from a variety of sources. These include legacy customer information and billing systems, call center customer contact systems, Web-based contact information, or any other point of contact where the company can collect customer information. This information is used in building the CRM database.

Managing data is an important part of any CRM system. As the system collects information about individual callers, the data are stored in a large data warehouse. This information can be analyzed and inferences made about your customers' needs and intentions. You can make these inferences at the individual customer level, creating a service plan for each one.

Developing a CRM strategy

In my opinion, CRM is first and foremost a strategy. The core of this strategy is a philosophy and plan on how you want to treat your customers, what you want to get from your customer relationships, and what you plan to give customers in return. All parts of the organization should coordinate in the execution of your CRM strategy — from marketing to call center operations.

The execution of the CRM strategy includes three components: people, process, and technology. As with many call center initiatives, it is very easy to purchase technology in the hopes that it will solve your problems and achieve your strategic goals.

Even with the best technology, the people in the call center need to see the value in pursuing the CRM strategy. Call center agents, who for a long time have been concerned primarily with call length and keeping the customer happy, must come to believe that collecting customer information and offering that customer new products and services — that is, selling — is good for the company, good for the customer, and good for the agent.

Changing old behaviors might take some time. The same can be said for various levels of management. Call center managers will need to believe that the extra time taken collecting data will be worth the investment in longer call length and increased cost per call. And senior managers will need to give the call center time to adapt.

The CRM process will not spring to life overnight. It may take some time and some trial and error before all the components come together in a successful and profitable CRM solution. Patience, however, does not come easily, particularly when companies have spent millions of dollars on CRM applications, training, and consulting.

Using CRM data

Data analysis should be part of your overall CRM strategy. This analysis can be as simple as preparing reports and conducting database queries, or as complex as building predictive models in an effort to forecast the future behavior of your customers. Your marketing department might decide to mail information to certain customers who are most likely to purchase a product, for example. Other customers who are considered less likely to make any changes to the products or services they consume might be targeted for little or no marketing activity.

In the call center, the collected customer information is used to create business rules. Some rules will guide agents in the handling of specific customer calls. For example, VIP customers can be identified by automatic number identification from their home phone, and their calls can be routed to your best agents. Once the customer's call is answered, agents will be prompted by the CRM tools to make specific offers that analysis suggests the customer will be interested in.

Similarly, your data analysis can produce a daily list of the customers who are most likely to stop using your products. You can then make a point of making a service call to these customers to see if there is anything that can be done to enhance their use of your product or service. This proactive "save initiative" greatly reduces customer cancellation rates.

CRM applications are not unlike the call center applications on the agents' workstation. They include ways to access customer information and deliver information to the customer. In a CRM environment they will have additional functionality, such as information on the customer's call history and preferences, suggested sales and service strategies, and even suggested scripting.

My advice, especially to smaller organizations, is to start small and simple.

NuComm gets a lesson in CRM

Several years ago, in my first call center, we were very concerned with the collection of data. Our interest was in statistical process control. We wanted to know as much about the process of work in our call center as possible. So we collected lots of data: when the customer called, why they called, how often they called, what they called about, what the result of the call was, what the customer liked or didn't like, what the customer wanted — lots of data. We did this with a very simple tool, built using Microsoft Access by a smart kid in our call center. It supported about 100 users and it wasn't very complex or expensive to run or build. We didn't really know what we were going to do with a lot of this information. However, fate lent a hand.

It was early December; we were approaching the end of the year. One of our clients was coming up to their year-end and it was very important that they meet their sales projections. However, it was clear to everyone that the sales projections were not going to be met. And we were sure that we were about to get fired.

During a business review, the client commented that if they had thought of tracking customers who wanted the company's product but were unable to get it because it was not yet available in their area, then they could have met their sales objective by finding out which customers could now receive the product and offering it to them before the year end. "Oh," I answered, "we have that." "Holy cow!" the client said (or something like that) — "How many do you have on the list?" I made a quick call and found that there were easily twice as many customers who wanted the product as the shortfall in the sales objective. So we gave our client the list. The client contacted these customers and easily signed up enough to meet their sales objective.

We were heroes, kept the business, and CRM at NuComm was born. Ever since, I've been a big believer in listening to customers and making notes on how we can help them in the future. That's really all it amounts to. And while there are a lot of great and complex tools designed to help companies in their CRM pursuit, the tools and processes don't need to be complex to get a lot of value.

The technology component of call center CRM addresses the handling of each customer contact. What do your data and intelligence on this customer tell you about their needs and preferences? How should you handle them? Do they get routed to the IVR? Which agents should handle your high-value customers? Once the call reaches an agent, the primary point of CRM applications is to provide the agent with the means to access information on the customer, including recommendations developed from your analysis, and to collect new information provided by the customer.

How to Recommend Technology

Okay, you're a technology genius and boy oh boy, have you found some technology that's going to make a big difference. So what's next? How do you go about getting approval so you can start saving the call center money? Well, my first piece of advice is to keep it simple. Try the one-page cost–benefit analysis.

The one-page cost–benefit analysis

The most appropriate and effective way to submit a proposal for technology enhancements is with a one-page cost–benefit analysis. It's easy, and only two specific rules apply:

- ✔ First, the analysis must easily fit onto one page of $8^{1}/_{2}$- by 11-inch paper, and
- ✔ Second, the argument for spending money on new technology must be communicated in one minute or less.

In my call center, if you can't make the case on one piece of paper and in one minute or less, then I don't want to see the proposal. Certainly, some proposals are going to be a lot longer than one page. The point is that the business case for new technology should be so clear and so focused on business objectives and drivers that it can easily be summarized in one page. And you know what? No one ever reads those other pages anyway.

The easiest way to meet both of these rules is to use the business model I outline in Chapter 2. The model says that all business activities go toward the key objectives of generating revenue, minimizing cost, or satisfying customers. To make the case for new technology, you have to define the benefit of new technology in terms of those key business objectives.

I cover this in much more detail in other chapters. See Table 5-1 for a detailed list of key business objectives and the drivers that affect them.

To make your business case, you have to show that the new technology will affect at least one of the drivers in a manner that results in a benefit to your company that is substantially larger than the cost of the new technology.

Case study — Our call center gets IVR

A few years ago, we considered implementing IVR in one of our call centers. We believed that some of our simpler calls could be handled through an automated IVR. The possibility of cost savings was appealing. Our goals in implementing IVR were to reduce costs and increase service — customers would be able to use automated services 24 hours a day, without waiting.

At the time, I spoke with reps from five companies with call centers similar to ours. All five reported that as a result of implementing IVR they'd reduced calls getting to their agent staff by between 5 and 10 percent — the IVR handled the calls so agents didn't have to.

To be conservative, I assumed that our IVR would reduce calls by 5 percent. I was conservative because my manager loves to attack the reasonableness of my assumptions. Whenever I say that a new technology is going to affect one of our drivers, I always get the question, "How do you know for sure?" So, I'd better have a fairly good body of evidence supporting my assumptions. The more conservative I am in my assumptions, the easier a time I have making my case.

The cost for our IVR was budgeted at $25,000 per year. Using a formula given to me by our analyst, I quickly did a cost–benefit calculation:

Calculating the cost benefit of IVR

	Before IVR	*After IVR*
A Contacts per customer (1 Year)	4 times	3.8 times
B Customer base	500,000	500,000
C Call length (seconds)	240	240
D Occupancy	80%	80%
E Agent utilization rate	70%	70%
F Variable cost per hour	$20.86	$20.86
G Fixed costs per year	$4,000,000	$4,025,000
Total = A × B × C ÷ 3600* ÷ D ÷ E × F + G	$8,966,667	$8,743,333
Change		**$223,334**

(*3,600 seconds per hour)

So my one-minute cost–benefit analysis looked something like this:

> *Project:* Interactive voice response
>
> *Benefit:* Five-percent reduction in calls offered to agents resulting in more than $200,000 in annual savings.
>
> *How I know this for sure:* I surveyed five companies with similar calls and applications. All have realized reductions in calls offered to agents of more than 5 percent.
>
> *Cost:* $25,000 per year.

The one-minute cost–benefit analysis might not always get the project approved right away, but you're sure to get your manager's attention with numbers like those above.

Of course, the technology manager won't spend all of his or her time researching new technology. A great deal of it is spent ensuring that the call center's current technology is working — and continuing to make the call center go!

Part IV

Ensuring Continuous Improvement

The 5th Wave   By Rich Tennant

CUSTOMER PHONE SERVICE AT DISNEY CORP.

In this part . . .

*I*n this part I cover recruiting, job expectations, training, feedback, and support, and provide a simple framework to guide your journey through managing the performance of the most important resource in your organization — your agents.

In this part I also explore the call center process and how to manage it. Most operations can benefit from a discipline of continuous process improvement — if only they knew what that meant. I include an examination of policies and procedures, and review the importance of understanding both legislation and employment law and quality and certification trends in the industry. I also discuss the role of management certification.

Chapter 10

Managing Agent Performance Part 1: Hiring and Training

. . . .

In This Chapter

▶ Reviewing the primary components that contribute to agent success

▶ Introducing a step-by-step process for managing agent performance

▶ Understanding the importance of employee evaluation in hiring

▶ Setting clear expectations

▶ Covering the basics of effective training

. . . .

*E*very agent is a miniature version of your call center — every efficiency, revenue, or customer gained or lost by each individual agent directly affects the overall efficiency, revenue, and customer satisfaction of the entire operation. Moreover, variation in performance among agents highlights opportunities for improvement with agents and processes. All too frequently, however, agent performance management is not done well, or not done at all. This doesn't need to be the case.

With an understanding of the basic principles for optimizing performance, and a simple process to guide you (as I outline here and in Chapter 11), agent performance management can (and should) become the primary tool for achieving results for your operation.

The Key Components of Optimal Performance

In virtually any human endeavor, the three primary components that contribute to an individual's success are skill, motivation, and opportunity. Only when all three are optimized for your agents will overall call center performance and results be maximized.

Here's a brief overview of these important components:

- ✔ **Skill:** The ability or aptitude to do the job. What the agent brings to the party ... and what you add to them once they're there.

- ✔ **Motivation:** Behavior, which is directed to a goal. What drives the agents? What drives them to join your company? You need to take level of motivation into consideration when recruiting your people.

  Agent performance is also impacted by what you do, as a company, to arouse, maintain, and direct your agents' internal motivation.

- ✔ **Opportunity:** No matter how skilled or motivated your agents are, there can be no success without opportunity. However, opportunity is a part of performance management that's external to the agent. The environment that you put your agents into creates their opportunity. Tools, marketing, company policies, work processes, competition, media, economy, and customers all impact opportunity. Generally, opportunity at any given time is equal for all agents.

  Certainly, lots of things can be done to improve opportunity for your agents, such as improving your tools (such as customer relationship management applications — see Chapter 9), improving your product, and improving work processes and company policies. All of these things, however, are for the most part external to the agent.

Think about how these elements of performance relate to athletes playing professional sports. They obviously need a certain level of skill — probably a higher level than the average person (I've always known that the only thing keeping me from making it to the big leagues was the fact that I run too slow). Professional athletes also need an appropriate amount of motivation, or as the coach often describes it, a "fire in the belly!". The best players tend to have a natural, inherent desire to succeed. Finally, players can't play if there's no opportunity. Without fans buying tickets, there would be no games being played — no games, no opportunity to show off all that skill and motivation.

Managing agent performance is a process of managing their skill and motivation in an effective and ongoing manner. Done well, skill and motivation continually improve. Done poorly, at best, nothing happens — at worst, agents become disenchanted.

The Quick Answer: Following a Simple Framework

Years ago I was asked for a quick answer on what employee performance management included. After some thought, I boiled down managing agent performance to what I now call the "quick answer."

The five steps to the quick answer are:

1. Hire the right people.

2. Tell them what to do and why.

3. Show them how to do it.

4. Give them feedback on how they are doing.

5. Make supporting them your number-one mission.

I cover the first three steps in this chapter; Chapter 11 carries on with the final two steps.

Step 1 — Hire the right people: Recruiting and testing

Sounds simple enough, but hiring the right people is very important. Perhaps you're thinking, "In a call center, who's the right person? Someone who can speak?" The truth is, if you hire a person who isn't a good fit (especially from a skill and motivation standpoint), then your call center performance will suffer. Hire enough people who don't fit and you'll be in trouble.

Imagine you were putting together an Olympic baseball team. You'd start by advertising for tryouts. When 10,000 (or so) people applied, you'd do some prescreening, asking "Have you ever played baseball?" and other stuff like that. Then you'd have tryouts (on-field competency tests) to see if the candidates had the basic skill requirements. You'd want to know if they could throw, catch, and hit the ball with a big wooden stick. After the initial tests, you'd do other more advanced testing until you had a team of the best possible candidates.

Now, imagine the same team if you made all of your hiring decisions based on résumés and interviews alone. (Come on, you know that people are perfect only twice in their lives — at birth and on their résumé.) Chances are you'd put together a team that would make the Bad News Bears look like the Yankees.

It's the same in call centers. You've got to field the most skilled team to get the best results. That includes people who bring the necessary *skills* to do the job — language skills, typing, problem solving, learning capability — and people who have the necessary *motivation* to do the job. If you hire someone whose life ambition is to live in his parents' basement by day and hop the clubs at night (Dad made him go out and get a job and he found you), then you'll probably find that "this hire doesn't inspire."

Making good hiring decisions involves testing candidates in a manner that predicts their level of success on the job. In doing this you'll test for the correct skill and appropriate motivation.

Evaluating skill

Testing for skill is the easy part. You can do many things to evaluate skill level. Here are some of them.

Résumés and interviews

There's no better predictor of future success than past success. If candidates have done well in the past on jobs similar to the one you're considering them for, then your life is easier if you can determine just how well. Easier said than done, however. Sometimes candidates exaggerate past successes on their résumé — shocking, I know.

When interviewing potential call center agents, you might want to consider doing the first interview over the phone. Tell the candidate you'll be recording the interview and be sure to ask for permission. A phone interview is an excellent opportunity to see how the employee sounds and handles him- or herself in a live call situation.

Reference checks

Getting a reliable reference can also be difficult, since a smart candidate isn't likely to provide you with a poor or mediocre reference. It's far more effective if you can dig up your own reference from the candidate's previous employer. Even that isn't all that easy, because many companies have policies against giving detailed references — lest they be sued by their former employee for interfering with his or her ability to gain employment. Still, it can be done. If the candidate comes from within your own company it should be easier to find a reliable reference.

Aptitude tests

If you can't predict a candidate's future success in the job through résumés, interviewing, and reference checking, then employment testing is the route to go. A large number of tests are available. Some of those we like best include

- Customer service aptitude tests
- Sales aptitude tests
- Computer skills testing
- Specific call center aptitude testing

These tests are readily available through recruiting agencies or by searching the Internet.

Make sure that a test has been thoroughly validated to prove it accurately predicts success on the job. In some places, using a test that hasn't been validated can expose your organization to lawsuits from people who feel discriminated against. A variety of tests are available and you should find the one that's right for you.

Reducing recruiting time using IVR

If you run a call center with a large number of employees, you're probably constantly recruiting new agents just to keep up with staff turnover. Some large call centers use interactive voice response (IVR — see Chapter 8), which helps to recruit effectively and quickly without tying up recruiting staff, allowing them to focus on personal interviews.

Interested job applicants simply call your toll-free number. In a typical scenario, the automated IVR system asks the applicant to enter a telephone number and other identifying information for potential callback by your recruiters. Then the applicant is walked through a brief introduction to your business, available positions are listed, and the caller is interviewed on education, qualifications, and other job requirements. You control the entire interview process and the questions asked. At the end of the automated interview, applicants get a reference number and the call ends.

The data collected are used to create reports that your recruiters can search or filter based on their preferred criteria. For example, you can select only those employees that have customer service experience or a certain education level, thereby eliminating those that don't qualify for a live interview. This system reduces the number of live interviews conducted and allows your recruiting team to focus on those applicants who are qualified for the job.

It's also a good idea to do your own internal validation to see which methods work best for your center's needs. If you're good at collecting data on agent performance, then all you have to do to validate your employment tests is compare your employees' success on the job to their employment test results. You probably have an egghead in your office who remembers how to do correlation analysis — if you want to be really precise, let him have at it and then send him back to his Star Trek Web site.

Evaluating motivation

Predicting skills and aptitude (the ability to develop skills) is the easier part. Understanding a candidate's motivation is much more difficult but equally important.

You can uncover some of this information at the interview and reference-check stages — assuming the candidate's previous job was call center–related. Did she like her previous job? How was his attendance? Did she advance? Why did he leave?

If the candidate's never done a call center job, you'd be wise to have him or her listen to some calls — maybe for a few hours. Ask, "What do you think of the job?" "Does it interest you?" "Can you see yourself being in this role for five years?" "How would this job help you with your life goals?"

Similar to skills, level of interest and motivation in past jobs is a good indicator of future motivation in the new job.

Testing for motivation

It should be illegal, but sometimes candidates fake it. "Hey, Dad said that I had to get a job or he's going to kick me out of the house — which means goodbye 500-channel universe, goodbye high-speed Internet access, goodbye Mom's meatloaf ... I gotta get this job ... wonder if I'll meet any ladies ... ya, this job is my life!"

While skills testing tells you if a candidate can do the job, motivational assessment indicates if she will do the job. Some form of motivational testing helps to supplement interviews and reference checks. Sometimes a motivational analysis is built into the skills test, while in others the two are separate. Either way, a motivational analysis can greatly enhance your hiring success.

Frequently categorized as personality profiles, good tests will have a mechanism for detecting any attempt to manipulate the test.

Whatever testing you do should be integrated into your overall recruiting plan or model. (Figure 10-1 illustrates a sample recruiting process.) Also, from time to time you need to assess your recruiting process against your employees' success on the job. If you aren't getting consistent results, then it's time to change the process.

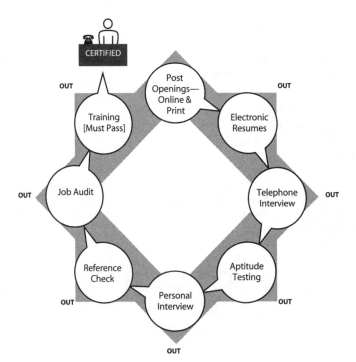

Figure 10-1:
Sample of a
recruiting
process.

Step 2 — Tell them what to do: Setting expectations

Trust me, one of the primary reasons why people don't succeed on the job is that no one's told them what to do — never mind being specific, clear, and measurable about it.

Your expectations for agents need to be clear on the first day they take responsibility for their job. Agents need to know what must be achieved to keep the job — and what they need to do to excel.

Perhaps it's a worn-out statement, but these expectations must be as measurable, specific, and observable as possible.

A good call center model tries to balance quality, cost control, and revenue generation. (See Chapter 2 for more on call center business models.) Likewise, when tracking agent performance you need a balanced set of measures. Call length, for example, is a cost-control measure, but to be thorough you'll need to track a complete set of quality, cost-control, and service measures. Table 10-1 shows some measures that you might consider. (I provide a more detailed explanation of measures in Chapter 2.)

Table 10-1	Typical Agent Expectation Measures and What They Tell You	
Business Objective	**Measures**	**What They Tell You**
Cost control	Call length / Schedule adherence	Together, call length and schedule adherence tell you what your agents are doing with their time.
	First-call resolution	First-call resolution tells you if agents are spending their time on calls effectively. If customers aren't calling back, it means they are.
Quality	Customer opinion	The customer's voice is the best indicator of satisfaction and quality. Call-review scores are great coaching tools, but don't confuse them with a direct indicator of quality. First, they're always subjective, and second, it's very difficult to get enough of them to get an accurate read on agent quality performance.
	Call-review scores	Use call reviews for coaching, and ask the customer about quality.

(Continued)

Table 10-1 *(Continued)*

Business Objective	Measures	What They Tell You
Revenue generation	Conversion (sales) per calls answered	Conversion tells you if your agent is getting results. Revenue per sale tells you about the scale of the results. Together they tell you how much revenue agents are delivering.
	Revenue per sale	Don't make the mistake of qualifying calls answered by taking out calls that you don't believe provide opportunities (wrong numbers, transfers, etc.). Everyone gets the same percentage of these calls. When you start filtering out calls, you open your call center data up to manipulation and unclear results. "Oh, we can include this call, but not that call ... that call? No, that call. Well, what about this call...."

Certainly you may consider other measures, but those in Table 10-1 are key because they all nicely drive your center's efficiency, service, and revenue objectives. In fact, they can be used to drive your model of operations throughout the organization. (Refer to Figure 2-1 for an illustration of an operations model.)

Keep it clear

If you were a new agent, here's an example of how we might explain minimum expectations:

"You need to handle customer calls in an average of 604 seconds or less over a monthly period, and no more than 10 percent of your customers can call back for the same issue within one month of talking to you. While doing this, the customers you speak to must give you a minimum score of 9 out of 10 or better when asked how satisfied they were with the service they received. You will need to sell one of our products to at least 15 percent of the people you speak to, and the average revenue per sale that you generate must be no less than $500.

"Of course, you'll have time to reach these minimum goals. Our experience is that it takes new hires one month to meet these minimums. After two months more than 85 percent of staff meet these goals consistently. Again, these are minimums; you and I will work together to make sure you meet them. Next, here's how you get bonuses and raises...."

Set actual expectations

Lots has been written and said about setting performance expectations. Most agree that performance expectations, at a minimum, need to be specific, measurable or observable, and realistic. Typically, call centers have no problem setting specific and measurable expectations. Making expectations realistic is more of a challenge. Frequently, expectations are set at the level where management would like to see performance. If expectations are set unrealistically high, staff will either ignore the expectation or become frustrated and demotivated in attempting to achieve it. If expectations are set unrealistically low, agents are likely to ignore the expectation because it's not a challenge. In both cases, the expectation fails to motivate.

A minimum expectation gives clear direction to your staff of the minimum they need to achieve. Because it's based on the average performance of the group, less one standard deviation (see Chapter 5), most will eventually achieve it without too much concern. Perhaps 15 to 20 percent of your staff will be conscious of the minimum expectation at any time. To motivate more of your staff and promote continuous improvement, it's useful to set a bonus level of performance.

I recommend setting the bonus level the same way that I set minimum expectations, except that for the bonus level of performance you calculate the group average performance and add one standard deviation. Like with minimum expectations, at any time approximately 13 percent of your staff will be achieving this bonus-level expectation — making the expectation realistic. There will be a number of staff performing just below this bonus level, and because they're close to achieving the bonus they'll be motivated to do "just a little better." This will result in improvement for these agents and the group as a whole — pushing up average performance, the minimum expectation, and the bonus-level expectation.

What's nice about setting minimum and bonus goals in this fashion is that it creates gentle pressure on the entire organization to improve.

To create expectations that are specific, measurable, and realistic, I like to use the historical performance of the agent group. To do this, I recommend using one standard deviation (see Chapter 5) from the average performance of the group to set the minimum — as illustrated in Figure 10-2. On the chart in Figure 10-2, the minimum expectation is set at approximately 603 seconds — one standard deviation above the team average of 589 seconds — while the bonus target for call length is approximately 575 seconds — one standard deviation below the average. That means that 87 percent of your staff will achieve this minimum. Those who don't achieve the minimum are targeted for extra help.

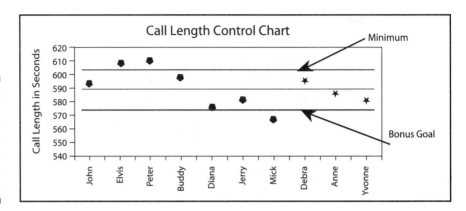

Figure 10-2:
Using a con-
trol chart to
set mini-
mum expec-
tations and
target goals.

Periodically, you'll need to change the goals to reflect improvements in process and agent performance.

Don't focus on one measure alone

In my discussion about setting expectations, I use average call length to demonstrate the setting of minimum and bonus expectations. Some of you will be saying right now, "Sure, but if all you manage is call length, then you're going to get fast, lousy service — and little or no quality." Fair comment. The same reasoning applies to any measure.

Concentrate your expectations on any one measure and you'll get what you asked for — great results in one measure, perhaps to the detriment of other areas of performance. What's needed is a balanced approach to setting expectations.

Some operations might need only to use a subset of the measures shown in Table 10-1. For example, if your call center doesn't do much selling then the revenue expectations might not be necessary.

When measuring agent performance you can use these metrics to create an overall scorecard — setting objectives (minimum expectations and bonus goals) for each measure individually and providing feedback (you'll find more details on feedback in Chapter 11), and rewarding performance based on how agents do against all the measures combined.

Every call's a sales call!

In Chapter 2, I mention that improvement in your call center's revenue generation can have a greater impact on results than improvements in cost-control measures. In larger call centers, small improvements in *retention rate* (maintaining customers who'd called to cancel service) can represent hundreds of thousands — or even millions — of dollars in saved revenue. Similarly, small improvements in selling and upselling can represent many hundreds of thousands of dollars or more.

Given that every interaction with a customer is a chance to enhance your business relationship, it's important that the expectation is set — and understood by all agents — that every call is treated as an opportunity to increase revenue, now or in the future. I provide a lot more details on general call handling in Chapter 14, and on handling sales calls specifically in Chapter 16, but if you just remember to treat every customer interaction as a make or break opportunity to win another long-term customer relationship you'll be on the right track.

"Dammit Jim, every call's a sales call!"

Create a balanced scorecard

I recommend using an overall performance index (OPI) — a single measure that rewards overall, balanced performance by mathematically combining the individual measures.

When establishing an overall performance index, I like to use the following calculation:

$$\text{OPI} = (3{,}600 \div \text{Call length}) \times \text{First-call resolution} \times \text{Schedule adherence} \times \text{Customer opinion} \times \text{Conversion} \times \text{Revenue per sale}$$

In the OPI calculation, 3,600 is the number of seconds in an hour. Dividing 3,600 by call length gives us a basic measure of productivity. Multiplying that by first-call resolution adjusts for agents who are getting through calls quickly but not completing the call satisfactorily (that is, the customer had to call back). This leads to a measure of overall productivity for which higher is better. Multiplying by schedule adherence adjusts the score downward for agents who aren't on the phones when they're scheduled to be — making them less productive. Multiplying by customer opinion adjusts the score downward for agents who leave customers less satisfied and higher for those whose customers are more satisfied. Multiplying by conversion rate and revenue per sale demonstrates how productive the agent is in generating revenue while processing customer requests. As you might have guessed, the higher the better.

Of course, you can always adjust the weighting of any one metric — giving customer opinion a higher weighting than the other measures, for example.

The agent who has the highest overall OPI is doing the best. They've balanced all their performance objectives into an overall optimum combination. OPI encourages improvement — improve performance in any of the key objectives, and OPI will improve. Improvement is always possible.

Now, you can chart OPI like you did with call length. The lower limit is a minimum and the upper limit indicates top-level or bonus-level performance. Direction to the agents becomes very simple: "Generate an OPI score that's above the lower band. If you exceed the higher band you'll get a bonus. You improve OPI by improving your performance in the underlying drivers. Do well in OPI and your life will be good."

Use an overall performance index ...

In compiling agent performance data for a rock-and-roll call center, management noticed that no one measure in itself tells the complete story about who is contributing more than the others. John has the lowest call length, but when the other measures are considered he comes out fourth in the overall ranking. John should focus on improving his first-call resolution. Maybe he tries to get through calls too quickly. Mick makes the most sales, but his average revenue per sale could use some improvement. Peter is our highest performing agent, because he has a high customer opinion and high average revenue per sale. Even though he had a higher call length than the others, his overall contribution translated into the highest overall performance index. Again, some will want to weight different measures in overall performance index to reflect their increased importance to the call center and the company.

Remember that these measures are derived from the call center's performance drivers that impact your business objectives. All of these measures are important, and it's important to consider them all when setting agent performance expectations.

... Oh, and also tell them why to do it!

When you tell your agents specifically *what* you expect of them, you're ahead of the game. When you tell them *why,* you're adding an extra level of motivational turbocharging that will kick-start continuous improvement.

Here are two good reasons you can give your agents for achieving their minimum expectations and stretch goals:

- ✔ **"Our department will meet its goals if we pull together."** Too often, the front line is left out of the big picture. Most people want to be part of a successful team. What's more, people want to know that their department (and company) is doing well and that their jobs are secure. Sharing department goals, how they work, and how individual results contribute to the overall goals is empowering and motivating.

> ✔ **"I'll reward you."** Raises, bonuses, commendations, opportunities for advancement — whatever the reward structure, it needs be tied into agents achieving their objectives. I once heard my favorite trainer say, "Every employee is tuned into the same radio station, W.I.I.F.M. — What's in it for me?"

Step 3 — Show them how to do it: Training and coaching

Okay, so you've hired very motivated and skilled people, and you've told them exactly what you expect of them.

If you stop there, you'll have some very frustrated high-performing people. (I wouldn't go alone into a room with a group of them.) Next, you've got to show people how to perform the specifics of the job they're being asked to do. Lots of companies train, but not all train in a manner that shows people how to excel at what's expected of them.

Plenty of material on effective training exists in the world. Here, I'll focus on a few basic rules to follow.

Make sure that the training you provide is targeted toward your agents' job performance goals. You've got to be able to answer these questions for your agents: "How will this help me meet and excel at my job expectations?" "How will this help me get ahead?" "How will this help me help the company?" Sounds simple, but it's important — especially if you want people to pay attention to the training you provide.

Keep it simple

Keep it SIMPLE ... Simpler ... simpler still. Research shows (I don't know what research, but hey, it sounds good) that a very high percentage of information that's delivered in training (maybe as high as 85 percent) is forgotten shortly after training ends. (Case in point: how much do you remember about high school calculus and algebra?)

You've got to stop fighting for the retention of information and focus instead on a few critical things for agents to remember — like, "How do I get my raises?" and "What must I not do if I want to keep my job?"

You should also focus on the development of critical skills for the job — how to use the database (which houses all the information that I really can't seem to cram into my head), for example — and call-handling skills.

Focusing on a few critical policies, call-handling skills (call control, customer service, sales, difficult situations) and knowledge tools will take your agents a long way.

Teach the basics: The key components of training

Here's a list outlining the key components that should be covered to make your call center training effective:

- ✔ **Individual goals and expectations:** Provide a recap of what's expected of your agents, how their goals impact the department and the company, and how training will be targeted to their goals and expectations.

- ✔ **Key policies and procedures:** Provide the critical information that agents need to know and tell them how they can access information on policies and procedures in the future.

- ✔ **Product knowledge:** What are all these customers calling about, anyway? What is it you're supporting? Your agents have to know this — at least the basics. In addition, teach your people how to look up information on your products. (If you're the call center for a major retailer, your agents aren't likely to remember the details of all 53,239 products that you sell.)

- ✔ **Call handling:** Teach and practice the skills that agents really need to do the job. Agents won't achieve mastery in the training class, but good skill development in key areas will help them through difficult situations — especially in the challenging first few days or weeks on the job.

  Call-handling skills include

  - Call control

  - Defusing anger: dealing with difficult situations

  - Customer service

  - Sales strategies

  Information and tutorials on call handling should also be accessible to agents through department systems. (I provide much more detail on call-handling tools and skills in Chapters 14 and 15.)

- ✔ **System utilization:** Your agents will need to know how to navigate all the various systems they require to do their job. (See Chapter 8 for examples and explanations of the call center technology used by agents.) Hopefully, one system or component includes a knowledge base or reference system that provides *walk-throughs* — a kind of graphic flowchart that illustrates the steps to completing a process — for all the other systems.

  Systems in today's call centers are becoming increasingly integrated and user-friendly. Still, some operations will continue to have a hodgepodge of older and newer systems. In these environments, remembering all the codes, toggles, back doors, and tricks can be very tough. Newer agents will need a tutorial or walk-through to help them along.

Keep it short

The sooner you get your agents out there and on the phones, the sooner they'll start developing the seeds you planted in training. And they are seeds — even the best trainers don't plant fully developed crops. Give them enough to make sure they aren't dangerous to themselves or your customers, test them to make sure they've got what they need, then get them out there. Training is a process, not an event.

I remember listening to an interview with the great Jack Nicklaus — arguably the most successful golfer of all time. During the interview he said that he was still learning about the game of golf, even though at the time he was in his mid-fifties.

It's the same with training for a job. You can give your agents a great start with new-hire training, but the process of learning about the job will never end. With this philosophy in mind, you can build in procedures to encourage continuous learning, such as

- ✔ **Weekly quizzes:** Quick weekly quizzes are a great way to test for ability in a specific area and, in the process, develop skill and awareness of the subject.

- ✔ **Regular coaching sessions:** Conduct one-on-one meetings with agents to review their strengths and weaknesses related to their job expectations. These sessions should be short and sweet and to the point.

- ✔ **Mystery calls:** Mystery calls are mock calls sent to your agents through the phone system, where a trainer or supervisor plays the part of a customer. It's a very quick and effective way to develop skills in problem areas.

- ✔ **Team meetings:** Team meetings are a great way to get new information (not too complex, though) or updates out to the entire team, and to celebrate successes. They can be a good way to develop some team bonding.

- ✔ **Updates training:** When skill development is more complex, classroom training might be needed. Again, our advice is to keep it simple and as brief as possible. Agents need to know the critical components of the new information — why it's so important and how it affects their job performance. Make sure that they also know where to find the procedures and policies on the subject.

- ✔ **Idle-time training:** A great development in call center training is the injection of training events in between calls. As an example, when idle times increase in our company agents receive mini training sessions through video, Webinars — seminars accessed over the World Wide Web — or audio learning. These sessions are tailored to each agent, and are generally short in duration but frequent. On a slow call-volume day, each agent might get a number of unique training sessions. Because idle time is used your cost is very low, and since the training is tied to agents' individual needs it's very effective.

Chapter 11

Managing Agent Performance Part 2: Providing Feedback and Support

● ●

In This Chapter

▶ Understanding the importance of various types of feedback

▶ Following a plan for providing feedback

▶ Reviewing the roles involved in giving feedback

▶ Using progressive discipline as a feedback mechanism

▶ Providing on-the-job and career/work–life support

▶ Realizing the importance of the call center supervisor

● ●

*I*n Chapter 10, I introduce the five-step "quick answer" to agent performance management:

1. Hire the right people.

2. Tell them what to do and why.

3. Show them how to do it.

4. Give them feedback on how they are doing.

5. Make supporting them your number-one mission.

Chapter 10 takes a look at the first three steps — the elements of agent performance management that will help you get your agents started off on the right foot, ensuring they have the potential to be successful.

In this chapter, I discuss what it takes to maximize that potential and bring your agents' success to fruition in the final two steps of the agent performance management "quick answer" — providing feedback and support.

Step 4 — Give Them Feedback on How They Are Doing: Providing Insight on Progress

Feedback is the process in which the output or results of agents' call-handling efforts are returned to them so that they can understand whether they've been successful in doing their job. Feedback is necessary whenever people attempt to achieve a goal.

Imagine how difficult achieving goals would be without feedback. Attempting to lose weight without the benefit of a scale, a mirror, or tight-fitting clothing might present challenges. Attempting to win a championship in any sport would be difficult without keeping score. Feedback is like the gauges in an airplane: it tells the pilot if he or she is flying safely and in the right direction.

I like to ask the question, "What's more important, feedback or training?" The truth is that both are very important, and ideally a call center should have excellence in both. However, over the long term good feedback is critical. My experience has been that with excellent feedback — and with even the most basic training — people will eventually produce the results that are expected.

In the opposite scenario, however — excellent training and little or no feedback — staff might get off to a good start, but ultimately it becomes more difficult for them to achieve excellence as they have no way to gauge their performance in order to make adjustments.

Feedback is a learning mechanism — a form of training — that provides people with a context for altering behavior to hone in on results. Without it, they're bound to miss the mark.

Understanding methods of feedback

Feedback is enhanced when expectations are well set, with measures of those expectations clearly communicated — as I discuss in Step 2 of the quick answer, "Tell them what to do and why," in Chapter 10.

The most obvious, and maybe the best basis for feedback, are the statistical measures (metrics) that you use to assess agent performance. The more accessible and up-to-date these stats are, the better. The stats are the "flight gauges" that you use to tell staff how they're progressing toward their target. An agent's performance expectations define the destination, or goal, while performance metrics define the measures for providing feedback as to whether the agent is moving toward that goal.

Ideally, agents will have access to a "dashboard" that provides up-to-the-minute readings on how they're doing. This might include performance for the day, week, and month to date (whatever is critical in their performance). Figure 11-1 illustrates an example of an agent's digital dashboard.

This dashboard is giving the agent feedback on his performance against performance expectations.

Figure 11-1:
A digital "dash-board" provides ongoing monitoring of agent perfor-mance.

	MTD Result	EXPECTATIONS Minimum	Bonus
First Call Resolution	75%	72%	80%
Schedule Adherence	96%	92%	96%
Customer Opinion	90%	87%	95%
Conversion	25%	18%	24%
Overall Performance Index	87	86	94

Again, it's best if the number of metrics is limited to as few as will capture the agent's performance. Adding too many metrics frequently confuses the message and runs the risk of confusing agents so much that they stop looking.

It's important that your agents are able to finish this sentence *at all times:* "Based on my performance, if I had my review today, I would...." If they're not meeting minimum expectations, then the answer might be, "... be drawn and quartered," or maybe, "... not get a raise." If they're doing very well, then the answer might be, "... get a great big, fat raise!"

Either way, the dashboard enables agents to see how they are doing and gives greater control over their destination.

Following a feedback-providing plan

Here's an example of how the process might work if you were a supervisor using an overall performance index (OPI) as a mechanism for providing feedback. (For more on OPI, see Chapter 10.)

Assume you're the supervisor of a team in a telecommunications call center. Looking at your team's month-to-date OPI results, you identify four agents who are working at the lower end of performance (Carl, Ken, Shelly, and Wendy). You also identify three agents who are excelling (Carol, Joanne, and Sally).

Start with the underachievers

The first thing you'd do is attempt to understand what is the critical weakness of each of the lower performers on your team — by looking at the individual results that make up the overall performance index.

Focusing on Carl for a moment, you learn that Carl's specific weakness is call length. (See Chapter 5 for more information on measuring call length.) His is particularly high when compared to the group, and it's having a large impact on his OPI. Upon investigation, two things become obvious. First, Carl hasn't been at this for very long — perhaps he's a new agent. Second, Carl is improving.

After gathering this information and doing this analysis, you're well prepared to give Carl some very specific feedback that will help him improve his performance. You'll probably meet with Carl, review his performance — which he's already seen, because he has access to his results and his relative performance against everyone else via his digital dashboard. You may decide to listen to some of Carl's calls, sitting beside him, to get an idea of what he's doing on each call to get the results that he's getting.

Then you'll give Carl some suggestions for improvement — an action plan. You might provide information on how to control a call better, or suggest that he attends additional system or product training, which you can arrange. After your meeting, remember to document your discussion. Give a copy of this documentation to Carl, along with a chance to sign off on the action plan you've agreed to.

Once you're finished with Carl (and your work with Carl really need not take much time) you'll move on to another victim — perhaps Ken — and repeat the process. (Ken might take a bit longer — he just hasn't been the same since Barbie dumped him.)

Move on to the peak performers

Once you're finished reviewing and setting action plans with each of your lower-performing team members, spend some time with the peak performers to understand what they're doing that makes them so good.

If, after listening to calls, you determine that a peak performer has developed some superior skills in a particular area, you may decide to pair him or her with one of your agents who's not doing so well in that area. The peak performer becomes a peer coach — an agent who provides specific coaching and assistance to other agents doing the same work (his or her peers).

Attend to the rest of the team

Finally, you may wish to scan your remaining staff's performance in an effort to find other opportunities for improvement. You might pay special attention to those who are almost at peak performance. Giving those agents a little bit of help might push them over the top in performance.

In general, I like to see a supervisor's attention divided 40/10/50:

- ✔ 40 percent with the agents who are having a hard time meeting the minimums — it's frequently the newer agents who need the most help. In general, fewer than 20 percent of the team will be in this group, so spending 40 percent of your time with them will be a good concentration of effort.

- ✔ 10 percent of your time should be spent with the peak performers. The peak performers will generally manage themselves to higher performance — especially if they have access to their performance data — but a little attention will be motivating.

- ✔ The other 50 percent of your time is spent with the staff that are neither underperforming nor overperforming. This will be about two-thirds of your team.

Table 11-1 provides a basic breakdown of how call center supervisors should spend their time.

Table 11-1   A Breakdown of the Supervisor's Feedback Schedule

Supervisor's Feedback Tasks	*Time Allotment*
Supervisor reviews statistics and identifies the agents most in need of help and the performance area most need of immediate help.	40 percent of supervisor feedback and in coaching time
Supervisor meets with agent(s) needing help, reviews performance, and works with staff to determine cause of weaknesses — listens to calls, talks to agent, reviews statistics with agent.	
Agent and supervisor agree to an action plan for improvement. Agent signs off on the action plan.	

(Continued)

Table 11-1 *(Continued)*	
Supervisor's Feedback Tasks	**Time Allotment**
Supervisor reviews statistics and identifies agents who are operating at a peak level of performance; determines where they excel the most.	10 percent of supervisor feedback and coaching time.
Supervisor meets with staff members to congratulate them and better understand what makes them so special. Peer coaches are born.	
Supervisor reviews the remaining agents, who are neither underperforming nor overperforming, and looks for anomalies in performance that, with attention, might help staff to improve.	50 percent of supervisor feedback and coaching time

Undertaking the performance review

The performance review can be a very effective form of feedback, or it can be a disaster for motivation and overall performance. The primary cause for the difference is how surprised the agent is by the results of the review — did they or did they not see it coming.

We believe the performance review should not reveal anything new about your employees' contribution and success in achieving their goals. The point is, agents should always know where they stand. They will if they take advantage of the methods of feedback throughout this chapter — most of which should be automatically available.

If agents always know where they stand, the performance review is just a recap of their performance over the last period and a formalization of the appropriate raises, bonuses, or corrective actions. The rest of the review can then be used to discuss the agent's future direction and goals.

The frequency of performance reviews varies from company to company. Many call centers do them annually — that's a long time to wait for a review. I like to conduct reviews quarterly. Quarterly reviews provide more reasons to celebrate and increased opportunities to motivate employees.

When successful agents have an opportunity to receive increases on a quarterly basis, it helps to provide continuing motivation and improved call center results.

The *probationary* review — the first review an employee gets — sets the tone for future reviews, and might be more formal. In many organizations it's done after the employee's been working for 90 days or less.

As with all staff, a probationary employee should always know where he or she stands. "If I had my probationary review today, I'd ..." "... be promoted to a permanent position" or "... not successfully complete my probation."

Giving one-on-one feedback

Most of an agent's performance statistics are provided automatically (or should be) and the agents should, to a degree, provide their own self-assessment. Still, employees need and expect a lot of one-on-one "face time" to discuss feedback and develop action plans for improvement.

One-on-one coaching and feedback isn't a requirement unique to call centers, and you can find many courses on how to do it well, so I don't get too exhaustive here, but here are some basics:

- **Begin with behavior.** Start by discussing the agent's specific behaviors, skills, and techniques that have attributed to his results in the period.

  You'll keep the agent more engaged in the discussion if you ask him to give his thoughts first before providing yours — and it's always best to start with the positive! Ask questions like, "What do you feel's been working well for you this quarter?" and then "What are some things you might have done differently?"

- **Review the results.** Next, show the agent how his behaviors have affected his results and the effect this will have on his job, career, and compensation. For example, "You've really been using the call control techniques we discussed last quarter very well, John, and you can see how your average call-handling time has improved — by 10 percent! That's enough to earn you a Level 1 bonus this quarter. Great job! Keep improving the way you have been and you'll easily knock another 15 seconds off your average call time, and next quarter you'll be getting the Level 2 bonus...."

- **Outline action plans.** Help your agents develop strategies for improvement by discussing specific skills, techniques, and behavior enhancements that will help them to improve their results. Explain exactly how success in these strategies will benefit their career.

- **Talk specifics and give examples.** This is a good time to review recorded calls, screen captures, and so on.

- **Keep it concise.** Stick to the one or two issues that will have the greatest impact, and keep the discussion results-oriented and to the point. After only five to ten minutes of discussion most agents are on information overload. Lots of 5-minute discussions are better than one 45-minute meeting. Keep it simple, and keep it short. Repetition works.

- **Document your discussion.** Please, oh, please — write it down! One of the many reasons to document all one-to-one feedback sessions is to have a record to go back to with the agent. There can be no doubt if it's in writing — especially if you have the agent sign off. Remember that

- Written plans or instructions tend to garner greater commitment than those that are given only verbally.

- The items discussed in these sessions provide good information for use in a performance review. "Here's what we did, here's what happened, aren't we smart!"

- If you ever get into a difficult situation and want to release the employee, having a well-documented record on file helps everyone. "Here's what we worked on, here's what happened (or didn't happen)," and so on.

Being nice

It should go without saying, but if you're in a role that requires you to give feedback, try to keep this important rule in mind: don't yell at people. And don't ridicule, mock, or be sarcastic. Treat your people with respect, just as you would expect to be treated and as you would want your employees to treat your customers.

The best managers and supervisors are nice even in disciplinary discussions — heck, *especially* in disciplinary discussions.

Every interaction you have with one of your staff is an opportunity to model the behavior you expect of them when dealing with your customers. Be professional, treat your people with honesty, dignity, and respect, and leave them feeling good about themselves, and they're more likely to treat others (including your customers) the same way.

Praising and punishing

Here's another adage that may be a little old and worn out, but will always be relevant: "Praise in public, punish in private." Celebrating success is almost always welcomed, and even shy folks like me enjoy the occasional pat on the back — especially when it comes in front of our colleagues and friends.

Public praising promotes teamwork and camaraderie too, and can have a very real motivating effect on the entire team. It's like handing out a treat to a child in a group — you're soon surrounded by a chorus of, "Can I have some?"

At the other end of the spectrum, it's important to conduct disciplinary discussions in private. Scolding or giving negative feedback publicly will embarrass your agents and put them on the defensive. They're likely to be more concerned with who's watching than with anything you're saying to them.

Think about a time you've seen a parent with a child who's acting out in a restaurant or grocery store. First thing the parent does is look around to see who's watching. People don't like to be the center of *negative* attention.

People feel bad enough about receiving punishment. Don't compound things by embarrassing them as well. Punishing in private allows your team members to maintain their dignity and feel good about themselves, even though they may not feel good about their behavior.

Using progressive discipline

Occasionally, things don't go as well with an agent as you'd hope. You've been coaching him, trying to steer his behavior and performance in the right direction, but you've found that he hasn't achieved satisfactory performance levels even after months of trying. Or, maybe you've found that he demonstrates a behavior that you just can't tolerate in the call center — like continually dipping Suzie's hair in the inkwell. At these times you're at the point where you need to start progressive discipline.

Progressive discipline is a process for dealing with behavior that doesn't meet expected standards. It's important to remember that the goal of progressive discipline is to get the employee's "buy in" that the performance deficiency is a problem, that their behavior has to be changed, and that they have the power to change it. The ultimate goal is to correct the incorrect behavior and get your employee back on track.

Progressive discipline is all about improving agent behavior and results — it isn't about punishment.

The steps of progressive discipline include increasing consequences for continuing the undesired behavior — hence the "progressive" part of the name. Here's a typical breakdown of how you would handle each of the steps:

1. First efforts to change behavior: Verbal discussion and warning.

2. Second efforts to change behavior: Written warning.

3. Third efforts to change behavior: Suspension of one to three days.

4. Final consequence: Termination. This final step is reserved for those people who won't improve.

At each step, you should help the agent to understand, at a minimum, these three things: The specifics of their inappropriate behavior, your company's expectations for appropriate behavior, and the further consequences (the next step) if the behavior continues.

All of your discussions should also include a "let's not get there" sentiment. After all, the goal is to change behavior — to get the employee on the road to great results, regular raises, and a long career in the company.

In most cases you won't get to the final step. In fact, if your agent is motivated a verbal warning is all he or she will need to get on the right track.

And once again ... please, PLEASE document your discussion after each round of progressive discipline and get the agent to sign off — even on the verbal discussions. As with other feedback and coaching, this documentation will provide a record for the agent's file of the efforts made to improve, while also creating a paper trail to show you've taken all appropriate steps prior to terminating the agent should that become necessary.

Reducing fear

An appeals process is a very effective way of ensuring that employee rights are maintained and, done well, will go a long way toward reducing fear. With an effective appeals process, the frontline agent is given the opportunity to appeal any discipline to a panel of peers who have been trained in the peer-review process. Typically, the peer-review panel considers the evidence pertaining to the situation and has the option of reducing, retracting, or agreeing with the disciplinary step taken. The peer panel does not generally have authority to change policy, only to decide if the punishment fit the crime for the specific case. Any appeals process needs to be well thought out and designed, and staff must be trained to use it.

Defining various feedback roles

The supervisor certainly plays a primary role, but many people and processes must come together to provide effective feedback to call center agents. All are designed to create a balanced system of feedback to both agent and supervisor.

The most important person in the feedback chain is the agent. A well-trained agent who has a very clear understanding of his or her expectations — how they're measured and how to affect them — will, to a great degree, manage his or her own performance; provided, that is, that the agent receives consistent feedback on that performance.

It's comparable to the way a professional athlete — a golfer, for instance — knows the score and knows how she's doing against par and against her competitors. She knows how far she hits the ball and her statistics relative to the rest of the game (putts, greens hit, success out of the sand). She knows precisely where she has to improve if she wants to win more often.

The supervisor: Guiding and motivating

Even though our golfer can do all that on her own, she still also has a coach — someone to supervise her practice and guide her improvement. The coach gives her more details on why she's getting the results she is and how she might improve. Other people — say, the scorekeeper or club manufacturer — give her even more specialized feedback. Finally, fans will provide some final feedback and motivation on the quality of her play. A number of people are involved in the golfer's feedback chain, but it starts with her looking at her own results and deciding what has to change.

It's very much the same in your call center. The agents know how they're doing relative to their goals. If the feedback process is done well, agents know specifically what part of their performance needs to improve so that they can become more successful.

The supervisor provides feedback and specific coaching on how to improve performance deficiencies. The supervisor is first and foremost the agent's performance coach.

As a supervisor, you'll want to check in with your agents (particularly at the beginning of their career in the call center) to make sure they're reviewing their statistics regularly, and that they understand what their performance metrics are telling them. You'll then need to work with agents on ways to improve their performance.

A good system of expectations presented to the agents will frequently promote a certain degree of self-management, especially if expectations have been well set and the agents are familiar with the system of metrics — what they are and how they work. (I talk about setting expectations in Chapter 10.)

The nice thing about setting up a simple group of metrics into an overall performance index, or OPI (you'll find more on OPI in Chapter 10) is that supervisors and agents are able to hone in on the area of performance where, through improvement, the agent could gain the greatest benefit.

Here's a recap of the OPI formula I use:

OPI = (3,600 ÷ Call length) × First-call resolution × Schedule adherence × Customer opinion × Conversion × Revenue per sale

Even the top performers will have a relative weakness in one (or more) of their responsibilities. A good supervisor will help the agent identify the relative weakness, and then show him or her how to improve in that area.

The quality department: Providing data-auditing and call-monitoring feedback

In the call center, your quality team is a separate department of people (or maybe just one person) who listen to agent calls and grade them according to company procedure and policy. The quality department will grade a call against a list of defined behaviors and procedures that the call center believes are important. Their assessments will be used to provide suggestions for improvement. See Chapter 15 for more on call quality control.

Ideally, your quality team should record and store the reviewed calls so your agents can listen to them to understand how they can improve upon future calls.

With the combination of listening to calls and monitoring data, the quality team and supervisor can catch errors and suggest improvements for call handling to the agent.

Using call-monitoring data appropriately

I recommend that you use call-monitoring data as a basis for feedback only — not to evaluate or reward agent performance. Assessments are always somewhat subjective — the only true test of the effectiveness of a call is the customer's opinion. The way an individual customer feels about how a call was handled is driven by interpersonal dynamics and not by overly simplified call elements, such as how many times the agent used the customer's name (a common quality monitoring element). Additionally, you'll have a hard time assessing enough calls to get a statistically significant sample of the agent's work — that is, if you intend to do it well.

On the other hand, call monitoring and assessments provide great insight that can (and definitely should) be used as a basis for feedback, and can be very useful when used for process enhancement and marketing research purposes.

Here's an overview of how call reviews can be used for each of these purposes:

- **Feedback:** When, as a supervisor, you review recorded agent calls with the goal of understanding how the agent's statistical results represent performance, feedback becomes more effective. For example, if the statistics show that an agent on your team has excessively long calls, you could monitor and assess some of his calls and then use the information you collect to provide feedback to help the agent understand exactly why he's not controlling his calls well. Perhaps the calls monitored show that he's letting customers control calls. You would also explain how this reflects in the call-length statistic.

    Perhaps the agent could listen to some recorded calls of agents who are getting better statistical results to show the difference in control.

    Similarly, you might review calls with another agent to better understand why customers are giving her low customer opinion scores. ("I've listened to a couple of your calls, Jane, and perhaps you should stop telling customers to 'shut up and listen.'")

✔ **Enhancing call-handling processes:** By listening to lots of calls — especially calls by specific type (billing, sales, general inquiry), management will get a view of the processes being used for handling customer calls.

By observing live call handling, you can make process improvements that directly affect the call center's performance.

✔ **Market research:** Marketing executives will find no better focus group than customers whose calls are being handled in a call center. What's better, this focus group is running every hour that the call center is running. Using call monitoring as a customer research tool contributes additional value to the organization — making the call center even more important.

Enough is enough: Monitoring the appropriate number of calls

You're probably already asking, "So how many calls do you need to monitor?" Our answer is, "Enough to achieve your objective."

If the goal of your call monitoring is to help your agents understand why they're getting the results they are and to show them how to improve, then you'll need to listen to enough calls to demonstrate that the agent is consistently behaving in a way that's leading to the results they're getting. That might require a couple of reviews, or a half-dozen.

You might use only one or two reviews, however, for agents who are already getting good results. So if you're coaching an agent a lot in a given month, you'll probably want to review more of his or her calls.

If, as a manager, you want to understand the call center process better, you'll need to listen to enough calls to see patterns emerge that illustrate how things are being done. Variations will occur, but generally after a pattern has been observed it won't change without some form of management intervention.

Finally, if marketing wants to understand customer opinion better, then they just need to listen to enough calls to hear a consistent message from the customer. How many is that? We don't know, what does the marketing consultant say? "What say we run it up the flag pole and see who salutes it."

Seriously, here's what we really recommend. Certainly you need to collect at least some calls for all agents — as many as you can economically do in any month — probably five or six at a minimum. If agents understand their performance goals well and are getting steady access to the reports that show how they're doing, they should also have access to call reviews (complete with commentary on how their call behaviors are affecting their performance statistics).

In most cases, we don't even think that the supervisor's involvement is all that necessary. Just make sure that the assessment is available for agents to listen to when they want (and their schedule allows).

It's best that you don't use call monitoring as a performance measure. The difficulty in acquiring a statistically relevant sample of calls combined with the subjective nature of call monitoring makes the process very contentious. Customer opinion scores are a better measure of call quality. Here's the bottom line on call monitoring: it's a great coaching tool, but a bad assessment tool.

The training team: Providing feedback as a training tool

In many operations, trainers stay with their group of trainees for some time after a session has ended — or the trainer might check in on the trainees from time to time — to assist in evaluation and coaching.

Trainers' feedback on agent performance can be very valuable, because trainers can link feedback to lessons taught in the training class and to agents' performance goals. Good trainers are also more natural at teaching, so their feedback tends to be constructive and results-oriented, and is therefore generally well received by the agents.

The customer: Providing the ultimate feedback

Of course, the customer is probably the best source of feedback — especially when customer feedback is taken en masse. The best assessment of customer satisfaction and call quality is the customer's opinion. Advancements in technology and using automated tools like IVR (interactive voice response — see Chapter 8) and Web response makes customer feedback somewhat easier to capture.

Try not to place too much importance on the odd customer comment here and there, however. When reviewing customer feedback, it's better to consider the overall picture painted by a lot of customer assessments. One comment might not be truly representative of overall performance.

Take the occasional compliment and tuck it away. Sure it feels good, so enjoy it, but don't get bummed out by the infrequent abusive customer (yes, they're out there). For tips on how to deal with these difficult situations, have a look at Chapter 14.

Some cautionary feedback tales

Feedback is almost always beneficial, but some sources of feedback should be avoided and some ways of using feedback can be dangerous. Here, I offer some feedback cautions.

First, you've got to be careful about accepting feedback from Jane, the agent beside you. Maybe she knows what she's doing, but then again ... maybe not. Accepting instruction and feedback from the call center floor has created more mistakes than the ballpoint pen.

It's also how informal and unofficial policies and procedures are born, and it's very difficult to rid a call center of these procedures once they've become ingrained. Go ahead — listen to Jane, but validate her advice through a supervisor, procedures manual, or trainer.

Please, please, PLEASE don't use anecdotal information from customer calls as a reason to change anything.

Consider this scenario:

One of your supervisors nonchalantly wonders aloud, "We seem to be getting a lot more calls today than normal. I wonder why."

She then goes to Jane (yep, it's that darn Jane again), and asks, "Jane, any idea why we're so busy?"

Jane's last call was from a customer who was confused about an advertisement that came out in the paper that morning. She'd had another similar call earlier in the day. So, Jane replies, "There's an ad in the paper that's confusing all the customers."

The supervisor tells her manager that marketing has put an ad in the newspaper that customers don't understand. The manager then calls her director: "There's an ad in the paper that's causing us a lot of problems. Why didn't we know about this?"

The director phones the vice president of call centers, exasperated, and tells him, "Marketing is messing up my service targets! Now I'll have to go over budget."

He, in turn, calls the vice president of marketing and demands, "You tell Mary [the president] that I'm missing my numbers because you guys can't communicate properly."

This, of course, upsets the marketing VP, and she shoots back, "What are you talking about? You call center guys do this all the time!"

Ultimately, this leads to a total breakdown of organizational cohesiveness and teamwork. The call center and the marketing department refuse to work together, resulting in huge organizational inefficiencies. The company begins losing money, and the president starts to make changes at the top.

All because Jane got a couple of calls about one newspaper ad. Jane, Jane, Jane ....

Doing it with data

Save your company! Any time you need feedback on what's going on, do it with data.

Here's the same scenario, revisited:

The supervisor ponders, "We seem to be getting a lot more calls than normal today. I wonder why?"

She then goes to Jane and says, "Jane, I saw your customer satisfaction statistics. You've made some great improvements. Nice work! Let's talk about them when we meet today."

Jane smiles and thinks what a wonderful company she works for. The supervisor continues past Jane and stops to see Mark in reporting. "Mark, how's it going? Hey listen, we seem to be taking more calls than normal today. Any idea what's going on?"

Mark turns to the supervisor and replies, "We were up a bit on billing information calls earlier, but that's evened out. We had a few extra agents in new-product training, which caused us to get busy for a few minutes, but we're back to normal now. That's probably what you're seeing."

"Oh, that makes sense. Thanks!" says the supervisor.

It ends there. Well, not really there — Mark and the supervisor end up dating, getting married, and having kids. They're very happy. The call center and the marketing department get along very well and the company is making lots of money. The president was moved to another division and the vice president of call centers took her job. The VP of marketing was very happy for both of them.

All in all, things turned out very well — all because you didn't use anecdotal information to run your business.

Step 5 — Make Supporting Them Your Number-One Mission: Removing the Obstacles

Okay, you've hired good people, told them what you need of them, trained them well (see Chapter 10), and given them lots of feedback — the only thing left is to give them a little help when they need it. Support amounts to clearing the way so people can achieve — allowing them to maximize their skill and motivation.

Poor support is a tremendous demotivator in any workplace, but it's multiplied a hundredfold in a large call center where so many agents can get together and compare notes on the lack of support they're receiving.

The two categories of support your agents need to be provided are on-the-job/process-related support and career/work–life support.

"Ahem ... Little help over here!" Helping agents do their job

Mature agents, those who have been doing their job well for a long time, aren't going to need a lot of on-the-job assistance. However, when they need it, you'd better give it to them fast.

Newer agents need a lot of on-the-job assistance. In the heat of the moment, they can't remember all the information that was covered in training, or even the tools and sources for finding information. And sometimes they're going to run into situations that aren't covered by standard processes.

If new agents find that they consistently can't get the support they need, they'll quickly become disillusioned and demoralized, and they might even leave.

Call center job support amounts to being available to answer questions, give suggestions, and provide guidance. Job support is different from coaching in that it happens immediately and it relates to specific situations — usually, when your agent has a customer on hold who's waiting for an answer on a difficult issue that the agent doesn't have an immediate answer for. In these situations support can't wait — the clock is ticking, loudly.

Agents usually can't get up to go look around for their supervisor, and support can't happen if the supervisors are in their office working, in a meeting, or in the cafeteria. They need to be in the call center and within reach.

And the nature of call center logistics — scheduling the right number of staff and meeting service objectives, while handling thousands of calls — means that supervisor support needs to be available within seconds.

Support that takes even a few minutes to get to the agents becomes a major bottleneck and will have adverse effects on levels of service, efficiency, customer satisfaction, and employee morale.

Here's how it looks in a well-run call center: At any time, you've got a supervisor within a few seconds' reach of any agent who needs help. If the center typically gets a lot of support requests, then you're going to need more supervisors to field the demand. If you have a very big call center with lots of demand, you'll have supervisors every few rows of desks available to give support.

Using a help desk to provide support remotely

Larger centers facing the issue of constant demand for immediate support frequently utilize *support desks* or *help desks* — essentially turning the process of providing support into a "call center within a call center." In this scenario, support staff (sometimes supervisors, sometimes highly skilled agents) man a special desk, perhaps called the help desk. When agents need help, instead of looking for a supervisor they call the help desk.

Just like customers, the agents' calls are answered on a first come, first served basis, and during peaks in demand agents are told to "wait for the next available supervisor."

If your call center has a large volume of support requests from agents, the help desk is a really good idea. Some of the benefits include:

- ✔ **Increased cost control:** In the same way that having customer calls queue up creates the basis for overall cost control (see Chapters 1 and 2 for more detail on improving cost control), having agents "wait for the next available supervisor" means that you can more easily staff the right number of supervisors to provide sufficient support.

- ✔ **Tracking of support statistics:** Having supervisors logged in to the phone system provides much greater reporting options (as I discuss in Chapter 8), including requests received, average time to process a request, and speed of service to provide support.

Some operations create applications that track the support questions and types of calls made by their agents. With these tools, call centers can determine what types of questions their supervisors are getting — perhaps targeting the most frequent questions for additional agent training. You can also determine which agents are asking for support the most, and for what questions — improving your ability to provide specific, targeted coaching on trouble areas.

Offering career and work–life support

Career and work–life support is less frequent than on-the-job support, but equally important. It happens when agents want to discuss work as it relates to them personally. Typical issues include vacation time, sick leave, doctor appointments, raises, advancement opportunities, disputes, conflicts, concerns, and so on.

These types of issues can't simply be put into a telephone queue to be answered by the first available supervisor: "Thank you for calling support desk, this is David, how can I help you?" "Well, David, I'm having a personal crisis at home, the baby isn't sleeping well and the hours that I have to work are killing me. Any suggestions?"

These situations are best handled one-on-one with the agent's own supervisor — preferably in private.

The biggest challenge with this type of support is making supervisors' time available from their feedback, coaching, and other duties, but you have to make it happen — for your employees' quality of work life and for overall staff morale.

Meeting the challenges of call center supervision

Given the responsibility to provide performance management and agent support, the call center supervisor is one busy puppy. Many operations find that one or the other of those two primary responsibilities gets sacrificed. This creates a problem, because to run an effective call center neither can be done poorly.

Can a single supervisor do both? In some call centers they do, but those who are successful pay careful attention to the scheduling of their supervisors' time. (I talk about scheduling agents in Chapter 7.)

Some operations split the roles of performance management and support. One supervisor, or group of supervisors (who might not be assigned to specific agents) provides on-the-job support. The other supervisor, or group of supervisors, is assigned the role of agent performance management — usually to specific agents to create the continuity and consistency needed for effective ongoing coaching and career support.

Determining the right number of supervisors

Whether or not you split the supervisor responsibilities, you need to determine how many supervisor resources are needed before you can start assigning duties. As with all scheduling, it starts with a view of the total demand on your supervisors' time. You need to ask, "How much supervisor time is needed to do all the required performance management?" and, "How much supervisor time is needed to provide job and career support?" Add the two together and you'll have a good estimate of supervisor demand.

Ask these questions to determine if you've scheduled sufficient supervisory resources:

✔ **Are you providing job-related support in a timely fashion?** If you've implemented a help desk or phone queue, your telephone reports will tell you this. Poor response time in the queue means that you don't have enough supervisors scheduled to meet the demand — more are needed.

✔ **Are you getting all the performance management done?** If coaching and performance management is well documented, reviewing the documentation will help determine the volume and quality of coaching being done. If documentation is sparse or poorly done, an opportunity exists for the manager to coach and develop the supervisor. Automated tools exist that are designed to record documentation, to flag potential coaching issues and create greater accountability for your supervisors.

In our centers we use a tool called "The Coach" to track agent performance management. Coaching sessions are automatically scheduled based on performance metrics, and aging reports are kept to track how much time it takes to complete coaching sessions and how long coaching sessions are left outstanding. After the coaching session, the discussion is documented for future reference by the supervisor or agent.

✔ **What do the supervisors have to say?** They'll tell you, loud and clear, if support or feedback is lacking. You can gather this information from your monthly employee opinion survey, from a survey designed specifically for this purpose, or by simply asking them — via agent focus groups, for example.

In working to optimize and improve call center performance one of the most powerful tools available is agent performance management — the process of managing and maximizing agent skills and motivation. In Chapter 10, I introduce the "quick answer" to effective agent performance management, looking at recruiting, setting expectations, and training. In this chapter, I complete the quick answer by examining agent feedback and support. Central to the idea of agent performance management is alignment between corporate and call center objectives and agent goals, objectives, and direction.

Done well, no other process will do more to achieve corporate and call center objectives than agent performance management.

Chapter 12

The Power of Process Management

*M*any call centers have fallen prey to what W. Edwards Deming called "instant pudding." Deming, a management guru whose theories led to the development of total quality management, was referring to the act of installing the latest technology or implementing the latest management fad with the hope that this alone would result in operational success.

Certainly best practices exist in the call center industry, but ongoing improvement and excellence don't come without internal examination and innovation.

Many organizations have realized that improving processes is a necessary step to continuous improvement and excellence. These organizations are increasingly hiring brighter and brighter business people for the call center, and those people are increasingly focused on the *process* of managing a call center. In this chapter you'll find an exploration of that process and ideas on how to manage it.

Managing Complexity: The Need for Process Management in the Call Center

Call centers have been around now for about 30 years — the same period of time during which the use of computer technology has become widespread, — so you can't really refer to the call center industry as a new business. However, the state of call center management is still extremely varied and inconsistent — something you might expect from a younger business. Examples of excellence in call center operations and results can be found, but unfortunately even more examples of poor results exist — from inconsistent service delivery to cost overruns, missed revenue targets, and poor employee morale.

Due to the impact that call centers have on their respective organizations in terms of revenue, cost, and customer relationships, bad results get quick attention. In fact, in response to corporate and customer dissatisfaction with call center performance, sub-industries and government watchdogs have sprung up during the last decade.

None of this should be terribly surprising; call centers are complex places integrating many business disciplines. Operators of call centers must be adept at

- Managing and motivating a large and diverse workforce who are tied to their workstations for eight hours a day by their headsets,

- Understanding the finance and managerial accounting,

- Understanding, recommending, and implementing increasingly sophisticated technology,

- Understanding, interpreting, and acting on sophisticated statistical techniques,

- Understanding the systems, products, and procedures of their organization and integrating them into the call center workflow, and

- Bringing all this together to produce a consistent, high-value result meeting customer, corporate, and employee demands.

Defining Process Management: What It Is and How It Helps

A *process* is a series of related actions that culminate in a result. *Management* is planning and control. So, *process management* is the planning, execution, and control of a course of actions, so that an intended result is achieved. We like to think of process management as a system of achieving "alignment" among the inputs, procedures, and desired results of the call center.

Call-handling process improvements decrease costs in a telecommunications company

A few years ago, I was helping a telecommunications company improve the cost of running its call centers. We focused our time on the process of handling various types of calls. This was a fun exercise where we pulled call center agents into a room and mapped out how they were handling the most frequent customer inquiry types. Up to this point, there had been no standardized approach for handling the various call types.

As we were identifying and documenting the general approach that was being used to handle customer inquiries, the agents began making suggestions for improvement. Two things resulted:

✔ First, we developed several new call-handling processes that were trained and went into effect almost immediately.

✔ Second, the agents defined a process for making ongoing improvements in the call-handling process.

Within a month, call length had declined by 15 percent, and the total cost per customer of running the operation was down by a similar amount. Further, management reported that errors and callbacks were also down. Months later, the improvements continued.

Alignment, in this case, means answering yes to the question, "Is this action or role supporting or driving toward one or more of your goals?"

The great thing about call centers is that many, if not most, of your goals can be clearly stated in terms of visible metrics — things like cost per customer, revenue per customer, customer satisfaction, and employee satisfaction. You can find much more about call center goals and metrics in Chapters 2 and 5.

Benefiting from process management

It's useful to think of process management in terms of what it does for the drivers of performance. If a process improvement positively affects a driver, performance (and results) will be enhanced — often in a very quantifiable way.

Here are some examples of typical process improvements you can make in your call center, and the potential benefits associated with each:

✔ A redesign of your call-handling process that reduces average call length by 10 seconds reduces cost per call, the total expense to run your operation, and the number of seats needed. It might also improve customer satisfaction as customers receive a faster resolution to their need. (I talk about call length in Chapter 5.)

✔ Creation of a new schedule, which improves speed of answer, can increase customer satisfaction. (See Chapter 7 for more on schedules.)

✔ Improvements in *off-phone* or *overhead* work processes — those not directly affecting agents on the phones — can result in a reduction in total support duties required and a corresponding reduction in the average cost per hour of call center services.

✔ A new interactive voice response (IVR) unit design — automated voice prompts that provide service to customers calling your center — reduces the number of callers needing to speak with a live agent, which in turn reduces contacts per customer, which reduces total cost, number of staff, and equipment needed. (You can find more on IVR in Chapter 8.)

✔ Developing a more effective way of presenting customer data to your agents during calls will help agents present purchase options to customers and can lead to a higher percentage of calls resulting in sales, or higher average value per sale.

Developing a culture of improvement

Process management will provide the greatest benefit when everyone involved in the process is involved in the improvements. No one will be better equipped to tell you the weak spots in your call-handling processes than your agents. Similarly, for non-phone/overhead work, your management team will quickly point to the roadblocks in these processes.

The people who work with a process every day are best able to tell you how things are actually done as opposed to how things are supposed to be done.

Aside from helping to improve results, involving all parts of the team in the process mapping/process improvement exercise is also a great team-building exercise.

The key is to involve the people who know the most about each process, and then acknowledge their commitment.

Process Mapping: Homegrown Process Improvement

Process mapping is a powerful and common management method for designing and analyzing business processes. Literally, a business process is graphed out in a *flowchart* — a diagram showing sequence of operations in a process such as the steps involved in a successful customer call — so everyone can see and understand the steps involved in producing a result. In Figure 12-1 I provide a sample call center recruiting and hiring process chart as an example for you to follow.

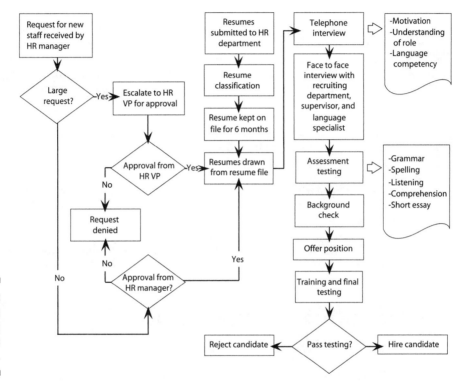

Figure 12-1:
Recruiting
and hiring
process
flowchart.

In my own call center, and to clients of my consulting practice, I recommend mapping out all key processes.

Process mapping and flowcharting is a well-defined discipline. I could spend dozens of pages outlining some of the standard conventions used in process mapping and charting, but I won't. Later in this chapter, however, I do provide some tips.

With a little time, some common sense, a pot of coffee, and a bunch of dry-erase markers, your management team can put together some homegrown process charts that you'll get lots of benefits from.

Involving the team

Process mapping is a tool that works best with collaboration, meaning that you should get everyone involved — including all levels of management and your call center agents.

While process mapping is fairly straightforward, it's worthwhile to spend some time with your team reviewing how it works and why it's important. A bit of upfront training will help prevent blank stares at the beginning of your process mapping exercise. It also helps to share the spoils of your process improvement success. It doesn't have to be much, just some form of recognition — a party, a platter of fine imported cheeses, whatever.

The important thing is to involve members from all parts of the call center team. Any and all input will help the process mapping exercise, while increasing buy-in and improving the quality of the results.

The act of charting out the steps of a process helps to simplify the process and clarifies potential problems, inefficiencies, or needed rework. If you haven't mapped out your processes before, give it a try — you'll be amazed. At some point you'll probably laugh out loud and ask the question, "What idiot designed that?" On second thought, you might want to keep that thought to yourself. The idiot might be sitting beside you ... or it might even *be* you!

Drawing the benefits: Gaining from collaboration

Benefits you'll realize from a collaborative exercise of process mapping include the following:

- ✔ Your processes will be simplified, resulting in efficiencies and reduced rework.

- ✔ Improvements will be implemented at an accelerated pace. You'll no longer need to use the "hit and miss" approach to managing improvement.

- ✔ Costs will be reduced as you find more efficient ways of doing things.

- ✔ More effective call-handling and data management processes will lead to enhanced customer satisfaction and increased revenue.

- ✔ New employees will learn their jobs faster with an easy-to-understand graphical overview of their work processes.

Charting the flow: An amateur's guide to process mapping

In a flowchart's simplest form, you just draw a picture of what happens in your work process, starting with inputs, identifying all actions and decisions associated with a process, and then finalizing your diagram with the output or goals. A little more discipline will help, without getting too complicated.

Here's a guideline outlining the steps for constructing a process flowchart:

1. Determine the process beginning and ending points.

2. List each step involved:

   i. Use action verbs to describe steps, and

   ii. Decide if you want a general understanding or want to list every discrete step.

3. Rough in an approximate order:

   i. Relationships and parallel steps will begin to emerge.

4. Place each step in the appropriate symbol. In Figure 12-1, for example, the diamond-shaped text boxes represent a step in the process where a decision is made — usually yes or no — while the rectangular text boxes illustrate an activity. The arrows show the direction of the process flow.

5. Add arrows.

6. Check for redundancy.

7. Check for missing elements.

8. Ask for a second (and third) set of eyes to review.

The purpose of diagramming is to understand the processes you currently use and ask yourself, "What's expected of us? What should we be doing to provide better customer focus and satisfaction?" The process map will identify the best practices you need to incorporate, and locate appropriate benchmarks for measuring how you can arrive at better ways of communicating your services.

As Dr. George Washington Carver put it: *"It is simply service that measures success."*

Identifying the Key Processes

You're not going to develop and analyze flowcharts for every process in your call center, so start with the big ones and add process maps as new issues become apparent. Some key processes to consider include

- Accepting new assignments from headquarters

- Working out organizational design

- Managing call flow, IVR, and call routing

- Establishing processes that drive contacts/customer, occupancy, call length, and revenue per call (I introduce key performance drivers and how to affect them in Chapter 2)

- Hiring the right people

- Training and certification

- Managing agent performance (there's more on hiring, training, and agent performance management in Chapters 10 and 11)

- Ensuring quality control

- Handling calls by key call types, including any type that you haven't created a call guide for (I discuss call guides in Chapter 15)

- Staffing and its effects on occupancy, call length, contacts/customer (see Chapter 7 for lots of detail on effective scheduling)

- Taking corrective action regarding missed targets

Doing It By the Book: Policies and Procedures

If it isn't written, it isn't real! Whether your call center's processes are good or bad, it's important to write them down and formalize them into some kind of procedures document.

You can create and agree to the greatest set of processes and procedures in the world, but if you don't write them down your people will probably stop using them.

Making it real! Documenting your procedures

By documenting your procedures and making them accessible to everyone in your center, you create a reference guide and training tool for people to govern their actions by. Written documentation also becomes a standard against which you can audit work processes. Probably the biggest advantage is that it serves as a baseline for future improvement.

When you do create a formalized procedures manual, you should keep some of the following things in mind.

Providing visuals: A picture paints a thousand words

Of course your documentation will contain primarily words, but use lots of photos, diagrams, and flowcharts as well. It's been said before, but a picture really does make things clearer.

Implementing a change process

You need to have a process in place for updating and changing the document. Make sure, also, that you have someone reviewing what your people are doing as compared to the procedures document.

In my group of call centers I have a person dedicated to procedures documentation, and another whose job it is to watch people work and attend meetings just to make sure that the company procedures are being followed. He also identifies procedures that aren't documented or procedures that need improvement or updating.

Ensuring accountability from the top

Overall responsibility and drive for updating and improving the procedures manual must come from a senior person in the call center — ideally the most senior person.

If the top person isn't involved, you run the risk of losing commitment and momentum in use of the document.

Keeping information updated: Paper will kill ya, kid!

If you can, put your procedures manual (and all other company documents) online — store them electronically, for example on an intranet. When a document can be found online only, it's common to everyone. If the information's out of date, then it's out of date for all — and is more likely to be noticed and rectified for all.

With paper documentation it's far too easy for someone to use an out-of-date version, which could be hazardous depending on the type of business you're in.

Paper is also cumbersome, messy, and harder to use. Sure, people like paper, but six months after committing all your resources to an online source (like an intranet) people will have adapted.

Yes, computer systems do go down occasionally. For the rare times that they're offline, you can have backup paper copies. But keep them locked up in a cabinet, and don't let anyone have them until the computers go down. Then you can crack the seal and hand out fresh, clean, identical copies. As soon as the computer is back up, grab all those paper copies and put them away.

Trust me — if you haven't already done this, you may find it's one of the most beneficial process improvements you can make.

Staying Informed: Legislative Considerations

Your procedures manual should include a section on policies. What's the difference between policies and procedures? *Procedures* are how you do things; *policies* are rules governing your behavior. Call centers write lots of policies — designed to protect worker safety, department performance, and company reputation.

It's also a good idea to include policies that ensure you work within the guidelines of the legislation that governs your call center operations, including legislation that addresses specifically how call centers operate and legislation that addresses the broader law, like individual rights.

Some legislation can be assumed away — meaning that you can assume that people know inherently what to do or not to do in these cases. For example, it's doubtful you should need a policy stating, "Thou shalt not poke anyone in the eye."

Law and order: Creating appropriate policies

A good rule is that your procedures manual should include policies for any legislation that could be violated by someone in your call center due to ignorance of the law. Examples might include:

✔ **Labor laws:** These are laws especially related to recruiting, working conditions, working hours, labor relations, discipline, termination, layoffs, compensation, harassment, and employment equity.

✔ **Call-center-specific legislation:** This includes legislation that directly or indirectly affects how your call center can operate — hours of calling for outbound projects, telephone solicitation, do not call lists, privacy of personal information, and others.

✔ **Legislated service levels:** Call center operations in certain industries have minimum service-level targets established by their local government. For example, in some U.S. states the cable industry has minimum speed of answer requirements for call centers. Failure to meet these minimums can result in a substantial fine to the cable operator.

All of these obligations are very serious and need to be considered in your operations. It's important that you create policies that address these legislative requirements, then filter your procedures through the policies and train the affected staff in the policies and underlying legislation. Failure to do this could land you in a heap of trouble.

Having a leg to stand on: Knowing the law

Probably the best place to start is with a good lawyer or two. You'll need a labor lawyer and a lawyer who specializes in the laws affecting call centers and/or telecommunications.

Give your lawyers copies of your policies and procedures and ask them to review and comment on them. Then, ask them to identify the areas of legislation that haven't been adequately addressed by your policies and procedures. They'll find lots of stuff — it's what lawyers do — and it'll be worth it.

Periodically, ask your lawyers to review any updates or to provide you with information on new legislation that affects your operations.

Other than employment law, the laws that affect your call center are often governed by a centralized government agency. Wherever you live, you'll want to be aware of and compliant with your local laws and, equally important, the laws of the country that your call center is doing business with. To give you an idea of the kinds of laws you'll need to be aware of, here is a list of considerations (specific to the United States, unless otherwise noted) that affect call centers:

✔ **Telemarketing and Consumer Fraud and Abuse Prevention Act:** Under this law, the Federal Trade Commission (FTC) adopted the Telemarketing Sales Rule (TSR), which prohibits misrepresentations, prohibits calls to a consumer after the consumer has asked not to be called, sets payment restrictions for the sale of certain goods and services, and requires that specific business records be kept for two years.

- **Telephone Consumer Protection Act (TCPA):** The Federal Communications Commission (FCC) places restrictions on unwanted telephone solicitations, automatic telephone dialing systems, artificial or prerecorded voice messages, and the use of fax machines to send unsolicited advertisements.

- **The Do Not Call Implementation Act of 2003:** This law gave the FTC the authority to create and enforce a national do not call registry, rules that the FCC has also adopted. Once consumers have placed their names on the national do not call list, telemarketers cannot make unsolicited sales calls to them. Failure to comply with the law can result in very large fines. While some exemptions apply, this law has greatly cut down the number of unwanted telemarketing calls.

- **Privacy laws:** Privacy laws in both the U.S. and Canada have been established to protect consumers' personal information by regulating how and when personal information can be collected, used, or disclosed. These laws also regulate the length of time personal information can be retained, how it must be secured, and finally, how it must be destroyed. Violations of these laws can result in fines and criminal prosecution.

- **State laws:** In addition to those above, many states have registration and bonding requirements for telemarketers as well as state-specific do not call lists and programs.

- **Canadian laws:** Canada regulates outbound telemarketing through the Canadian Radio-television and Telecommunications Commission (CRTC). The CRTC issues regulations called Telecom Decisions, including calling time restrictions, disclosure requirements, and prohibitions on calls to consumers who have asked not to be called. Current regulations include identification and caller ID requirements, as well as the maintenance of a company-specific do not call list.

  Organizations that conduct unsolicited telemarketing activity must honor a consumer do not call request for three years. Canada does not have a national do not call registry, but in late 2004 the CRTC introduced legislation to create such a list. Violations of CRTC rules can result in the termination of telecommunications services to the call center.

- **The Personal Information Protection and Electronic Documents Act (PIPEDA):** PIPEDA governs the collection, use, and disclosure of personally identifiable information by companies in Canada. All organizations engaged in commercial activity must designate a privacy officer or contact, have written policies and procedures outlining how personal information is handled and protected, and train employees on data-handling procedures. In addition, PIPEDA is deemed to meet the requirements set forth in the European Union's Data Protection Directive, thereby allowing Canadian-based organizations to handle data about consumers in EU member states.

- **European laws:** The European Union (EU), currently comprising 25 member states, has two primary directives that impact call centers. The first, the Distance Selling Regulations of 2000, protects consumers who buy goods and services at a distance throughout Europe, whether or not companies selling these goods or services are located within the EU. The regulations cover sales made by mail order, Internet, telephone, and all other means of distance communication. They require suppliers to give certain information to consumers; offer the right to cancel the contract within seven working days of receiving goods or concluding contract for services; meet set deadlines for delivery of goods/performance of service; and offer consumer protection against fraudulent use of card payments. The regulations also prohibit inertial selling, which is the practice of sending unrequested goods to customers and sending them an invoice for the goods in the hope that they will pay it.

The second EU directive relates to data protection and establishes how and with whom personal data can be collected, used, disclosed, held, and destroyed, whether within or outside of a member state. Consumer rights under both directives must be implemented into each member state's national laws and these national laws vary from state to state. Eighteen of the 25 EU member states have established preference services that include do not call lists. Requirements regarding do not call laws also vary from state to state.

Maintaining compliance

If you have a large call center or if you run an outsourcing call center (as I do), you may want to consider creating a compliance officer role in your operation. The compliance officer is responsible for making sure that your company is compliant with all the legislation affecting your call center.

The best part of having a compliance officer is that he or she is the person who has to talk to the lawyers!

Chapter 13

Quality Programs: Ensuring Process Improvement

● ●

In This Chapter

▶ Providing certification for your management team

▶ Developing a quality control program

▶ Finding call center support services

● ●

*I*n the service world, and the call center industry particularly, the meaning of *quality* has changed from the original definition of "an inherent or distinguishing characteristic of something (or someone)." Quality has come to mean something of superior grade, as in a quality wine. So, when people talk of improving quality, it's kind of like saying seeking perfection — or, as I'm defining it here, continuously improving.

Quality control, meanwhile, is defined as "a system for ensuring the maintenance of proper standards," which I interpret as a system designed to ensure continuous process improvement. I define and discuss process improvement in some detail in Chapter 12. In this chapter, you'll find suggestions and resources to help ensure process improvement happens in your center.

The Importance of a Management Certification Program

Certification involves taking your existing, new, or potential call center management through a training program that covers call center definitions, concepts, and practices. Your goal is to produce a management team familiar with call center operations and skilled at managing call center processes so that each of their operations achieves excellent results.

Call center management certification is not all that new, but its popularity has exploded in recent years — a good thing, because certification is a very good idea.

The increase in demand for this type of program is largely in response to a shortage of supply in skilled call center management. The diversity of skills and knowledge required — from managing service level and occupancy (see Chapter 5) to labor relations and the psychology of motivation — make call center management a fairly specialized skill.

A good certification program can take smart people and develop them into competent call center operators.

In-house versus external programs

Certification programs come in two varieties, home grown and external. It's a mistake to assume that a program is no good just because it was developed in-house — good programs can be created internally or purchased externally. It can be beneficial, however — not to mention a lot easier — to get external help from people who've already gone through the process of creating the course.

You'll find a handy-dandy reference of certification program suppliers in Appendix 2.

A course is a course, of course, of course...

To develop a good program, you should assume that participants know very little about call centers. Starting with the basics is important because your certification course will be used as indoctrination for managers new to the call center environment (that is, smart people hired to perform call center management functions).

Going beyond the basics, you may want to create a general call center management certification program, targeted to managers and executives who need an overall understanding of how the call center operates.

Here are some topics you might include in your certification course:

- Call center definitions
- Call center business objectives and metrics
- Unique call center concepts — such as managing service levels and occupancy
- Call center logistics — location, building, setup, and so on

- ✔ Technology in the call center and how it helps
- ✔ Supervision and agent performance management — including labor relations
- ✔ Forecasting and scheduling
- ✔ Quality assurance
- ✔ Process management — including policies, procedures, and best practices
- ✔ Legislation affecting the call center

Courses providing a general overview like this could take a week to complete. However, in each module you can go into a great deal of depth, making the course considerably longer.

A more feasible approach would be to create separate certification courses for the different disciplines within the call center, including forecasting and scheduling; supervisor and agent performance management; analysis and reporting; and technology management. You could then prioritize the courses as optional, suggested, or required for specific roles within your center. For example, forecasting and scheduling would be a required course for the folks on your resource management team.

Who should attend management certification courses?

Certification programs are useful for smart new managers brought in to run all or part of your call center operations. They may have been transferred from other departments within the company and have good management credentials, but little or no call center experience.

Senior managers who have call center operations responsibility will also benefit. These might be executives who've just been given the responsibility of running the call center, or executives who've been in call centers for some time and want to make more sense of the operation and why it causes so much fuss and attention.

Finally, certification will also help call center agents, supervisors, and junior managers who want or need a better overall understanding of call center operations.

Getting your call center certification can be a great career move, setting you up for advancement after successfully completing the course.

Quality Control: Instituting a Quality Program

You can do a great deal on your own to improve processes (see Chapter 12) and ensure quality control within your call center. Still, there are people out there who do this for a living, helping businesses to better understand their processes and build systems of improvement.

The benefit of turning to one of these organizations is that you don't have to reinvent the wheel. They bring time-tested methodologies that can be quickly implemented into your organization. You can then start working at improving your operation sooner, with what's likely a better-defined approach than if you'd built a quality program on your own.

Someone senior in your organization generally sponsors these programs, so getting resources to get the work done can be less difficult.

In this section, we discuss some of the quality control programs most commonly used in the call center industry.

The International Organization for Standardization — ISO 9001/2000

A good place to start is ISO 9001/2000, an international standard for the creation and maintenance of a quality assurance system within a company. ISO provides your company with a template for building and documenting your quality system.

Key elements of ISO include standards for training employees, maintenance of equipment, record keeping, inspection of processes, customer relations, and continuous improvement. Adherence to ISO standards is ensured by an annual audit, which is conducted by a third-party, ISO-accredited auditor.

It's important to note that ISO certification does not assure your company that your products or services will be of a high quality. ISO merely provides a means to ensure that you've documented and are following your internal procedures — including procedures for correcting problems and improving processes. "Say what you do and do what you say" is a common ISO motto.

ISO certification brings immediate results to marketing services call center

A while ago, I was working with a really great group of people at a marketing services call center. They seemed to have it all: smart, talented, motivated people; great technology; a culture based on improvement and learning; and a really good understanding of how to run a call center. Yet, in spite of all their advantages, they produced inconsistent results — sometimes great, sometimes not so good.

The problem seemed to be that, like so many operations, they had several ways to complete any task. Even their definitions were a mess. It was difficult having a conversation with many of them because they could use three different words to describe the same thing.

One of their frustrations was that even after they'd found a really good way of doing something they would eventually abandon that approach to try something else, ultimately forgetting and losing some of the practices that made them successful.

I encouraged this company to pursue the ISO standard and it did. It took more than a year and a large financial investment to reach certification. What ISO did was force the company into standardization and documentation. It drove this group of innovators a little crazy, but they were even forced to follow a rigid process for making improvements. It didn't take long for the organization to see improvements in consistency. And that was all this group really needed, because they were already good.

Criticisms of ISO

The application of ISO certification to call centers has received some criticism. Some suggest that it's a manufacturing standard and isn't suited to service operations like call centers, while others argue that ISO doesn't focus enough on measurable outputs, especially quality outputs.

A further criticism is that companies can simply fake their adherence to ISO — running around like lunatics at audit time to cover up the fact that they haven't been faithful to their quality system — just for the purpose of marketing the fact they are an "ISO shop."

While all of these criticisms are legitimate, they're probably not fair in their assessment of the standard. Like many business practices, if you use ISO as a framework in a sincere attempt to build a structure for documenting work processes then it's a great tool and can lead to substantial process improvements in your organization. It certainly has in ours.

ISO can be tailored to the call center environment, integrating measurable outputs of success. It's up to you, as the user, to determine what those outputs should be.

If you agree that it's a good idea to standardize and document work processes, then ISO is a great way to go. However, ISO is the beginning, not the end of process management and control. I talk about process management in Chapter 12.

If you're interested in using ISO, be aware that it is not a quick process. It might take a year or more to convert your processes to the ISO standard. The more you have documented already, the better.

You'll need a consultant and a registrar. You'll find some suggestions of where to find them in Appendix 2.

Customer Operations Performance Center

Customer Operations Performance Center Inc. (COPC) was created in 1995 by a group of users of call center services.

The focus of the standard is on measurable criteria in the areas of customer service, customer satisfaction, operational efficiency, and the application of effective processes in those areas. A committee made up of industry professionals from high-profile users and purchasers of call center services maintains the COPC standard.

COPC used the Malcolm Baldrige National Quality Award as a framework to develop a standard unique to the call center industry, originally intended for evaluating third-party providers of call center services. It has evolved into a standard used by both in-house and external/outsourced call center operations.

COPC is the only group that can certify your organization to the call-center-specific, COPC-2000 standard. In addition to call center auditing, they offer consulting services, training, and industry forums.

Six Sigma

Six Sigma is a business system that uses data and statistical analysis to improve efficiency and control and reduce variation in business processes for the purpose of increasing profits, customer satisfaction, and employee morale.

Six Sigma literally means "six standard deviations" and refers to the reduction of errors to six standard deviations from the center of process output, which translates to about 3.4 defects per million outputs. (Approximately none!) Imagine your call center having fewer than four bad calls per million customer interactions.

Knowing your call center defect rate

In the call center, a *defect* occurs when a customer call ends without the desired outcome — probably resulting in an unsatisfied customer. Indicators of call defects include abandoned calls, repeat calls, customer complaints, low customer satisfaction scores, and errors discovered in call monitoring scores. Defects occur because of inadequacies with the call-handling process and with your call center agents.

Understanding what your levels of defects are, then grouping them by cause, is the start to reducing these defects and creating improved customer satisfaction.

Airlines fly safe flights at a Six Sigma level of quality, but not many businesses or industries consistently work at a this level. Service-oriented businesses frequently run at a much higher level of defect — one sigma or perhaps two (about 340,000 defects for every million opportunities).

For your organization, the point of Six Sigma is to manage and control the process of work so that the consistency of output increases — meaning errors decrease.

Six Sigma is a rigorous discipline of process management that makes use of problem solving, project management, and statistical analysis. It aligns the needs of your customers with the strategic priorities of your company to focus on the company's financial results — the ultimate goal of any business process.

The most critical factors of Six Sigma that forge success include:

- ✔ **Well-trained problem solvers (Black Belts):** When starting Six Sigma, you can expect lots of training. Your internal Six Sigma experts — called "Black Belts" — will receive approximately five weeks of Six Sigma training. Everyone else in your call center will receive some Six Sigma training — from several hours to a couple of weeks, depending on their roles.

- ✔ **Data-driven, problem-solving methodology:** Six Sigma is very data heavy. (I talk about the process in the next section.) Part of the appeal of Six Sigma is gaining an understanding of what drives the results of your operation. You'll be very confident of this understanding because of the rigor put into statistically validating the cause-and-effect relationships.

- ✔ **Alignment:** The goal of Six Sigma is to align the needs of your customers with the strategic priorities of your company, with a focus on financial results. The ultimate outcome of Six Sigma is better results.

Defining the Six Sigma improvement process

The centerpiece of Six Sigma problem solving is the RDMAICR model. (That's pronounced R-D-M-A-I-C-R. Catchy, eh?)

1. **R — Recognize:** The company, or call center, identifies a problem or area for improvement in process outputs.

2. **D — Define:** Six Sigma projects are identified, personnel are assigned to the project, and the financial impact of the project is estimated.

3. **M — Measure:** The current state of the process is measured. Baseline measurements are taken, the process is mapped out, and the existing process is evaluated.

4. **A — Analyze:** Data are collected on process inputs and outputs and analyzed to determine cause-and-effect relationships. Insight is gained into what affects variation among the variables.

5. **I — Improve:** Controlled experiments and tests are conducted to understand the direct relationship between inputs and outputs (or results). The goal is to understand the exact correlation between things you can control and outputs.

6. **C — Control:** During this phase, the newly gained understanding of how to maximize results is put to work. Process improvements are put into place so that the results of the process are maximized. These improvements are formalized and documented so they can be handed over to the people who'll be working with the process day-to-day.

7. **R — Realize:** This is the good part. The process is handed back to the people who'll be working with it. The project is tracked for a period of 12 months to quantify the actual results.

The Six Sigma payoff

In your call center, Six Sigma will provide a number of benefits. First, it brings discipline and structure to understanding, documenting, and controlling call center goals and work processes. Second, you'll gain understanding of the controllable variables that drive customer satisfaction, profitability, employee morale, and quality.

Additionally, your people will have a high level of comfort that the understanding gained is "right" because of the rigor that Six Sigma uses in statistically validating its findings.

The act of engaging the entire call center in the Six Sigma improvement process is also beneficial. A Six Sigma implementation is as much a cultural change as it is a new business process.

Ultimately, Six Sigma provides a steady, methodical way of driving toward operational goals.

While Six Sigma was originally designed for use in manufacturing, it's gaining rapid acceptance in call centers — because it works. For the many call centers that do not have well defined process management discipline, Six Sigma is very good.

It's not for the faint of heart, however. Understand that when you start down the Six Sigma road, it's a lot of work; done well, however, the work can pay off nicely.

Finding Other Sources of Help

Over the last decade call center management has become a discipline and industry unto itself — a very large industry. As a result, subindustries have developed solely for the purpose of providing call center support. Here are some sources where you can find support to help you meet your call center goals.

Consulting firms

Call center consulting services have become readily available and cover everything from general call center management and technology to very specific consulting disciplines, such as call handling, location selection and development, recruitment, and scheduling.

You'll find that most of the large consulting firms have a division of experts who'll be able to help you with your call center projects.

A lot of smaller, independent call center consulting and support companies are also available. These shouldn't be overlooked, because some are very good — particularly those that specialize in specific disciplines within call center management.

I provide a list of some places to look for call center support in Appendix 2. An Internet search under "call center consulting" is a good place to start.

Trade shows

As the call center industry has grown, so has the number of call center trade shows. You'll find them taking place around the world and often specializing in specific trends in the industry. Of course, call center trade shows have benefits and drawbacks similar to those of any industry — they're busy and fun and often located in some far-off exotic location.

Trade shows offer three primary sources of call center learning:

> ✔ **Sessions run by speakers who have some experience or expertise within a particular topic:** Often these can be very good — and sometimes they can be disappointing. It often depends on the conference — whether they've screened the speakers, paid them well, reviewed the content, and so on.

✔ **Exhibits:** The exhibit is where vendors of call center services and equipment set up booths so they can talk to you and tell you about their offerings. It's an excellent opportunity to see a huge cross-section of vendors and learn about the latest and greatest call center everything. Consistently, I find the trade show exhibits to be the most valuable part of any call center conference.

✔ **Networking:** Some of the industry's leading experts attend the larger and better-known trade shows. Usually, these experts are more than happy to spend a few minutes with you discussing the industry and your business. You'll also find a lot of people like you, who are working in or running a call center and are just looking for ideas.

The networking that you'll do at a trade show can help you build an informal and free system for support, information, and advice. I met my wife at a call center trade show. See, they work.

Trade magazines

Trade magazines are much cheaper than trade shows, and they're full of great and current information on the call center industry.

Everyone who's responsible in any way for the operation of a call center — or a department within a call center — should subscribe to call center industry and related magazines. A good trade magazine will cover every hot issue, trend, and discipline of running call centers over a one-year subscription. Even the advertising is good, because vendors strut their latest and greatest developments.

For the cost, you won't get a better source of information than call center trade magazines. Some that we like include

✔ *CallCenter Magazine*

✔ *Customer Interaction Solutions*

✔ *Communications Convergence*

Part V
Handling the Calls: Where It All Comes Together

The 5th Wave   By Rich Tennant

SCREW-U
Screws 'n Screwdrivers
CUSTOMER SERVICE

Screw-U! How can
I... Hello? Dang!

Another, hang
up Dave? Just
a tip—next time try
answering with a smile
on your
face.

In this part . . .

Part V gets down to the basics of call handling. I review a straightforward plan of attack that agents can follow when speaking directly to customers.

The most critical relationship in the call center is that of agent and customer. If your agents handle calls well, you'll be blessed with lots of happy customers. If they don't, you might want to start planning for your going out of business sale. I share vital (and in some cases, seemingly obvious) tips and techniques — on topics from call control and anger diffusion to customer service and call center selling — to ensure that agents are efficiently and effectively handling this most important interaction in the call center.

Chapter 14

"Thank You for Calling...": Call-Handling Skills and Techniques

....

....

None of the work done in your call center — hiring great people, creating schedules, developing great processes, and investing in the best technology to get calls to your agents — is worth a hill of beans if the agents don't know how to handle the calls when they arrive.

In the call center, when your agents speak to your customers is truly where "the rubber hits the road!" How your customers' calls are handled can, quite literally, make or break your operation.

In Chapter 15 I discuss how calls might be structured. In this chapter I offer more specific tips and techniques that'll help your agents when handling calls.

Following the Golden Rule of Call Handling: Just Be Nice!

Somebody (actually, I think it was me) once said to talk to your customers as if you were speaking with your grandmother — or your priest, minister, rabbi, or guru. Treat people with respect and dignity, with common sense, and with good manners — like your mother always told you to — and you'll be rewarded in kind.

The most effective rule to follow in order to provide world-class customer service also happens to be the simplest. Just be nice! After years of listening to calls, I still believe that it is the most important basic.

Every customer call is another opportunity to make or break the perception customers have of the service your company provides.

Here are five *golden rules* that are vital in helping to ensure a more positive experience for your customer.

- ✔ Be polite.
- ✔ Use empathy and understanding.
- ✔ Use the customer's name.
- ✔ Take ownership of the situation and the solution.
- ✔ Use positive, "can-do" language.

These rules aren't the kinds of things for which customer-service legends are made. Customers aren't likely to ask to speak to a supervisor to rave about the service they've received just because you follow them (although a lot of agents wish they would). But these simple rules are what will leave the customer thinking, "That was a really nice call," even though they may not put their finger on exactly why.

The rules are simple and, you might say, based on common sense; however, in the average call center they're not as common as they should be. Let's look at the rules one by one.

Be polite

Always say please when asking a customer for something; whether it's an e-mail address, telephone number, or just permission to put a customer on hold ... please say please. And don't forget to say thank you every time a customer gives you something you've asked for.

> You: *"May I please have your email address?"*
>
> Customer: *"joeschmo@mexico.com"*
>
> You: *"Thank you."*

When you're polite customers feel respected and valued, and it shows that you appreciate the time they've taken to speak with you.

Use empathy and understanding

Put yourself in your customer's shoes. Try to understand where the customer is coming from and think about how you'd feel if you were experiencing their situation. This is particularly important if a customer is angry or annoyed. Your intent should be to relieve the customer's stress by providing him with an ally.

> *"I can understand how you must be feeling. I certainly appreciate your frustration...."*

Don't add fuel to the fire agreeing with an upset customer by saying something like, "You're right, our service *is* terrible." Empathy is showing concern for the customer's situation and feelings without agreeing or disagreeing with what the customer is saying.

Use the customer's name

"There's no greater music than the sound of one's own name." Calling customers by name lets them know you value them and helps make them feel more comfortable. When you personalize the interaction, customers feel like they're talking to a real person, perhaps even a friend.

> *"Thank you for bringing this to my attention, Mr. Jones."*

Take ownership of the situation and the solution

Customers call your call center because they want their questions answered or their problems resolved. When you answer the call, you own the situation and are responsible for finding a resolution. It's your duty to do everything you can to help the customer — or to find the most qualified person who can.

> *"I'm glad you called me today, Mr. Smith. I'd be happy to look after this for you."*

Don't pass the buck to your manager or blame another department. Treat each customer as if she is the only customer your company has, and you're the only person in your company.

Use positive, "can do" language

Always tell the customer what you *can* do for her, rather than what you can't do. Of course, there'll be times when it's not in your power to grant a customer's specific request. Rather than focus on the negative — "I'm sorry, I can't help you with that" — show the customer that you're committed to helping her by focusing on what you *can* do.

> *"Thank you for bringing this to my attention, Ms. Brown. I can put you in touch with the specific person who has all the information needed to resolve this for you. Do you mind waiting for a moment while I transfer you, or would you prefer I give them a call and have them contact you?"*

Doesn't that sound a whole lot better than

> *"I'm sorry, I can't do that."*

Or worse,

> *"That's not my job."*

As long as you're contributing to customers getting what they wanted (their questions answered or their problem resolved), then you *are* helping them.

When you incorporate these golden rules with a structured call plan like the one I outline in Chapter 15, you'll be well on your way to providing extraordinary customer service that will meet and exceed your callers' expectations.

Dealing with Difficult Situations: Successful Anger Diffusion — "Passion before Reason"

In customer relationships, or just about any interaction between people for that matter, passion comes before reason. Pierre Trudeau, the famous Canadian prime minister and philosopher, argued for "reason before passion" in decision-making. While this might be great philosophical advice, it's not such good advice for dealing with customers.

When customers are passionate, you'll have a hard time reasoning with them. You'll find it increasingly challenging to work with customers until you've addressed that passion. This truth leads to one of my favorite call-handling expressions: "Deal with the emotion first, then deal with the problem."

That philosophy is especially important when handling a call from a customer who's upset, angry, or frustrated.

Consistently following the golden rules described in this chapter while speaking with a calm, friendly, and helpful tone of voice will dramatically lessen the number of irate customers you find yourself dealing with.

Deal first with the emotion...

Even the friendliest, most passive customer service agents, however, occasionally find themselves speaking with a customer who's angry. Remember that an angry customer has become angry for a reason. Something has happened to cause the anger; something that usually still needs resolution.

So, when dealing with difficult situations, it's important to realize that, in effect, you're dealing with two separate issues — a problem that needs resolving, and the strained emotion of the customer. It's imperative that you deal with the emotion first, before you can even clear the air enough to get to the problem.

Here's a step-by-step process to assist you when dealing with these difficult — and highly stressful — situations.

1. Ask the customer to tell you about his entire experience

"Please tell me about your experience, Mr. Johnson."

Let the customer vent, without judging his interpretation of the details, and never interrupt. Interruptions sound accusatory and will put the customer on the defensive. On the other hand, feel free to show that you're listening with short verbal cues, since the customer cannot see you. "Uh huh," "I see," or "Please go on, I'm taking notes."

Think of the situation as a balloon filled to capacity with air — it's ready to pop at any minute. By allowing the customer to vent, some of that air will be released and it's less likely to pop. Two minutes is usually the maximum that anyone will rant and rave.

Take notes, including some of the customer's specific words, as he is recounting his story. Later you can use these exact words to emphasize the fact that you've been listening.

Corral the "OK"

Did you ever catch yourself saying "okay" as someone tells you a story? Saying "okay" is a benign way of acknowledging that you understand what's happening. This unintentional acknowledgement can be a problem for some customers. Don't say "okay" when customers vent. Some customers might turn this against you and say, "No, it's *not* okay!"

It's better to say something like "I understand" or "I see."

2. Empathize with the customer, using "feel, felt, found" phrases

"I can certainly understand your frustration, Mr. Smith."

"I'm sorry you had to experience that, Mr. Jones."

"I would feel the same way if I were in that situation, Ms. McGillicuddy."

I talk more about using "feel, felt, found" phrases in the next section.

Avoid the temptation to push back!

Try this exercise to illustrate the importance of allowing the customer to vent, and in using empathy when attempting to defuse an angry customer. You'll need someone to help you with this, so please find a friend. Go ahead ... I'll wait.

Thanks for coming back. Okay, ask your friend to hold one hand up in the air with his palm facing you. Now you place the palm of your hand against his and begin gently pushing. Slowly increase the pressure applied against his hand. As you do, he'll invariably push back in resistance.

Now, reverse roles. Hold your palm in the air facing your friend, and ask him to gently press against your palm. As he does, move your palm back away from him, so he is virtually pressing air. In all likelihood, he'll attempt it again, trying to push harder, or moving his hand more quickly, but again, simply pull your hand back so there

is no resistance. Eventually, he'll give up, because there's nothing for him to push against.

That's kind of how it works when dealing with angry customers. If you push back on a customer who's upset, she's bound to push back on you even harder. Soon everyone is pushing back and no one's dealing with emotions or problems.

Instead of pushing back, if you go with the customer and don't fight her emotions you'll be able to more effectively defuse the situation. You must resist the temptation to push back. Let the customer get it off her chest without interrupting or becoming defensive.

No matter how much your heart rate increases and your temperature rises — along with your stress level — remain calm, empathetic, and helpful, and avoid the temptation to push back!

Using empathy this way doesn't mean you're agreeing (or disagreeing) with what the customer has said; however, you're showing that you care about how the customer feels about the situation. You're simply acknowledging his feelings, not saying where the blame lies.

3. Review the emotions and facts of the complaint and empathize again

> "If I understand you correctly, this is what happened..."

> "...and this is how it made you feel."

If possible, use some of the same words the customer did to describe the situation and his feelings about it.

> "...Is that correct?"

> "Is this a correct summary of the details, Mr. Johnson?"

When the customer responds yes, you've proven that you listened, that you are on the same side of the fence, and that you're interested in solving the issue.

In addition, you've just taken more air out of the balloon because he feels as if he's found someone who cares and who'll find a resolution he's satisfied with. At this point, why would he get angry with you and jeopardize his chance at resolving the problem?

... Then deal with the problem

4. Offer a solution and sell the customer on that solution

> "What I'd like to do for you right now, Mr. Johnson, with your permission is..."

Sell the solution by explaining to the customer specifically what you're going to do and how it'll help in resolving the issue. When the customer is sold on the solution, he is less likely to call back to try to find someone else who'll do something better for him.

By asking permission you involve the customer in the solution, and increase the chances of gaining their agreement.

5. Bring the conversation to a close

> "Mr. Johnson, it appears as though we're making our way toward ensuring you don't have to experience this again."

Leave the customer feeling you care about him and that you're doing everything you can to help. Talk to the person's feelings rather than the problem.

Sure, it's true that you can't guarantee this issue will never arise again, but you can leave the customer feeling that if something were to happen again, he'd be able to call you and receive the same prompt, courteous resolution to the problem.

6. Wrap up the conversation

"Mr. Johnson, I would like to thank you for calling and allowing me to help you with this situation. I'm very sorry you had to go through this experience..."

Thank the customer and apologize for the problem. This is the final impression you'll leave with the customer. Make sure it's a good one.

The intention is not to say that you or your company did anything wrong, but simply to acknowledge to the customer that you understand and care about how they feel.

Done well, an angry customer can be defused in minutes. Done poorly, it can take hours and may cost you the customer in the future.

Coming to Your Emotional Rescue: Feel, Felt, Found

Many techniques exist for handling calls from concerned customers — those callers who might take issue with something they believe you or your company have done. Some of the techniques are quite complex.

In the call center, however — since a primary goal is to get through the call quickly, and because there's often a great deal of disparity in the level of call-handling sophistication among agents — it's important to keep your call-handling methodology simple and efficient.

An effective way to deal with concerned callers is the "feel, felt, found (FFF)" method. Yes, it's old and worn, but it's easy to remember and it works.

It works because it provides a communication framework and addresses a person's emotions.

Using "feel, felt, found"

It's important to understand that the term "feel, felt, found" is intended only as a template to guide you in handling the caller's concern. The intent is not — as too many agents (and trainers and supervisors) assume — for the words *feel, felt,* and *found* to actually be used in every case.

"Feel, felt, found" is just an easy way to remember the most important aspects of what you should say when dealing with a caller's concern. In the breakdown below, I include a typical phrase to illustrate the purpose of each step. My suggestion, however, is that you do not use these phrases word for word, because customers — particularly those who read this book — will see your attempt to deal with their concern as a trick or technique.

Remember, you're supposed to be having a conversation with the customer, so use natural wording that keeps all parts of the conversation — even when you're dealing with a customer's issue — well, conversational.

1. **"I understand how you *feel*."** You first need to identify with the customer and validate her concern. It doesn't mean you're agreeing that it can't be dealt with, just that it's a concern to that customer and you appreciate her bringing it to your attention. (And, frankly, you *should* appreciate it!)

   It's only when you really understand the customer's concerns and deal with them that you can provide the appropriate resolution to the problem or inquiry.

   A similar statement, which serves the same purpose, would be to say something like, "I can certainly appreciate your concern" or, "I know where you're coming from." That way you avoid the rebuttal from those savvy customers: "Don't you feel-felt-found me!"

2. **"Others have *felt* the same way."** Next, you need to empathize with the customer. A statement expressing your empathy helps break down a potentially confrontational barrier and puts you on the customer's side of the fence.

   Instead of taking a defensive posture and facing off with the customer, using empathy is like stepping over the fence and standing beside her, putting your arm around her shoulder, and saying, "Hey, this isn't about you versus me, it's about you and me versus this issue."

   Essentially, you want to show the customer that she's not alone in how she feels, that her concern isn't so daunting, and that it's certainly not something that hasn't been dealt with before. The customer must feel confident that her concern can be satisfactorily overcome before she will agree to commit to your proposed resolution.

   Note that I suggest the same technique when dealing with an emotional customer. Similar statements achieving the same result might be, "Another customer I spoke to this week had a similar concern," or "I've been there myself."

3. **"What they *found* was..."** Finally, you need to provide a suggested solution to the customer's concern. You use the *found* statement as a bridge to help further the customer's confidence that this solution you're suggesting is tried and true — it's worked before when someone was concerned with a similar issue.

In essence, the purpose of this step is to show the customer how her concern is outweighed by the benefits of the solution being offered.

Found statements that might flow with the *feel* and *felt* phrases above might be, "When we really looked at the situation, we came to the conclusion that..." or, "What I realized was that...."

The point is that it's not about using the words *feel, felt,* and *found;* it's about connecting with, relating to, and engaging the customer and genuinely caring about helping her deal with her issue.

Most people (including me) have faced a situation at some point in their lives where they've found themselves consoling a friend in need — perhaps dealing with the death of a loved one, for example. Think about what you might say to him. Probably something like, "I can appreciate what you're going through, John. I know how difficult it was when my family was dealing with the same thing. You know, one of the things that really helped us out was...." Sounds a lot like "feel, felt, found," doesn't it?

Avoiding confrontation: No buts about it

A common error made by agents, and an easy trap to fall into when facing a customer with a concern, is to become defensive or confrontational. The easy rebuttal to an issue is, "Yes, but...." It's also an easy way to lose customers.

I talk about how to deal with the customer's emotions earlier in this chapter.

It's vital that all call center agents understand you should never, ever, ever say "yes, *but*" to a customer! The word "but" — especially when it comes right after a customer has stated an area of concern — tends to devalue everything the customer has said. Even if you politely say, "I certainly appreciate your concern, Ms. Jones, *but...*" it doesn't matter what comes next; the customer will feel her concern is not truly appreciated.

The word "but" suggests disagreement. It sets up a confrontational stance; precisely the thing you want to avoid when helping to deal with a customer concern.

The BUT stops here!

If you want to see how fast a conversation can go downhill and become confrontational when someone uses the word "but," try this little exercise. I use it sometimes when training agents how to deal with customer concerns, and when training supervisors on giving performance feedback to agents.

You'll need two volunteers. Ask them to imagine that they've just sat down at a table in a nice restaurant and are looking at the menu. Have them simply carry on a typical conversation discussing what they'd like to order. The one proviso is that each of them must begin every statement they make with, "Yes, but..." irrespective of what the other person has said.

Watch how fast the two participants become frustrated and defensive with each other.

Next, have them repeat the same scenario, this time prefacing each statement with, "Yes, *and*...." The difference is remarkable. The tones become more serene and the participants more agreeable — even when they attempt to disagree.

The word "but" creates confrontation, and although this exercise usually generates a lot of laughs, it shows — sometimes dramatically — how quickly a conversation can get heated when it feels as though the person you're speaking with constantly disagrees with you.

When dealing with customer concerns, keep your but to yourself!

Maintaining Control of the Call: A Question of Questions

A great way to maintain control over any call is the LAMA statement/question technique, taught to my staff and me a number of years ago by Judy McKee of McKee Motivation in Escondido, California. LAMA stands for **L**isten, **A**cknowledge, **M**ake a Statement, and **A**sk a question. It relies on the principle that the person in control of a conversation is the one asking questions.

LAMA is a very customer-friendly, non-confrontational, and effective technique for maintaining control of a call as you guide the conversation through your call strategy. It helps you guide the direction the call is going without attempting to manipulate or control the caller. Here are the highlights of the steps involved.

1. Listen

The first part of LAMA is to listen to what the customer has to say. As it relates to the business at hand, it might help to take note of any details that will help you in working through the specific issue.

2. Acknowledge

After the customer has told you something — anything — acknowledge what she has said. When talking over the phone the customer can't see you, so nodding won't do. It's important that the customer knows that you're listening.

Acknowledging what the customer says can be as simple as saying, "Yes" or "I see" or "I understand what you're saying." Even if what the customer has to say is negative you have to acknowledge that you've heard her, perhaps with something like, "I can understand why you'd feel that way" or "I'm sorry that happened."

Acknowledging what the caller has said is a very powerful customer satisfier and call-control tool. It shows respect for the customer and tells her that you've heard her and that she is valued.

3. Make a statement

Making a statement allows you to reframe the discussion and begin taking it in the direction that you need it to go. Your statement can be a proposed solution, or a feature or benefit of your product or service. "Well, if I can help you through this procedure of rebooting your computer, I think we'll be able to solve the problem and your service should be back up and running in no time."

4. Ask a question

A simple rule of call control is that the person asking the questions controls the call. The final part of the LAMA technique is to ask an appropriate question that solidly brings control of the call back to the call center agent. "Do you know where your computer is plugged in to the electrical outlet, Mr. Smith? Would you unplug it for me, wait 30 seconds, and plug it back in, please?

I recently saw a great example of call control using LAMA in one of our centers. Kim is a technical support agent. I was sitting with her, listening to calls, when she received what seemed like an impossible call to control. After introducing herself, Kim was greeted by a very nice lady who really wanted to talk — about everything. The customer started the call by asking Kim where she was from. Kim politely answered, which may have been a mistake because the lady seemed to know everything and everyone in Kim's hometown. Now it wasn't busy on the phones, and the woman on the other end of the phone really was a customer, so there wouldn't be any harm in indulging her for a moment or two, but Kim clearly wanted to show me that she could handle this situation.

Soon, Kim found an opening. When the customer said that she and her daughter had visited Kim's hometown, Kim asked her, "Does your daughter live with you?" To this the customer said yes. Kim went on: "Does she use your computer?" And with that, the call moved back to the topic of technical support. The customer wasn't going to make it easy and continued to try to discuss many other subjects, but Kim simply continued to acknowledge the customer's questions and comments, following each with a question of her own to pull the conversation back on track. It was far from easy, but Kim managed to wrestle control from the customer, achieve the call objective, and make the customer happy at the same time.

Practice Makes Perfect: The Role of Role-playing

Call-handling strategies are not complex, but they do require a certain amount of practice. It's a good idea to role-play call-handling techniques a great deal — maybe hundreds of times — away from the phones. Practice it in your personal conversations too, and when talking to friends on the phone. It works. See Chapter 15 for more details on call strategies and script aids.

More formal role-playing can also be used as an effective training technique. I cover the specifics of call center training in Chapter 10, but suffice it to say that the more real-life call simulation you're exposed to before going on the phone, the greater the likelihood you'll be successful sooner — and a lot less stressed.

Although it's difficult to simulate the actual call-handling experience perfectly, role-playing — especially in a training class, with your trainer or another trainee — certainly gives you a chance to practice your call-handling skills and the use of any call guides and script aids you'll be working with.

I recommend that agents demonstrate their grasp of call-handling tools and techniques before going "live" on the phones. An effective way to do that is to implement a role-play certification program — having your agents role-play with a trainer or supervisor, and grading them on their effectiveness at following the call strategy, using the appropriate call-handling skills, and utilizing any necessary guides or script aids (as I discuss in Chapter 15).

Chapter 15

Call-Handling Strategies and Tools

. . . .

In This Chapter

▶ Understanding the importance of call control and a structured call plan

▶ Developing and using an appropriate call strategy

▶ Utilizing call guides and script aids

. . . .

As the facilitator of the call, you need some kind of plan to get you and the customer where you need to go. In this chapter I talk about tools, such as planned call strategies, call-flow guides, and script aids that help to provide structure and a plan for your interactions with customers.

The better the plan and the more skilled you are as a facilitator, the easier it'll be to get to your goal — a mutually satisfactory conclusion to the call.

Why Do These People Keep Calling Us? Understanding Callers' Issues

People do business over the phone for myriad reasons — to enquire about a bill or statement, seek customer service or technical support, make a purchase, reply to a promotion, and so on. Think about the last time (or any time) you dialed a 1-800 number or e-mailed a customer support desk. All of the reasons why customers contact your call center can essentially be categorized as one of two things: they want their problems resolved or their questions answered.

You want it when? Acknowledging callers' urgency

When you picked up the phone or sent the e-mail, what was your expectation about when you would gain a resolution? Sooner rather than later, right? Most everyone lives an increasingly busy life and has a lot of things to do; calling a call center is not the highlight of a person's day.

Customers contact call centers because they want a quick, efficient resolution to their problem or question. All too often, I hear agents suggest that, "I can't have short calls while still providing good customer service." This simply isn't the case.

If the customer calls for information regarding your product or service, then helping them to make a quick and informed purchase decision is exactly what they want. An efficient, complete, and pleasant sales call is an example of *great* customer service. Therefore, it's the duty of the call center to provide exactly that, in a courteous and professional manner.

I'm not suggesting that you rush through every call and push the customer off the phone. What I am suggesting is that you don't dawdle. Take all the time that the customer needs, but stay focused on the purpose of the call and get to the point. I've heard too many calls where the agent allowed the call to drift off topic only to take a long time and never satisfy the customer's original request.

Handling Calls Efficiently

One of the most common problems I see with call handling is that no one's driving the bus. Customers don't know where the conversation will lead, so they can't be in control. The agent must control the call for it to end successfully.

The fact is, it's okay to control calls. It doesn't mean that you're taking control of customers or making decisions for them; you're simply facilitating the flow of calls. One might say you go from being a call service representative to becoming a call *facilitator* representative. So, agents on the whole need to develop their facilitation skills — this is the essence of modern call handling.

A well-controlled call drives the conversation to an efficient and successful conclusion — meaning that customers end up getting what they wanted, while at the same time feeling valued by the company. The company achieves its goals by maximizing service, revenue, and efficiency.

A well-controlled call is efficient because it takes no more time than is necessary to achieve the goals of the call and the call is complete — meaning the customer will not have to call back to clarify missed or poorly communicated information.

Controlling the uncontrollable call

So what do you do when the customer doesn't want to let you control the call? You know the type — they want to know where you're from, what the weather's like, or they want to tell you about their weekend at the coast. For these people, the process of doing business is more social and leisurely. You can't shut them out or ignore what they're talking about. At the same time, you have an objective to work toward. In this situation, call control becomes very important — the customer will let the conversation drift all over the place.

It's up to you to keep the call focused, and to maintain a friendly and courteous air at the same time.

I provide some specific call-handling techniques to help in circumstances when you need to regain control of the call and get things back on track in Chapter 14.

Perhaps the most significant thing to keep in mind, and what should be considered the first rule of call control, is that the person asking the questions is in control. People in general feel morally and psychologically bound to answer a question when asked. You do too, don't you? See, gotcha … you're nodding, aren't you? Ha, you did it again! Seriously, most people find it impolite not to answer a question asked directly of them.

The simple act of asking questions alone will help you gain greater call control. You certainly don't want to make the customer feel uncomfortable or manipulated, so you have to make sure your questions are appropriate and relevant. Sounds reasonable, doesn't it? I provide details of the LAMA call control technique, which relies on this principle of asking questions, in Chapter 14.

Having a call plan

How long should calls be? I don't know and I'm not sure that anyone else really does, either. One of the first things you should look for, however, is how much variation exists in average call length among all agents.

Why focus on call length? Well, not only is call length a major driver in call center outputs, as I discuss in Chapter 5, but it's also an excellent mirror of process. Given that all your agents are using the same tools, working with the same products, and speaking with the same customers, it stands to reason that variances in call length are the result of different work processes and skills among the agent population.

Tracking the amount of variation that exists in call length is a good way of tracking variation in approach among agents. Surprisingly, most call centers see variation in average call length in hundreds or thousands of percent. Think about this. The agents are all doing something very different!

With a high degree of variation in agent call-handling approaches, it's difficult to determine which strategies are most effective. Your goal is to build an approach that consistently produces great results, and then teach that approach to all your agents. (I talk about training in Chapter 10.) Over time your approach will evolve and improve. As this happens, your results should also improve.

Comparing call length with customer satisfaction

A little while ago, my company implemented the use of post-call customer satisfaction surveys. After a few months of collecting data, we attempted to determine if there was a correlation between call length and customer satisfaction.

We learned that the lowest customer satisfaction scores came from agents who had very high or very low call lengths. The very high call lengths didn't surprise us, but the very low call lengths did. Some of the agents with the lowest customer satisfaction scores were also our most skilled. Some agents with very low call lengths also had excellent first-call resolution and call accuracy scores. Yet these same agents had low customer satisfaction scores.

We ultimately learned that while these agents were very skilled, they did not take the time to relate to the customer and make them feel valued and involved. They didn't facilitate the call; they took the customer hostage.

We also learned that the agents with the highest customer satisfaction scores tended to have similar call lengths. These call lengths were efficient, but not too low. These agents tended to have it all — high customer satisfaction scores, modest call length, high first-call resolution, and high call accuracy.

Your first goal is to increase the consistency of the call-handling approach. You do this by documenting the call-handling process, training agents on the process, and then coaching agents on how well they follow the standard approach. (I talk about how to document process in Chapter 12.) Your quality control department will listen to calls and evaluate them for conformity to the standard call-handling approach.

Over time, you'll see (and, as I discuss in this chapter, your quality department will report) improvements in consistency among your agents. When this happens you'll notice improvements in the consistency of call length.

With consistency great things start to happen. It becomes easier to determine a correlation between call-handling approaches and other metrics, such as call length, conversion rate, customer satisfaction, and others. (See Chapter 5 for more on metrics.)

It also becomes easier to implement incremental changes and improvements in call-handling process. In fact, the call-handling process will start to continually evolve and improve. As changes are made, you'll look for and capture incremental improvements in your performance metrics.

The remainder of this chapter and the next focus on call-handling strategies that will result in good performance and consistency.

It's easy to overcomplicate things. Keep in mind that research done by my company suggests customers want the same thing you do: an efficient resolution to their call. So keep it simple, don't rush them, but do get to the point — and just be nice!

Following a Structured Call Plan: Keeping Customers Happy

Not everyone likes the idea of a defined script or call guide. Stereotypical call scripting smacks of hard-core cold-call telemarketing. The "follow the script at all costs" approach used in some outbound cold calling is not effective as it isn't two-way communication, it's a commercial — one that usually ignores the customer.

Still, the *concept* of a call strategy or script is a good one. When planning an important meeting or presentation, even the best speakers typically plan out what they're going to say — some even write down their words verbatim.

A call guide or script is simply a way to help you with your thought process and to make your calls more structured, professional, and successful. I take you through the steps of calls later in the chapter.

Choosing the appropriate tool

A *strategy* is a general approach to a call. Strategies can be fairly standardized, with common elements such as *greeting the customer* or *closing the call,* and some customization based on the customer's reason for calling or answers to questions.

In my call centers, we use a call strategy (which I outline later in this chapter) that includes an introduction, a problem-solving phase, a solutions phase, and a conclusion. The skills I discuss in Chapter 14 are used throughout the call strategy.

A call *guide* is a basic outline of the call, with structured bullet points for agents to follow. Guides don't tend to tell the agent what words to use, but they do give the agent a path to follow on the call — often including lots of product and procedural information.

Lots of call centers use call guides. Figure 15-1 illustrates a sample call guide.

PIZZA PIZZAZ Customer Order Call Guide

Step 1. Enter Telephone Number
Step 2. Click "Enter"

Step 3. Repeat Previous Order and ask:
         "Would you like to have the same order again," *Customer Name?*

         Yes? Go to Step 4.   No? <u>Click Here</u>

Step 4. Ask:
         "Would you like that deliviered?"

         Yes? Go to Step 5.   No? <u>Click Here</u>

Step 5. Confirm Address
Step 6. State price of order
Step 7. State time. Inform the customer that their order
         will be delivered in 45 minutes.

Step 8. Ask:
         "Is there anything else I can do for you today?"

         Yes? <u>Click Here</u>   No? **"Thank you for calling PIZZA PIZZAZ"**

Figure 15-1:
A call guide.

A *script* tends to be much more detailed — often suggesting the wording that an agent should use. With the development of customer relationship management (CRM) software, scripts are becoming increasingly dynamic — integrating responses to customer questions and offering customized solutions. Some operations will integrate policies and procedures, such as product information or pricing, right into the script. Changes to procedures or policies might then also be integrated.

As a call center agent, in this case, in order to follow procedure you have to follow the script because you might not know what the system's going to tell you next!

You'll find more about scripts, including an example, later in this chapter.

The Call Strategy: Keeping Calls on Track

A structured call interaction helps you quickly identify what your customer needs and wants, and helps the customer make a decision or find a resolution to their issue in a shorter period of time. Every good call has a plan. In my call centers, we call our structured call plan the "call strategy." It's a plan (or process) you can use to control calls and maximize your results.

The call strategy is a conversation template, designed to provide the agent with a track to run on to maintain control of the call while simultaneously tailoring the call — and the features and benefits of the specific product, service, or solution — to the needs of the customer.

In addition, the call strategy is generic enough to be customized to virtually any call type, from customer service to technical support — and, of course, sales, both inbound and outbound.

Identifying the required elements of the call strategy

A call strategy is a good tool for helping agents get through a call, and for evaluating agents' call-handling effectiveness. Each section of the strategy can include tips and suggestions for maximizing success, and management may include certain required elements in each section so that the call center complies with legislative requirements.

Call center quality control guidelines can also follow a call strategy, including a scoring system that grades how well the agent follows the required elements in each component of the call.

Key components of a call strategy include

- ✔ **Introduction and rapport:** Introducing yourself and finding out with whom you're speaking. These first few seconds are critical to establishing a friendly relationship.
- ✔ **Needs analysis:** Listening and asking questions to understand why the customer called.
- ✔ **Solution:** Telling the customer what they want to hear — hopefully!
- ✔ **Closure:** Getting agreement on the call completion.
- ✔ **Summary:** Reviewing the call with the customer to make sure that you understand one another.

Table 15-1 illustrates an example of some required elements for each component of the call strategy used in my call centers.

Table 15-1	Required Elements of the Call Strategy
Component	**Required Elements**
Introduction	Address the customer by last name.
	Ask for the customer's home phone number.
	Retrieve the account information as soon as you've identified the customer.
	Verify that you are speaking with the account holder.
	Use a standard introduction: "Thank you for calling XYZ, this is John speaking, how may I be of service to you today?"
Needs analysis	Use closed questions to uncover specifics of the customer's need.
	View the customer's account for updates, problems, or new service offerings.
	Input the customer's need into the customer issues database.
	Identify the customer's need and repeat it back to the customer to verify understanding.
	Use the phrase, "I can help you with that."
Solution	Target solution/offering.
	Verify the services and offerings that the customer qualifies for.
	Suggest an offering to the customer, giving them the benefit statement of your solution.
	Ask the customer if your solution satisfies his or her need.
	Gain acceptance. If not, go back to needs analysis.
Closure	Confirm with the customer that your solution will satisfy his or her need.
	Input the solution into the customer information database.
	Get the customer's commitment to do his or her part in satisfying the need.

Component	Required Elements
Summary	Summarize what has happened, what you will be doing, and what the customer will be doing.
	For sales, read the sales validation script.
	End with, "Thank you for calling XYZ. Have a nice day."

An overview of the call strategy and each of its components for a typical sales call is illustrated in Figure 15-2 and described below.

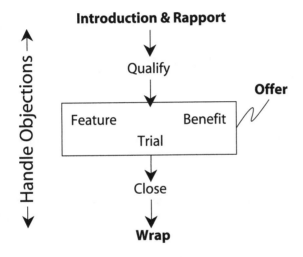

Figure 15-2: Call strategy for a sales call.

1. Introduction and rapport: Starting off on the right foot

The purpose of this portion of the call, as the name suggests, is for you to greet the caller, introduce your company and yourself, get to know who's calling, and set a friendly, trusting mood and tone for the call. I liken it to handing your business card to the customer and greeting him or her with a warm smile and a firm handshake. This takes only a few seconds.

A couple of important additions to the introduction that should be considered when conducting outbound telemarketing and inbound sales calls include rules that are legislated for telephone sales. (See Chapter 12 for more on these rules.)

On an inbound call, the customer is the one initiating the contact, so they (almost always) know who they're calling and the specific reason for the call; but on an outbound call you have to inform the customer of your name, your company name, the purpose of your call, and the nature of the goods or services you're promoting.

In some areas, legislation also exists insisting you ask the customer for permission to continue with the call once you've introduced yourself. Again, I think it's a good idea to do this whether it's legislated or not, out of respect for the customer's time.

It's vital that your call center understands the specific laws pertaining to calling in your area and the areas you service (including do not call legislation and the Telemarketing Sales Rule). I cover general call center legislation in Chapter 12.

2. Needs analysis: Asking the right questions

Needs analysis is asking questions (and really listening to the answers!). In sales, this is frequently called qualifying. Needs analysis is finding out the specifics of the customer's needs so you can match the benefits of your product or service to those needs.

Whether selling a product or solving a problem for a customer, it's important to ensure that the solution you suggest is based on the customer's specific wants and needs. The only way to understand those wants and needs is to ask questions.

Asking good, timely, and relevant questions helps you build trust with the customer, because they see that you're interested in them and their specific issue. If you don't ask questions, the customer feels (appropriately) that you're forcing a generic solution on them without truly taking them into consideration.

Think about needs analysis this way. Imagine for a moment that I had an unusual pain in my chest one morning. I call my doctor and he suggests I come in to the hospital right away for a visit.

I tell him about waking up with the pain. He says, "Sit tight for a moment," and disappears out of the examination room. He returns and says, "Okay, Réal, I want you to go upstairs to get some blood work done. I've got you booked for open-heart surgery this afternoon."

WHAT?! How much trust am I likely to have in this suggested course of action? Well, I can assure you, I'd be looking for a second opinion!

Is this scenario likely to happen? Of course not. What's more likely? Well, my doctor will probably ask a whole lot of questions. Perhaps things like, "When did you first notice the pain? Have you ever experienced this type of pain before? Is there any history of heart disease in your family?" — and, most importantly, "What did you eat for breakfast this morning?" To which I will reply, "A double-onion beef burrito supreme with hot peppers, why?" At this point, the doctor will no doubt suggest that I take two antacids and call him in the morning. Do you think I'd be likely to have a much greater level of trust in the doctor in this case? Absolutely.

The point is that doctors generally don't suggest a solution without first asking a lot of good questions. The proper treatment is based on the patient's needs and the specifics of their situation. That's exactly how the agent must handle the customer call.

Before you can administer the appropriate medication (product, service, solution), the patient (your customer) must be diagnosed.

3. Solution

Once the customer's needs have been diagnosed (analyzed or qualified), the next step is to find and offer a solution. Solutions come in a variety of formats, depending on the purpose of the call. They can include a simple answer to a customer question, a diagnosis and solution to a complex technical problem, or a suggested purchase.

It might be necessary to explain to a customer the *benefits* of your proposed solution, particularly in a sales call and especially when the customer needs to invest further in your product or service.

Even for non-sales calls (like technical support or customer service), if you believe that you're proposing the best course of action for the caller it will help to move the call along if you also provide to the customer the *benefits* of the course of action you're proposing.

Benefits illustrate to customers how the solution will help *them* specifically, based on the needs you uncovered in the needs analysis, and they help you gain the customer's buy-in to your solution.

Here are some examples of solutions offered for different call types:

- **Service call:** "If we can have a service technician visit your home next Friday at 10 a.m., then we can have him connect your Internet service right then, and you can be using the Internet that same day."

- **Technical support call:** "If you take a few moments to turn your computer off and on, our changes should take effect and your computer will be running again."

> ✔ **Sales call:** "If you buy our high-speed Internet product, those delays that you've been experiencing will go away. You'll find that you spend less time waiting for the Internet and more time using it. It's always on, so you won't even have to wait for the service to start up."

I provide more detail on the benefits of stating benefits in Chapter 16.

4. Closure: Asking for commitment

Once you've presented your offer and given the customer the confidence that what you've suggested is the best course of action, the next step is to ask for a commitment from the customer. Bringing closure to a call is an important part of call control. In sales, closure means simply asking for the business. With other calls, it involves asking the customer to accept the conclusion so you can move on.

This step is generally stated as a question, intended to confirm the customer's satisfaction with the proposed solution and suggest the next course of action needed to complete the interaction.

Here are examples of typical closure questions that might be asked after offering the solutions provided above:

> ✔ **Service call:** "Shall we go ahead and book a service appointment, Mr. Jones?"
>
> ✔ **Technical support call:** "Now that your computer is working again, are we finished for today or is there something else I can help you with?"
>
> ✔ **Sales call:** "Is this something you feel you'd like to purchase, Mrs. Smith?"

I explore the close for sales calls in more detail in Chapter 16.

Whether you're on a sales call or any other type of call, the key to a good close is that it's clear and unambiguous.

5. Summary: Recapping the call

The primary purpose of the summary is to recap what's been agreed to, what's been done, or what future action is to follow. The summary is also a good time to ask the customer if he or she has any other requests.

Your goal is to provide a basic summary of the call, and, in combination with the close, complete the call in such a way as to ensure the customer feels valued and his or her expectations are met or exceeded. One of the key objectives of the summary is to make sure that the customer doesn't have to call back for the same or a related issue.

In the case of a sales call, the summary may include some statement that legally must be read by the agent to ensure the customer understands completely what she has agreed to, and that she hasn't been misled in any way.

This brief recap and clarification of understanding increases the level of overall customer satisfaction, while at the same time increasing call center efficiency by reducing call volume because it helps to ensure that the customer doesn't need to call back. To that end, at the very least, the summary should offer additional assistance by asking a question such as, "Is there anything else we can help you with today?"

Of course, since leaving the customer with a good impression is another goal of the summary, at the completion of every call it's important for the agent to thank customers for their call, their business, or maybe their patience — whatever's most appropriate.

Handling objections

A lot has been written on handling objections — it's a difficult and sometimes controversial subject. It's important that you don't try to manipulate or trick customers into agreement, so treat your customers with respect and dignity and handle their objections the same way.

Naturally, some objections are temporary and can be addressed. For example:

> *Caller: "Well, yes I like your service, but I only buy from stores in my area."*

> *You: "As it happens, we have a store within a mile of your house..."*

This is a good use of objection handling. In fact, as you can see, objection handling is just part of the dialogue between customer and agent.

But here's where objection handling goes bad: when you make the assumption that "No" means that the caller just doesn't get it yet; or, when agents have to hear a standard number of no's before they can give up on a customer. This is when handling objections becomes manipulative.

Even when customers call you, sometimes the answer is no.

Talk to the customer — treat the interaction like a conversation. (After all, that's what it is!) Explain the benefits of your product or service, and if a legitimate objection comes up, answer it as part of the dialogue. If customers say no, listen. If they mean no, then thank them for their time and move on.

Finding the right time to handle objections

You'll notice in the illustration of the call strategy in Figure 15-2 that *Handle Objections* is shown along the side, with arrows pointing from the top of the strategy to the bottom. Why? Well, because the only time to deal with an objection is as soon as it comes up!

Objections are showstoppers. A conversation cannot move forward if a customer objection or concern is left unanswered.

Of course, if possible you'd like to deal with an objection *before* it comes up. When you ask good questions in your needs analysis, uncovering and identifying the customer's real needs and emotions, and then satisfy those with the appropriate solutions, customers will have fewer objections.

Using the call strategy in real life

The great thing about using a generic call structure such as the call strategy described in this chapter is that it can be used as a template for virtually any call, no matter why the customer is calling.

To understand this, review the illustration of the call strategy again (Figure 15-2) and relate it to a typical telephone conversation you may have had recently with a friend or relative.

For example, imagine you're phoning a friend to invite him or her to see a movie with you — the conversation might go something like this:

1. **Introduction and rapport:** You'll probably start by saying something like, "Hi John, it's me," sharing a few pleasantries and telling your friend why you've called — because you're thinking about going out to see a movie.

2. **Needs analysis:** Next, you'll ask John some questions about what types of movies he likes and what he's seen recently to find out what might be of interest.

3. **Offer solution:** You'll suggest the movie you'd like to see and why you think it'll be great, and add something like, "How's that sound?" or "What do you think?"

4. **Closure:** "So, shall I pick you up around 6:00, or would you rather see the late show?"

5. **Summary:** "Great! I'll drive, and you're buying the popcorn. I'll see you at 6:00."

6. **Handle objections:** Not that your friend is likely to object, but let's say John suggests he doesn't have any extra money and can't afford a movie. You reply, "Hey, I feel your pain. Things are pretty tight at my place, too. Listen, I was actually thinking about going tomorrow night anyway because tickets are half price. I really think this is a show we've got to see while it's still on the big screen — I hear the cinematography is amazing. So, what do you say?"

Implementing a structured call plan such as the call strategy is not the end of the process. Words are still required that speak to the specific product or service being represented in the call. You'll always have certain specific questions that need be asked, points that must be made, benefits that should be stated, and information that should be provided to the customer.

It's not advisable to rely completely on the imagination of your individual agents to come up with all of these statements on their own (especially given the state of some agents' imagination!). That's where call guides and scripts come in.

Creating Call Guides: Developing the Call Strategy into a Tool

If the call strategy is the track for the call to run on, then a call guide provides the direction. The call strategy should be integrated throughout the call guide. Refer to Figure 15-1 for an example of a call guide.

A good call guide is dynamic and relies on logic and decision making to — yes — *guide* the agent through needs analysis and create a solution for the customer. If it's really good, it integrates customer-specific information so that the agent can present a tailored solution for each customer.

An Internet (or intranet)-based call guide can also include links to policies and procedures.

One benefit of very detailed guides is that they reduce training time for agents. Training can focus on the basics (call handling and product knowledge) and how to use the call guide or any non-integrated tools. Agents can then gain proficiency by listening to calls and practicing working with the guide.

Call guides also increase consistency in approach. Everyone in your call center should be using the same procedures and information. The call guide ensures everyone is (literally) on the same page.

Scripting: Not Just for Telemarketing Anymore

Scripting, at least the way I recommend it be used, is really just an extension of the call guide with suggested and required wording added in the appropriate places.

Sophisticated scripts can also include logic branches: based on customer requests and information, the agent takes different "branches" of the script to arrive at the appropriate information and solutions for each customer inquiry.

Scripts can be of significant help when dealing with more complicated situations, such as diagnosing complex problems or covering off legal requirements.

One of the key ingredients of effective scripting is to ensure the language is user-friendly. The words must sound natural coming from the person saying them.

I suggest consulting with agents who are working on a given call-handling job to assist in the development of appropriate scripting. Whether your call center solves technical problems or sells widgets, your agents will run up against it all. Giving them a process to tell you what the script needs by way of solutions and language will make for better scripts in a shorter period of time.

Write your scripts in language that your agents can actually use without sounding like they must've swallowed a thesaurus. The best way to make this happen is to let the agents help in the development of the scripting, and to ensure they understand that the scripting is intended as a template for an actual conversation, not a commercial designed to bulldoze the customer into submission.

In Figure 15-3, I include a sample of a typical script aid developed for an inbound sales-and-service call center for high-speed Internet.

Effective call handling is paramount in driving the call center's primary business objectives of efficiency, revenue generation, and service. Scripts that have been well thought out with involvement from call center agents can increase the effectiveness and consistency of call handling in any project.

START WITH ENERGY AND ENTHUSIASM

Comments	Script
INTRO	Thank you for calling OKAY Cable. This is ___________speaking. How are you doing today?
Mandatory qualifying questions	**Q** May I please have your telephone number, so I can check your current account information? (Verify address and check for serviceability in that area) (Review current account status to provide information to identify customer needs) **Q** May I ask where you heard about OKAY Cable Services? (Source of awareness) <Enter information into database> √ OKAY Cable offers a lot of great entertainment at a great value. In order to help me discover exactly how we can benefit you, I'd like to ask you a couple of questions…

CREATE MOUNTAINS OF VALUE

High Speed Data

Choose a maximum of 2 - 3 FBT's and ASK FOR THE BUSINESS!!!

Feature	Benefit "What this means to you is…"	Trial
Q Do you mind if I ask how many people in your home currently use the Internet? **Q** Have you ever had a situation when someone's been on the Internet, and someone else needed to use the phone?		
Ready and waiting connection with no dial-up required	√ You'll never have to worry about missing an important phone call. √ Someone could be on the phone, AND on the Internet, AND watching TV if you wanted! √ You'll have a world of information at your finger tips with just the click of the mouse, like turning a channel on your TV.	How's that for convenience?
Q What would you say are the main reasons the Internet is used for in your home? **Q** Have you ever noticed a time where someone in your family was staring at the computer screen, because they were waiting for something to download?		
Blazing Speed	√ Downloading videos or music files will take you seconds, instead of hours. √ Your children will get more done in less time when they're online, so they'll be able to spend quality time with you.	That sounds pretty nice, doesn't it?
Q Other than yourself, how many people in your home use e-mail? **Q** Do you ever receive information through your e-mail that might not be appropriate for your children to see?		
Multiple e-mail addresses	√ Everyone in the home could have their own personal e-mail, all of which can be password protected. √ If there were children in the home, this would help avoid the little ones viewing e-mails that might not be suitable for sensitive eyes. √ You could also have have separate e-mails to receive thing from family and friends or from business associates, or to separate all thee junk e-mails we sometimes get.	That kind of peace of mind would be great, wouldn't it?
Q Have you ever used the Internet to look at websites; for example, for new updates on scores, etc? **Q** What if you had your own personal website?		
10 MB of tree web space	√ You could create your own or family web page, perhaps to display your own personal hobbies and interests. √ This is also a great way to keep in touch with friends and family. For example, you could download recent pictures of your children, and create a virtual photo album for your loved ones to enjoy.	Isn't that amazing?

ASK FOR THE BUSINESS

CLOSE	We can have this setup for you in a couple of days, would you prefer a morning or afternoon installation time?

WRAP IT UP

RECAP	Follow the scripted recap, covering each of the following points: • Numbers of outlets • Wired or unwired installation—explain the difference • Due to time constraints, technicians will not be able to install extra outlets
WRAP	Review the scrioted wrao checklist items Finish the call by saying, "Thank you for calling OKAY Cable."

Figure 15-3: A script aid for selling high-speed Internet.

Measuring Call Compliance: Using the Strategy for Quality Control

Your quality control group is a very important part of managing and improving the call-handling process. Their job is to listen to calls and evaluate how well agents are doing in following the standardized approaches.

Your quality control department is the keeper of the call-handling standard and needs to include the following roles and responsibilities:

- ✔ **Process owner:** The person or people responsible for keeping and evolving the call-handling standard.

  Your center's call-handling standard has to be well documented and communicated. Standards that are vague create confusion and frustration. You need to be as specific as possible in what should be in a call.

  Communicating changes to the standard is also very important. If significant changes need to be made, training and on-the-job coaching might be required.

- ✔ **Call auditors:** The people who listen to and evaluate calls for consistency — they look for variation away from the standard.

  Approaches vary by company. In some, auditors give feedback directly to the agent and supervisor, while others send the feedback to the supervisor and agent expecting that they'll review it together. Either way works. The important part is that feedback against the standard happens.

If the call auditor's feedback can be tied to deficiencies in performance results, then it's even more effective.

Feedback needs to be provided as soon after the call as possible. Ideally, it'll include sample voice recordings from the actual call, and possibly screen captures of how the agent navigates through the call.

How the auditing is done will depend on the type of call strategy used by your specific call center. Where call centers use very prescribed scripting, the auditor will follow the script and check for deviance.

For less prescribed call strategies, the auditors look for, and grade on, required elements. Generally, they'll follow a call strategy or call flow set by the company.

Even the most generalized call strategies should have a defined flow with required elements throughout the body of the call. For example, the standard call flow might require the use of a standard greeting. Should the agent not use the standard greeting, they'd be penalized (or receive a lower score) on that part of the call.

Tone of voice is difficult to script and it's less tangible than words. However, as I discuss in Chapter 16, agent tone has the largest impact on what is communicated to the caller throughout the call. At the point of evaluating tone, call auditing becomes more subjective.

However, even tone can be defined to a degree, and with calibration meetings (where supervisors, auditors, and trainers get together to compare how they grade calls) a measure of agreement and understanding can be achieved. Certainly, very good or very bad tone can be agreed upon. Every call review and every part of a call should also be evaluated for the use of tone.

Chapter 16

Handling Sales Calls

• •

• •

*T*he world of call center sales is evolving. For a long time, many call centers were seen only as a cost for their companies. They were a necessary (but not always appreciated or understood) cost associated with looking after customers.

The Way We Were

Many call center operations were separated along the lines of sales and service. One department generated revenue, and the other served customers and generated costs. Selling was seen as a necessary evil, and lip service was paid to delivering great customer service while pressure was applied to improve efficiency and cut costs.

Cost cutting can be easily quantified. It is more difficult to quantify the benefits of a balanced strategy, which maximizes each of cost, revenue generation, and customer satisfaction. (I talk about how you can make all these work together in Chapter 2.) In extreme cases, too much emphasis on cost cutting results in reduced customer service and revenue-generating capabilities.

Fortunately, research is beginning to show that selling, far from being a bad thing (from the customer's perspective), can actually strengthen a customer relationship. What's more, with the right tools in place your agents can do more than one task at a time, so every agent becomes a sales agent for the company.

Other research shows that service can affect whether a customer continues to do business with your company. So you're faced with a whole new paradigm — balancing efficiency, revenue, and service.

Turning Call Centers into Profit Centers

Cost is still a concern, but this cost is increasingly looked at in terms of the total return that is realized for that cost. A slightly more expensive call center that generates much more revenue and retains far more customers is much more valuable than a barebones, low-cost operation. Good news: your call centers are now profit centers!

For many call centers, this is great news. Moving from being a sales center to a profit center gives the call center much greater importance within the organization. With profits, you can justify investment in better tools and training.

However, customer service call centers and agents have gone (and are going) through something of a culture shock. They've gone from being directed to "Answer the phone and keep call length low" to "Use the customer relationship management system to identify the best bundle of products and services for the customer and sell them something." (I discuss customer relationship management systems and other call center technology in Chapter 9.)

For many call center staff, selling is a new skill. In this chapter, I provide the basics to successful selling in today's evolving call center environment.

Understanding the Key Ingredients to Call Center Selling

I have a very basic philosophy for selling over the phone. The key ingredients are really just those that are required for successful customer service in any environment. (I talk more about providing great customer service through call handling in Chapter 14.)

Whether selling over the telephone, in a retail environment, in big business, or door-to-door, there are certain selling fundamentals that are needed in every sales interaction:

- ✔ Develop a good rapport with the customer.

- ✔ Provide good two-way communication.

- ✔ Make a valuable offering.

- ✔ Ask for the business.

- ✔ Don't overcome objections; answer questions.

Although they're certainly most easily related to sales calls, these rules can (and should) be utilized in every call situation. These simple concepts are basic, common sense customer-service fundamentals that apply in virtually any situation where you're consulting with someone with the hope of coming to a satisfactory resolution.

Developing a good rapport

You have to develop a trusting relationship with your customer from the beginning of the call. You need to build rapport with the customer at every step, from the first words out of your mouth during the introduction through to the conclusion of the call.

I provide advice, tips, and techniques for providing world-class service in Chapter 14, and discuss the elements of the call strategy and other call-handling tools in Chapter 15 — all of which will help tremendously in developing rapport and trust.

Here are some of the things you can do to build rapport:

- ✔ Start each call with rapport building.
- ✔ Listen to the customer and acknowledge what the customer says while controlling the call. LAMA, a technique discussed in Chapter 14, is an excellent guide to building trust and controlling the call.
- ✔ When dealing with difficult situations, deal with the customer's emotions before dealing with the problems.
- ✔ Just be nice.

When selling, there are other things that you can do to maintain and build trust, which I'll discuss in this chapter.

Trust is a vital element in every sales interaction. The customer has to trust her own ability to make the right decision — a decision that is largely based on discussion with you.

So, the customer also has to trust that you have her best interests in mind — or at least that you're not attempting to take her for a ride. The importance of trust is magnified when doing business over the phone, because the customer doesn't have the ability to look you in the eye, or to sample your product.

You can't establish trust unless you're trustworthy, so you need to understand and accept that you're going to do what's right for the customer. You have to believe that you're the expert, but also understand that the customer is the ultimate decision maker. If your customer says no, then no is the answer.

Having said that, you should do what you can to build on any already successful relationship with the customer. Just be aware that if you start selling too early (before you've established rapport) you won't be successful. An attempt to sell without gaining trust gives the impression that you're not sincere.

Go through the process; seek to understand your customer's questions, needs, and emotions, and deal with each (emotions first, of course — as I discuss in Chapter 14). As part of the solutions you offer, or as an add-on to your solutions, always look to continually develop the relationship with the customer.

At every step of the way, you must show that you're interested in helping and working with your customer.

Communicating with your customer

Good selling demands a strong two-way dialogue. You want the customer to be engaged in what you're saying, not just waiting for an opportunity to get off the phone. This means that when selling you have to stick to all the good call-handling skills I discuss in Chapter 14. If you haven't already you may want to review them, but here are some highlights:

- ✔ **Control the call**. The person asking the questions controls the flow of the call. It doesn't mean you're controlling the customer, or their decision making, you're just trying to take the call down the right path — to arrive at the appropriate destination more quickly. Asking timely and relevant questions geared toward discovering the specifics of the customer's needs and wants will allow you to more quickly analyze those needs and come up with an appropriate solution.

- ✔ **Involve the customer**. Make sure your questioning doesn't come off sounding like a survey — or worse, an interrogation. Acknowledge and address the customer's questions, emotions, needs, and wants.

- ✔ **Use a call strategy and/or script**. As I discuss in Chapter 15, these will help to keep your discussion focused and on track, and will help to ensure that you don't leave out any important information.

- ✔ **Mind your tone**. A very good strategy for any type of call center communication, and one that is particularly effective for sales, is to control the pace and tone of your speech. As I discuss in the next section, over the phone it's not only what you say, but how you say it.

The importance of tone

Someone once told me (and I believe them) that the majority of telephone communication is done through the tone of your voice, while only a minority is through the words that you use. It makes sense. In face-to-face communication you have the advantage of body language — both you observing your customer's and the customer observing yours — *and* you can use visual aids, such as brochures, to enhance your presentation.

When communicating over the telephone, your body language must be made evident through your tone, and the only visual aids you have are the pictures you paint in the mind of your customer. So if you want to communicate enthusiasm to a customer about a product or service, then it needs to come out in your voice.

Even agents with a lesser degree of product knowledge will have success in capturing a customer's imagination when speaking with a positive, enthusiastic tone of voice.

I first saw the impact of enthusiasm in my own call centers a number of years ago. We were running an inbound sales program for a client that had been with us for about six months. The project was growing and a group of new agents were in their first week on the phones. In reviewing our performance statistics I saw that one of the new agents, Angela, had been outperforming all other agents on all measures, including sales and quality — in her first week! I decided to sit with Angela to get a better idea of where the magic was coming from. What I found was a young lady who was having a great time. She loved the job and it came through in her tone. Sometimes she fumbled with product knowledge — she was new, after all — but eventually she found all the information she needed and was so enthusiastic about what she was talking about that her enthusiasm was frequently transferred to the customer, who would make a purchase. I asked Angela for her secret to such early success. "I don't know, but it's a lot of fun," she said. For a long time that became my call center mantra: "I don't know, but it's a lot of fun."

Since meeting Angela many years ago, I've seen this phenomenon a number of times with new agents. They join the company, go through new-hire training, hit the call center floor, and right away they're getting great customer satisfaction scores and fantastic sales levels. When you ask them how they're doing it, many simply answer the same way Angela did.

Unfortunately, the power of new-hire enthusiasm frequently fades. The performance of many of these same agents drops off after time — customer satisfaction survey results go down, and their sales go down. They may even tell you they're in a slump, but it's not really a slump at all. When you join a new company, everything's new and exciting and this comes through in your voice. Once you're settled in, your tone drops down a few notches and presto: your results drop as well.

If you want to make an immediate improvement in your results, change the tone and pace of your voice. Sound excited to be talking to the customer. It works. Remember, though, that most customers will pick up on fake enthusiasm. Fake enthusiasm will have the opposite effect — destroying trust and preventing any chance you have of making a sale.

So, sincerity is important. The best way I know to develop sincere enthusiasm for a product is to spend time understanding how the product can provide more value to your customer than the cost you will be asking for in return. To do this effectively you need to understand not only your product but also each customer you're speaking to. These are all good sales technique that I discuss more later on.

Controlling your tone

To provide immediate results that ensure you come across with a more positive, enthusiastic tone, you need only focus on a few simple things.

To control your tone of voice, it helps to be aware of the elements that affect how you sound to the customer. Three of the most common are speed, volume, and inflection.

When you're speaking about something you're excited about, you tend to increase the *speed* and *volume* of your speech. So, if you're attempting to get a customer excited about a feature of your product, service, or solution, a slight increase in speed and volume helps. On the other hand, when you want to emphasize a particular point you may lower your voice — in both volume and speed — sometimes to almost a whisper, in an attempt to draw in the person you're talking to.

Inflection is the natural modulation of tone you have in your voice. Entertaining people tend to speak with a great deal of inflection. Their voice tone and pace goes up and down as they speak. People who speak with little or no inflection (monotone) tend to sound bored, disinterested, or uncaring, while those who use more inflection sound engaging and interesting.

By varying the rate of speed and volume of your speech and using appropriate inflection, you can greatly improve the way you sound and, consequently, the customer's perception of the level of service you provide.

Everyone uses speed, volume, and inflection naturally when speaking, but being aware of their impact and how best to use them allows you to raise the level of enthusiasm in your voice and more easily engage customers in conversation, even on the days when you're not feeling particularly enthusiastic.

Posture can also have a dramatic impact on how you sound. Although customers may not see poor body language over the phone, they can certainly hear its effects. Your voice will not project as well when you're lying back in your chair as it will if you're sitting up straight. Aside from the physiological effect of suppressing your vocal cords and diaphragm, a posture that is overly relaxed tends to dampen your natural enthusiasm.

If you find yourself in a bit of an enthusiasm slump, try sitting up, or even standing, while taking calls. It can have a very positive effect on how you sound.

Perhaps the most significant impact on tone is your mood. A bad, sad, or depressed mood can be an enthusiasm killer. Some days, it's tough enough just dragging yourself out of bed, let alone trying to sound energetic and enthusiastic. A poor mood can be a tough thing to overcome.

I don't believe you can ever totally check your baggage at the door, slap on a happy face, put on your headset, and present a picture of positivism to your customers when you've got a lot of *stuff* going on; but it's when you're having *one of those days* that, as a call center agent, you have to "fake it 'til you make it." It's on those days that it's important to pump up the volume and speed of your voice, making a concentrated effort to use a little more inflection and sit up a little straighter.

Just a few minor adjustments can have a major impact on your tone, and your mood — and don't be surprised if they have a positive effect on your results too!

Creating a valuable offering

If you don't believe that your customer will benefit more from the product or service you're offering than what it's going to cost them to get it, it'll be very difficult to sell anything.

The customer has to believe it, too. Customers will make the decision to buy only when they believe the value provided by your product or service is greater than the cost to them. Imagine it like a scale (or balance), with the weight of the value of your product or service on one side, and the weight of what it's going to cost the customer on the other (as I illustrate in Figure 16-1.) The value side has to outweigh the cost.

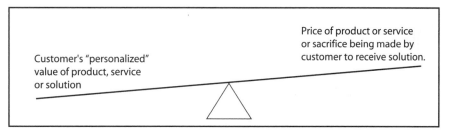

Figure 16-1: Balancing the decision to buy.

Customer's "personalized" value of product, service or solution

Price of product or service or sacrifice being made by customer to receive solution.

Your job of enhancing or adding to the customer relationship is different from stereotypical selling and it starts with a fundamental belief that the customer will benefit from your product or service.

You're in it for the long run

When you sell something to a customer, you're trying to make the relationship more valuable in a long-term way. Selling something that the customer just cancels in 30 or 60 days doesn't help anyone. The customer becomes irritated, and the company spends money processing the sale and then more money processing the cancellation. No one wins.

Ya gotta believe!

I'm very comfortable selling our call center services. Whether call center business or consulting, our services are not small-ticket items. Still, I know that the services we offer to our clients have generated and saved their companies millions of dollars over the years. It's easy to sell to your customers when you know that what you're selling will provide them with tremendous benefits. It ceases to be selling and starts to become counseling.

Trust me, over the years I've seen companies that have built a business around selling lots and lots of low-value stuff to their large client base. Many of those companies aren't around anymore.

So, for the first step to creating a valuable offering, you have to see how the customer is going to benefit from your product or service. You can't do this if you haven't spent a few minutes listening to and talking with the customer, gaining an understanding of her needs. In the call strategy I introduce in Chapter 15, this part of the interaction is called *needs analysis*.

Once you're convinced that you have a product or service that the customer will greatly benefit from, you're in a position to discuss and demonstrate that value. In the most important part of the sales process, you'll work with the customer to demonstrate as much value as you can.

When customers don't buy (and often they don't) it's because they didn't see enough of a return in value for parting with their money.

Creating "mountains of value"

Mountains of value means a lot more value than you're asking for in return. Your job is to create "mountains of value" for each specific customer.

For example, for some customers you might create enough value to convince them to purchase your high-speed Internet service by simply explaining how they'll be able to download games 20 percent faster than with their existing service.

However, if you demonstrated to the customer that by purchasing your high-speed Internet service their children will have a faster, more reliable access to the greatest store of knowledge that the world has ever known, and that with your service their kids will be better equipped at school so they can learn faster and easier and compete better with other students around the world, and that this advantage is a tool that they'll use to succeed in life, you'll have created a lot more value.

Avoid the info-dump!

Regrettably, agents who have a great deal of knowledge about their product or service often feel obliged to share ALL OF IT with the customer. This is not necessary, or advisable. Attempting to impress the customer with your wealth of knowledge is likely to turn them off. In fact, you'll often talk yourself out of a solution or sale by overwhelming the customer with unnecessary details.

By asking questions about the customer's needs, listening, and addressing him or her specifically, you're showing that you value the customer and care about their needs and desires.

"People don't care how much you know, until they know how much you care."

The benefits of benefits

You may have heard about features and benefits before. In any form of communication over the phone, it's important to understand the difference.

A *feature* is an element or individual characteristic of a product, service, or solution. Air conditioning, for example, is a feature of a new car.

A *benefit* is the value that a person would take away from a feature — it should describe how the customer would gain from utilizing that feature. "A comfortable environment inside the car, even on the hottest day," is a benefit of new-car air conditioning.

Personalizing value with benefits

Benefits are personal. What may be very valuable to you might not be valuable to me. This is why it's important to involve the customer in a two-way dialogue to better understand what he needs and values. If you determine that the customer is sensitive to heat, then air conditioning is a feature with a large benefit. If the customer loves the heat and fresh air, then air conditioning is a feature with a smaller benefit.

Benefit statements help to answer the customer's question, "So what?" or, "What's that mean to me?" People buy benefits, not features.

The biggest mistake that salespeople who talk mostly about features make is to assume the customer will automatically understand the benefit of the feature being discussed. This does not create mountains of value. To create mountains of value for a customer, you've got to talk in terms of the specific benefits *that* customer will receive from the product's features.

Speaking of benefits...

Last summer, my wife and I decided it was finally time to replace our aging BBQ. I went to my local hardware/outdoor goods store to check out the various models. The clerk began to tell (not ask) us about some of the great *features* of the particular BBQ we were looking at. The first thing he mentioned was that it had 40,000 BTUs and a stainless steel burner with dual controls.

Now, I don't know about you, but I was pretty proud of myself for remembering that BTU stands for British thermal unit — however, I sure don't have a clue what it means or what 40,000 of them are likely to do! Obviously the look on my face gave me away, as the clerk, after a short pause, slowly added, "So ... basically you've got heat enough to cook for a large family and adjustable heat distribution so your food will cook more quickly and evenly." That, I understood! We bought the BBQ.

People make buying decisions based on their specific, "personalized" value, or what they believe the product or service will do for *them* — how it'll solve their specific problem or satisfy their need or want.

To create more personalized value than you're asking from the customer in return, you must ask timely and relevant questions to uncover the customer's specific needs and then tailor your solution to emphasize the *benefits* that respond to those needs. The more you can build up the customer's personalized value, the more success you'll have in gaining his or her trust and commitment.

Some might refer to this process as consultative selling. Fine. Today, that's what call center selling is all about.

No one wants the old-fashioned, telemarketing, hold-them-hostage-for-ten-minutes sales pitch. In the world of high-value customer relationships, it doesn't work anyway.

Asking for the business

You can get entire books on how to ask for or "close" the sale. One idea is constant throughout: it's important.

As you're creating value, some customers will come right out and say "I want this, please arrange it for me," but a surprising number are more reserved and are politely waiting for you to tell them what the next step is. Well here it is: "If you think this is as good an idea as I do, then you can buy it right now if you like."

As a customer, you expect the sale to be closed

Recently, I went into a shoe store. I was greeted by Joe, a very friendly and enthusiastic sales clerk. Joe asked me what I was looking for, showed me some shoes that he had on the shelves, asked me about color preferences, then suggested that I try some on. I found a pair and told Joe, "I like these." Joe immediately picked up the shoes, showed me to the counter, and said, "Will that be cash or charge?" I bought the shoes. Now, I wanted the shoes, but I hadn't been overly clear with my "I like these" comment. It occurred to me that what Joe had done, what all shoe store clerks do, is to close the sale

by asking, "Will that be cash or charge?" I got to thinking that it would have been very strange and perhaps awkward if Joe had not closed the sale. When shopping in a retail store we *expect* a sales clerk to close the sale.

It's exactly the same when doing business over the phone. The customer expects you to help them finish the process and complete the transaction. Problems arise when you don't do an adequate job of creating value for the customer, which makes it seem unnatural or uncomfortable to ask for a commitment.

When a call's been done well, the close is the natural and obvious conclusion to the consultative selling process — but most of the time you've got to do it. It is absolutely true that if you don't ask for the business usually you won't get it. Don't be afraid to ask — especially if you've done a good job.

Keeping it simple and to the point

I like obvious, unambiguous closes, like, "Would you like to buy this?" Other variations exist, but the point is that you come right out and, in a nice friendly manner, ask the customer to buy — no tricks, no manipulation.

Sure there are other techniques, like the assumptive close: "I just need some information for our records...." A few minutes might go by before the customer realizes that you're closing the sale. These techniques can be seen as tricky and manipulative. And sure, sometimes customers stick around, but often they quickly cancel the service, after a seed of doubt creeps in and they start to feel that maybe they've been bamboozled. In the process, they've developed a sour taste in their mouth.

It's okay to ask again...

As long as the discussion continues to be open and honest and involving the customer, it's perfectly natural to ask more than once if the customer would like to buy.

Remember, you're after long-term, high-value relationships. The best way to create these is through an open, two-way dialogue where you work to understand the customer's needs and provide a product or service solution that adds a lot of personalized value.

Checking for interest: The trial close

A *trial close* is a useful communications tool used to test someone's interest in a product, service, or idea before asking for his or her commitment. It's a way of getting feedback from a customer and helps you to avoid early-closing rejection.

Whether talking to a customer, a friend, or your mother, you want to avoid putting people in a position where they're wrong or have to correct a previous decision. Having to change your position creates a roadblock in communication, and therefore in sales interactions.

You don't want customers saying no to a sales presentation before they have all the facts. Asking for the business too early in a conversation can severely dampen sales results.

Trial closing stops short of asking for the business but tests the customer's interest in what you're saying. A trial close uses noncommittal questions or phrases that invoke a response — "Isn't that great?" or "Isn't that a good idea?"

Use the trial close to test the customer's interest level. If it's high, then you should ask for the business directly and simply. If it's not high, continue to build on the features and benefits of the product or service to the customer. Build value with the customer until he or she shows lots of interest, you have nothing else to say, or the customer has had enough.

At this point, make an attempt to close the business. If the customer says yes, great! If she doesn't, fine, you know that she's heard and understood all the benefits of your suggestion and decided against it. Relationship intact.

I like the trial close because it continues to engage the customer in a two-way communication. Here's an example.

I have a swimming pool in my backyard. The pool is 30 years old, and some beautiful large trees frame it. It looks very nice, but you can imagine how often I'm cleaning leaves out of the pool — spring, summer, and fall. After a particularly bad stretch, I told my wife that I was about to buy a chainsaw and cut all the trees down. She suggested that I first call the pool store for advice.

When I called, the owner said to me, "We've got an automatic pool cleaner that sits in the pool and does the cleaning for you so you don't ever have to worry about doing it again ... isn't that great?"

Are you kidding me? I totally got the trial close and it didn't take me any time at all to indicate that this was the answer to my prayers. "Yes, yes, yes, that's what I need. When can I get it?" At this point, I didn't even know the price.

Well, the pool guy was good. He told me when he'd be by to install the vacuum and show me how to use it, which I agreed to. And before we said goodbye he summarized the call, telling me again when he'd be by and saying, "and the price will be $400." I guess I'm just lucky that the price wasn't $4,000.

The pool owner did a great job of using the trial close. In my case he picked up that I didn't need any more convincing and that he should go straight to closing the sale. If I had waffled when he said "isn't that great," he probably would've asked some more questions and presented more benefits, building value until I was more committed to buying.

Handling objections

An objection is a reason the customer gives for not wanting to buy right now. Some typical examples of objections include

- "I have to talk to my spouse."
- "I don't have the money right now."
- "I don't have the time."
- "I don't like red."

The first and most important thing to consider when dealing with objections is to respect them. The customer is stating the objection for a reason and it's not your job to try to show him that he's wrong. I talk about techniques for handling objections in Chapters 14 and 15.

If you get the impression that the customer wishes to close the conversation with the objection, let him. Preserve the relationship at all costs.

Sometimes a customer objection is just part of the dialogue. If the customer is open to continued dialogue, it's appropriate to *answer* the objection, remembering to respect what the customer has just said.

- "Would you like me to call you and your wife back tomorrow?"
- "Would you be interested in our payment terms?"
- "Would you like me to call you back when you have more time?"
- "I'm sorry, I should have mentioned that it comes in other colors."

R-E-S-P-E-C-T

You'll find that some objections are just part of the dialogue and process, provided you treat the customer and his objection with respect. In these cases, you'll make some sales after the objections happen, *and* you'll keep the customer relationship intact in the long term.

Forget all the stuff that you've heard about aggressive techniques for overcoming objections, including

- ✔ "No is just one more step to yes."
- ✔ "Only three no's mean no."
- ✔ "Turn a no to an on."

If you had a friend who took an approach like one of these in their relations with you, I'm pretty sure you wouldn't be friends for very long.

These techniques are pushy, manipulative, and disrespectful and show no understanding of how to build long-term customer relationships.

Why Doesn't Everyone Sell This Way?

Why doesn't everyone sell this way? Well, many call centers are starting to.

Another answer is that they just can't help themselves. They're stuck on the high-volume, quick-revenue treadmill. It's like a drug. Pressed by shareholders to constantly improve, companies are putting pressure on all areas to find revenue — *any* revenue. Company executives in turn press the call centers to generate more and more sales. So the company pushes the call center, the call center pushes its agents, and the agents then push the customers.

While companies demand more and more revenue from call centers, they often also squeeze more and more cost out of the call centers. As a result, call centers begin cutting costs — which means less training for agents, lower pay, and sometimes compensation based on commissions only.

Eventually, the call center becomes so focused on low cost that virtually all skill and capability are gone. The only thing left to do is fire up a predictive dialer (Chapter 8 introduces this and other call center technology) — the more names you've got, the better chance you have of generating revenue — then start cold-calling, push the customers, trick them once in a while, and sometimes even manipulate them.

It's the most vicious of vicious circles and it takes real commitment to get out of it.

First, you need to invest more in the skills and tools in your call center. Second, you need to accept that short-term revenue might go down, but if you do a good job of building value customers will stay, sales will stick, and mid- and long-term revenue will grow.

The cost of call center services may increase, but you'll receive a tremendous return on that investment.

Summarizing Successful Telephone Selling

Here's a list of the important points to remember that will help you be more successful in today's evolving, customer-focused, solutions-oriented world of call center sales.

1. **Build a good rapport with the customer.** This starts in the introduction of the call and includes being friendly, courteous, and professional. An upbeat and enthusiastic tone is one of your most powerful sales and communications tools.

2. **Keep all customer contacts conversational.** Involve your customer in two-way dialogue. Use the call control tools and techniques and call-handling skills and tips described in Chapters 14 and 15 to keep the call focused.

3. **Show the customer your product's tremendous value.** Match the features and benefits of your product, service, or solution to your customer's specific needs. The most important part of successful selling is to create much more value through the benefits of your product than you're asking from the customer in return. Use trial closes to test customer interest and readiness to buy.

4. **Ask for the business in a clear, unambiguous, and confident way.**

5. **Treat objections as questions, where appropriate.** Always respect customer objections.

6. **Accept that sometimes no means no.**

In Table 16-1, I offer a quick comparison highlighting some of the differences between the old ways of selling to those of today.

Table 16-1	The Evolution of Call Center Selling
Sales the Old Way	*Today's Sales*
Mass-marketed, volume-based	Targeted presentations
Overcoming objections	Answering questions
Assumptive, manipulative closing	Unambiguously asking for the business
Tightly scripted pitch	Two-way dialogue with script guides
Free offers and price discounting	Value creation
Low skill	High skill
Low cost	High return

A final word on scripting

In Chapter 15 I discuss call guides and scripts and how they can be used to effectively control calls. Scripting still has a place in telephone sales, but how scripts are used is evolving. Unfortunately, you'll still find lots of examples of the tightly scripted, one-pitch-does-it-all sales call.

Thankfully, with the aid of the CRM (customer relationship management — see Chapter 9) movement, a more dynamic, guided approach to sales scripting is evolving. These operations provide a dynamic, changing script based upon the unique attributes of each customer. Scripts are more suggestions than requirements, but it's still a good idea to have suggested scripting, particularly for newer or less experienced agents.

Give your agents the ability to tailor presentations to each customer using suggestions from the scripts.

Many scripts aren't really scripts at all — they're guides providing the agent with suggestions in a manner that provides structure to the call and helps the agent bring the call to a successful conclusion.

Part VI
The Part of Tens

The 5th Wave   By Rich Tennant

"...for technical support, press 7; for product information, press 8; if you're bored and just want to argue with someone, press 9..."

That's me...

In this part . . .

Here, you find a collection of quick hits from the call center industry that will give a boost to your company's revenue and efficiency, employee morale, and customer satisfaction. The Part of Tens is a fast and easy way for you to brush up on the main points listed in this book — while picking up some new tips and techniques.

Chapter 17

Ten Ways to Improve Agent Job Satisfaction

In This Chapter

▶ Maximizing agent job satisfaction

▶ Creating a better working environment

*I*n the business world, it's a generally accepted principle — one that I agree with — that companies with happier employees tend to have happier customers. By improving your agents' job satisfaction, you're likely to improve your customers' satisfaction as well.

In this chapter you'll find a list of things you can do to maximize your agents' satisfaction with their jobs.

Recruit People Who Value the Work

When recruiting, you need to look for two things in a candidate — skill and motivation. (For more on recruiting, see Chapter 10.) Most employers are good at finding the skill, but motivation is more difficult.

Remember that finding employees who value the work means you'll have employees who continue to be motivated after the honeymoon is over. In some cases, this might mean accepting a candidate with fewer or lesser skills. I'd take the person who's slightly less skilled but highly motivated, every day of the week.

This can be tough in some places. The knee-jerk reaction is to hire the most skilled person who knocks on your door. However, you often end up hiring a highly skilled person who's "between jobs." It should be no surprise when the person quits as soon as they find something that he or she considers better.

A more disconcerting situation occurs when the unmotivated agent doesn't find something better and ends up resenting your call center work for under-challenging them. They "quit" emotionally, but stay on the payroll.

Clarify Expectations

Tell your agents what's expected of them and what they'll get for meeting and exceeding those expectations. (I talk more about developing and communicating expectations in Chapter 3.)

One of the reasons why employees fail to do what's expected of them is that they aren't *told* what's expected of them. Being clear in your expectations — even before they accept the job — is one way to make sure that your agents aren't disappointed (and you aren't, either). Confusion about roles and contributions frustrates everyone.

Clear expectations set the road for achievement and, even if the rewards of meeting those expectations are intrinsic to the employee, enhance job satisfaction.

Provide Good, Job-Specific Training

Train your agents in the skills they need to be successful. Lack of skills is a roadblock to success and job satisfaction. (See Chapter 10 for more on training.)

Imagine trying to order dinner in a country where you don't speak the language, and nobody else speaks yours — you might go hungry. You'd certainly be frustrated.

Having the right skills, and an adequate level of ability in those skills — some of which are critical, such as call control, anger diffusion, sales, product and system knowledge, and policies and procedures — improves agent achievement, which is motivating. With a solid foundation of skills your agents can become skilled professional achievers.

Tell Them How They're Doing, Often

Good or bad, people need feedback; it tells them whether they're getting closer to their goals. (I talk more about feedback in Chapter 11.)

In the absence of feedback, agents will be frustrated because they don't know how they're doing or may feel their contribution is unappreciated. Failing to provide sufficient feedback can spoil a lot of your planning and managing.

At a very minimum, feedback tells your agents that you notice them and appreciate what they're doing.

Remove Roadblocks to Success

Obstacles occur in almost every endeavor, and your agents are likely to run into lots of them. Obstacles aren't, in themselves, de-motivating for staff; if, however, management does little to help remove these roadblocks, they can become very de-motivating.

Examples of roadblocks might include processes and tools that don't work, customer-unfriendly policies, or unhelpful management.

It doesn't matter how controllable or uncontrollable the roadblock is, if it's not removed it will eventually frustrate your employees. You've got to do something about it — your employees need to see you're trying to improve the situation.

Remove Fear

W. Edwards Deming, the famed statistician and business consultant, said that the "Economic cost of fear is appalling...."

Call centers can easily become scary places for employees. The level of accountability is very high, and in an increasingly competitive world the drive for results is only increasing. Poorly trained or bad managers compound the problems of fear.

Fear makes people shut down. It dampens their enthusiasm and prevents innovation and improvement. A lot of good people leave call center jobs because of fear.

Your management team must step in to ensure that hard-working employees need not fear for their jobs. This implies a fair workplace with a strong culture governed by a strong set of values.

You need to adapt policies to ensure accountability goes both ways. Agents are accountable for doing their best and management is accountable for contributing to the agents' success.

Regular (at least monthly) employee opinion surveys are a tool you can implement to ensure that a fear-free culture is maintained. Management should be responsible for the job satisfaction of their staff. Also, exit interviews will help to determine how successfully management is driving out fear.

An appeals process is a very effective way of ensuring that employee rights are maintained and, done well, will go a long way to reducing fear. With an effective appeals process, the frontline agent can appeal any disciplinary action to a panel of peers. The appeals process needs to be well thought out and designed, and staff must be trained to use it.

Don't Ask Them to Do Anything You Wouldn't Want to Do

If you can't see yourself doing something, then don't ask your agents to do it — including handling angry customers or making cold calls.

Have your managers do the frontline job from time to time — it's a worthwhile exercise. Some of the very best managers that I've seen will sit down in an agent's seat and say, "Watch me." This is a very fast way to get the respect of your call center agents. It shows that you're willing to do the job and, if you're good, might even give them some tips on how to do the job better.

Communicate the Good and the Bad — Be Straight and Honest

Effective communication is critical to agent job satisfaction.

If you've worked in a call center for any length of time, you can probably attest that call centers are rumor machines. It's not surprising, when you consider that so many people are brought together in one place. Furthermore, call centers abhor a vacuum — so if you're not communicating the truth, the rumor mill will fill the void.

My experience is that you can't communicate too much — the more, the better, including good news and bad. The more information you communicate, the less room there is for the rumor mill.

The great news is that today's call centers have lots of ways of communicating. From team meetings and e-mail to internal Web sites and chat sessions, you can communicate openly and honestly — and a lot.

Ask for Feedback

Communication needs to go both ways. On a regular basis (I suggest monthly) you should be asking employees for their feedback on how well management is doing at creating a healthy and effective workplace. You can, and should, ask a number of questions, but the one that's most important asks employees if they value their job.

You should also provide a mechanism for employees to give open-ended comments and suggestions. You may have to make the survey anonymous — even in the best environments some staff will not be comfortable completely opening up.

You may find a lot of harsh criticism. In any operation you're going to have some less satisfied employees, and they will be vocal. The important thing is to listen to the overlying trends.

It's important to work at either improving the most critical areas, as defined by your employees, or communicating why these things are as they are.

In subsequent months, you'll want to add specific questions regarding key areas of dissatisfaction to see if your staff feel you're improving.

Tying part of your managers' rewards to employee satisfaction is also a good idea, because it engages the entire management team in improving job satisfaction.

Be Positive

Call centers are great environments for tracking accountability, and in the quest for constant improvement it's easy to focus on finding things that aren't right. However, if this becomes too narrow a focus, you and your supervisors will soon find yourselves concentrating mainly on "catching people doing something wrong." While well intentioned, this management style is inherently negative and can dampen enthusiasm and morale.

Constant improvement is a worthy goal. When your suggestions for improvement come in a predominantly positive environment, they'll be received much more enthusiastically. (I talk more about process improvement in Chapter 12.)

As basic as it may sound, I subscribe to the idea of a ten-to-one positive to negative ratio. People in the office should be given ten pieces of positive reinforcement for every suggestion for improvement. Even suggestions for improvement can be framed in a positive manner: "Jane, you're already good at this — imagine what will happen when you start following the troubleshooting guidelines!"

I like to ask supervisors to tell me ten compliments and pieces of encouragement that they've given out to staff during the day. This should be easy: catch people doing something right! If it isn't easy, then we're not doing enough to create a positive environment.

I'm not suggesting a withdrawal from holding people accountable. What I am suggesting is accountability in a very positive environment.

Chapter 18

Ten Questions Every Call Center Manager Should Answer

*M*anaging a call center can be a rewarding and exciting job. If you want to be a successful call center manager, you need to know the answers to these important questions.

How Does Your Call Center Fit in to the Bigger Corporate Picture?

It's easy to forget that the call center is a cog in the corporate wheel. Everything starts with understanding how the call center fits into the big picture and answering the question, "What does the company need the call center to do?"

If you run a corporate call center, then your direction comes from the senior executives you report to. If you run an outsourced call center, then your direction comes from your client. In either case, you need clearly defined marching orders, ideally detailed in some form of service-level agreement.

With direction from the corporation, you can define optimal service levels, the types of support that you offer to callers, the types of skills your employees will need, and the kinds of tools that you'll need to fulfill your mission. No matter what type of operation you run, you'll work through these issues with your client and get the funding to create the operation the corporation needs.

When you understand what success looks like, you and your boss can define specific operating capabilities and performance targets: customer satisfaction levels, service-level objectives, cost per customer to deliver the service, and revenue generated per customer. You can then use this information to establish internal goals and operating procedures designed to achieve your desired results. (See Chapter 5 for ways to measure these targets.)

Remember, you can only get where you're going if you know where it is.

Why Are People Calling You?

Once you determine the top reasons why customers call, drill deeper into each reason to better understand its nuances. For example, if the top calling reason is for "billing" information, then billing could be broken down further into the specific types of billing calls: the customer did not understand the bill, the bill was late, the bill was wrong, and so on.

As a manager, your goal in this simple analysis is twofold: first, understand why customers are calling so you can create an effective call-handling process that satisfies customers' needs the first time they call. Second, determine which calls could have been avoided with improvements elsewhere in the company or call center.

Avoiding unnecessary calls improves call center efficiency, and resolving issues in fewer calls means happier customers.

For example, you might find that late processing of customer payments results in a direct increase in customers calling to enquire why their bill doesn't show their previous payment. With this knowledge, you can calculate the cost of handling those unnecessary calls. Investing in better payment processing will, at a minimum, result in capturing savings in the call center.

Understanding historical call types also helps with forecasting staffing and the facilities' needs. (I talk more about forecasting in Chapter 6.) The call center scheduler uses call types to forecast future demand — especially important in the short term. On any given day, call volume may be higher or lower than forecast. The more you understand why volume is high or low, the better your chance of determining what to do about being understaffed or overstaffed.

What's Your Ideal Service-Level Objective?

Setting a service-level objective — a call center term meaning your target for the percentage of calls you answer within a specified time frame of callers calling — that balances costs and service is critical, but it's an area that is often given little thought. (I give it a lot of thought in Chapter 2.)

Often call centers "go with the crowd" and set the service-level objective at whatever the industry is doing. Frequently, 80/20 (80 percent of calls answered within 20 seconds) becomes the default target — basically, because so many companies use it a lot of others do as well.

Keep in mind that 80/20 is a good level of service, but it might not be appropriate for your company. For example, a company running at 80/20 can expect customer calls to be answered in an average of 12 to 20 seconds — that's two to three rings. It's also an *average*. Some calls will be answered immediately, while some — maybe as many as 1 percent — could be answered in as long as one to three minutes, depending on the specific characteristics of the call center.

For some businesses, this might represent fine service. However, if yours is an emergency response call center, then 80/20 isn't good enough. Or, if your call center provides a very popular and free service for which callers are willing to wait to get through, then 80/20 might be too costly.

Setting the right objective is a matter of strategic consideration for each operation. Knowing what your ideal level of service is gives you a powerful argument in favor of getting the resources you need to achieve that level of service consistently.

In Chapter 5 I discuss how to set the ideal service-level objective. Understanding this analysis arms the call center manager with the knowledge not only of what the right level of performance is, but also of why that level of performance is important.

What Does It Cost to Run Your Call Center for One Hour?

When you know the total cost of running your call center for an hour (it's important to consider *all* the costs, and not just direct labor), you can quickly assess the benefits of a variety of business solutions, from cost of IVR (interactive voice response) to outsourcing.

Understanding the components of this cost per hour is a powerful cost-management tool. I discuss cost per hour in more detail in Chapter 5.

Are Your Employees Happy?

Maybe you've seen this happen — I certainly have. The best plans and programs flop, and call center results falter because employees aren't happy.

Sometimes, employee unrest comes on suddenly, brought on by a management decision or action; other times, it's a slow decline. Either way, the adage is bang on — if your employees aren't happy, then they won't be at their best when working with your customers.

This isn't to suggest that every day needs to be a love-in. However, the work environment does need to be fair and rewarding.

The topic of understanding and affecting employee morale is a large one, and could probably fill an entire ...*For Dummies* book on its own. A good place to start is to conduct regular employee satisfaction surveys (I like to do them monthly). These surveys provide feedback to management on changes to employee morale, and should track overall employee satisfaction with the job and satisfaction with specific elements of the job.

They should also capture employee comments so that issues causing employee dissatisfaction are identified. I suggest you make these surveys anonymous, because although you might get some harsh feedback, you also get the truth without sugar coating.

As I said, employee surveys are a place to start. Once you start measuring employee satisfaction, you know what the general mood is and you can see when sudden changes occur — a certain sign that attention is needed.

What Does the Future Look Like in 12 to 18 Months?

Most call center forecasting and scheduling focuses on the fairly near term — from tomorrow to a few months from now — but, as the call center manager, you need to keep the slightly longer term in mind as well. (I talk more about forecasting in Chapter 6.)

Major changes in caller demand, process, or products offered require a good deal of planning, particularly if the changes require expansion, training, or new technology.

Failure to prepare well ahead results in a last-minute urgent rush to adapt, which results in stress on the call center and degraded levels of customer service — and the larger the change, the greater the impact of being unprepared.

It's conceivable that your call center could deliver months of poor service because of a failure to plan for a major change in demand or requirements. Obviously, the costs of this are high. Lost customer goodwill, overtime costs, outsourced vendor costs, and contractor costs will be higher when you haven't planned for change in the longer term.

Forecasting for the long term doesn't need to be difficult. It starts with regular meetings with key people in the organization who might know about mid-term changes that could affect the call center — the senior executive in charge of the call center, someone in marketing, or a fortune teller. With a broad understanding of what might be coming, you can work with your analyst and scheduler to determine the impact of the changes. You can then prepare your proposals or business plans for presentation to the senior people in the organization.

What New or Existing Legislation Affects Your Call Center?

Call center management is becoming an exercise in risk management. This is definitely true; you need look no further than the legislation affecting the call center industry that has been tabled or passed.

Some of this legislation comes with hefty fines for violation, and not knowing about it is not an acceptable excuse.

And don't think that your organization is big enough to handle a few fines. These fines are significant, and they're on a per incident basis — meaning that if you have a large call center and there are many such incidents you're going to get a great big fine for violation. I'm talking a "the CEO just passed out!"–sized fine.

So, you need to know about these new laws and take steps to make sure that you comply with them. Better yet, hire a compliance officer and make her responsible for understanding the laws and making you comply. Better yet, get a compliance officer *and* a good lawyer. Some areas of the law that you need to be concerned with include

> ✔ Privacy
>
> ✔ Telephone sales
>
> ✔ Labor
>
> ✔ Human rights

I talk more about call center legislation in Chapter 12.

How Does Existing and New Technology Affect Your Call Center?

The developers of new technology are becoming increasingly creative at addressing the demands of the call center, bearing in mind that well-trained, motivated people and good processes are still necessary for success. As I describe in Chapter 8, better IVR platforms, better tools for the agent, and better training applications are a few examples of the technologies that are helping call centers.

If you understand your call center process, and the numbers and how to influence them, you can quickly identify the technologies that can improve your call center and drive results.

Call centers have such a large impact on customer relationships they often generate huge amounts of revenue and have tremendous staffing budgets; so, a well-placed technology can generate significant returns. It's not uncommon to implement technology that pays for itself in one year.

You need to look for opportunities in the old and proven technologies as well as the new or developing ones. You're not going to implement everything, but a few well-placed investments can make a big difference.

Of course, some caveats should be considered. Firstly, you need to understand how the technology is going to affect the drivers of your operation — call length, calls per customer, occupancy, cost per hour, conversion rate, revenue per sale, and customer satisfaction. With this knowledge you can calculate the benefits of the new technology.

Secondly, you need proof that the technology will get these results. Who has done this before? What results did they get? How do you know for sure? A lot of expensive technology that has never realized its promise is sitting in call centers. Excitement over unsubstantiated claims can lead to a premature purchase.

Finally, most technology can't be effective if it's implemented in a vacuum. People in the call center will need training on the technology, what it does, how it works, and how they need to interact with it.

With the proper understanding of the technology and its goals, managers and agents can participate in making the technology successful. The full creativity of the team will be brought to the new technology project. For example, people in the call center will find new uses for IVR technology, and call center agents will better adapt to scripting and customer profiling software if they understand how it works and what it is supposed to do for them.

What's Your Disaster Recovery Plan?

Ask some people what a disaster recovery plan is, and they envision some type of futuristic James Bond scene where the camera pans over a secret underground call center lair — probably under a volcano. "Yeah baby, bring it on, we're getting our calls handled!"

Sure, you could do that, but you can also make it simpler.

You need to consider how important it is to remain operational: some call centers might be able to live with temporary outages. For example, if you operate the information line for a local shopping center, people will understand if a hurricane shuts down your site for a few days. On the other hand, if your call center is the hub of a telephone banking operation, you'll need to keep the lights on.

You start by planning for temporary outages — perhaps due to power failures or inclement weather. You then progress with your planning until you've determined what you're going to do during prolonged outages, which might happen if the call center is involved in a natural disaster, fire, flood, or plague of locusts. (I discuss instituting a disaster recovery plan in Chapter 4.)

Depending on the severity of the outage, you want to have an escalating series of actions that are either automatically executed or that management initiates.

What Are Your Three Initiatives for Improvement?

I like to see effectively run call centers. But what I like even more are call centers that are always evolving and improving. In the long run, the call centers that have a culture of learning and improvement seem to do best.

The managers of these centers frequently have ongoing initiatives, the things they're working on or planning to that will lead to improvements in call center results. For example, they might be planning Six Sigma training, or a new management certification course, or better analysis tools, or new technology, or ISO registration — it doesn't matter.

The point is that managers who generate a culture of improvement and innovation always seem to have a few projects on the go that are designed to create improvements in call center results. And there is frequently a sense of excitement around these initiatives, almost like they can't wait until the initiatives are implemented and running. Of course, some initiatives work and some don't — but the ones that do make these call centers leaders.

Chapter 19

Ten Ways to Improve Call Center Costs and Increase Efficiency

* *

In This Chapter

▶ Improving efficiency and reducing costs while maintaining service

▶ Understanding the importance of mapping processes

▶ Eliminating unnecessary calls

* *

*G*enerally speaking, call centers provide a very efficient way to communicate with a large number of customers. However, since call center expenditures are frequently one of the larger line items for corporations, the costs are usually closely scrutinized.

In this chapter, I provide some tips for improving efficiencies and decreasing overall call center costs.

Improve Call Control

In most call centers implementing a better call control strategy will have an immediate impact, because reducing call length without sacrificing service is an effective way to reduce costs.

Most agents work hard to provide good service, and perhaps to sell additional products or services to customers, but many lack a structured plan for guiding the call to a successful conclusion. Some agents feel that if they're controlling the call they're not delivering good service — some even consider it rude. As a result, their calls frequently wander. Training your agents on simple call-control techniques makes a significant difference. I talk more about training in Chapter 10.

A good way to help agents with call control is through the development of a call guide. Call guides can be as simple as an outline of the general flow and content of each call — perhaps on one piece of paper — or can be very complex, using sophisticated scripting software and logical branching to guide agents through the most complicated calls.

Good call guides will help agents to control the call, reduce call length, and increase customer satisfaction, and can also reduce training time.

Map and Improve Call Processes

Mapping your processes for handling various types of customer calls is another useful exercise. For a more complete discussion of how to map processes, see Chapter 12.

Start by identifying the 8 to 10 primary reasons why customers call. Then, sit down with a group of agents, perhaps a supervisor or two, and a trainer to map out (on paper or in software) how each call is to be handled.

Once you've mapped the top call types, you can ask the group the question, "How might this be done better?" Simplifying and improving call processes can result in tremendous improvements to call length and other call objectives.

Do a Cost–Benefit Analysis of Your Service-Level Objective — Then Hit It!

A good service-level objective (a target set to measure how fast your call center answers the phone) creates a balance between the benefits and the costs associated with answering the phone faster. See Chapter 5 for more on assessing your service-level objectives.

Understanding the "sweet spot" — the point where customer satisfaction is maximized while costs are minimized — is a great way to control costs. In Chapter 5 I describe how to do a cost–benefit analysis to find your optimal service-level objective (the sweet spot).

Once the optimal rate is achieved, efficiency comes from delivering this level of service as consistently as possible — the less deviation from the optimal service level, the better. As a result, your call center occupancy will increase and your costs will decrease.

Make Your Call Center Bigger

You can increase occupancy without sacrificing customer satisfaction or service level by making your call center bigger. As you can read in Chapter 5, bigger call centers are more efficient than smaller centers. In larger centers, you'll have a higher level of occupancy for the same level of service.

The easiest way to make your call center bigger is to work together. If your call center is running separate call-handling groups (customer service and collections, for example), then by merging these two groups you'll take advantage of the economies of bigger call centers.

Blend Work

Another way to make your call center bigger so you can benefit from improved agent occupancy is by *blending* work into your call-handling queue. A classic example of blending is mixing outbound telemarketing into an inbound sales or service queue. In this case, you make use of agent *idle time* — time agents spend waiting for incoming calls — to do your outbound work. As a result, your agents are busier (more occupied) overall. Should inbound volumes increase or spike, your agents stop making outbound calls while they handle the inbound calls.

Outbound collections calls and customer-service "welcome" calls can also be used for blending, perhaps as an alternative to telemarketing. Or, other types of work could be blended in, such as answering e-mail or regular mail.

Using skills-based routing

Skills-based routing — sending calls of specific types to groups of agents based on their skills — is a great technique and, used properly, can give you a lift in occupancy while allowing you to create groups of specialized skills. I talk more about skills-based routing in Chapter 8.

However, be careful not to go overboard. Keep in mind that skills-based routing still amounts to the creation of separate call-answering groups and is not as efficient as one large pool.

The closer you move to having one skill group, things will be simpler and your overall occupancy higher — provided your staff can handle the added complexity.

Turn Idle Time into Training Time

Even in larger, more efficient call centers, idle time will make up 15 percent or more of an agent's time on the phones. In an agent's standard 8-hour shift, spending 15 percent of his or her time idle equates to more than one hour doing nothing but waiting for calls. That's a lot of time.

Recently, a few companies have experimented with turning some of this idle time into training time. To do this, a training application, using CTI, *(computer–telephone integration* — technology used to integrate your computer system with your telephone system) monitors the activity of agents working in a call-answering queue. When agents have sufficient idle time, the application sends training material to the agent's desktop and headset. If the application is sophisticated enough, material can be customized to the needs of the individual agent, and testing can also be added.

Since we've implemented idle-time training in my call centers, in addition to improvements in skills and performance we've seen reductions in off-phone training time and a reduction in the requirements for dedicated trainers.

See Chapter 10 for more on training.

Eliminate Unnecessary Calls

Unnecessary calls come from a variety of sources, including calls handled poorly on the first attempt, confusing marketing materials, incorrect or confusing invoices, misdirected calls, and so on. Reducing them is a call center efficiency basic. Here are three quick fixes for reducing the number of unnecessary calls in your call center.

✔ **Implement an IVR.** As I talk about in Chapter 8, using *interactive voice response* — automated voice prompts used to service customer contacts — offers customers a fast and efficient means of self-serving their calling needs for simple applications like account balances, general information, and even for ordering products and services. An IVR can increase the service you provide, as it can handle calls 7 days a week, 24 hours a day.

Depending on the environment, an IVR can offload between 5 and 25 percent or more of your call center's call volume. The payback is tremendous, making IVR one of the best investments in the call center.

✔ **Use Web pages.** The use of company Web pages to provide customers with self-service options probably has a brighter future than even IVR. Self-service through a company Web site is cheaper than IVR, it's generally always available, and the complexity of transactions that can be done through the Internet is greater than IVR.

✔ **Analyze why customers are calling.** A slightly more complex way to reduce unnecessary calls is to track the reasons for the calls. Tracking in detail, why customers call, highlights the number of call types that are unnecessary and avoidable. Examples might include billing errors, confusing marketing material, or failure to handle the call completely in the first place. Sometimes the fixes to these situations are as easy as a conversation with the right person, other times the process is more involved.

In either case, it helps to do the math to calculate the benefit — in terms of reduced costs to the call center and the company — of eliminating these unnecessary calls.

Learn What a Change in Agent Utilization Costs

You can't chain your agents to their desks; they need time for breaks, meetings, training, and coaching. In most operations, you'll also find a certain amount of time that's unaccounted for. This missing time happens for a number of reasons and is probably acceptable so long as it doesn't get out of hand — no more than a few percent, for example.

In my operation, every manager knows that every percentage reduction in *agent utilization* — the percentage of time agents are actually logged in to the phone systems, compared to the total time they're being paid for — costs the call center so many thousands of dollars per month. So, when we're planning meetings, training, and so on, it's done with the cost–benefit in mind. (See Chapter 5 for more information on measuring agent utilization.)

By consciously thinking about every use of off-phone time, your long-term use of human resources will become better controlled and costs will go down.

Spend More on Staff

Most call centers, at some point fall into the trap of focusing too heavily on cost of labor as a means to reducing overall call center costs. In fact, much of the outsourcing industry has been stuck in this dilemma.

It goes like this: Senior management, or the client, wants the lowest possible cost of call center service. As a result, your call center reduces wages. You then spend more time than usual sifting through recruits trying to find the best cheap labor. You might even spend a lot of time training this cheap labor, but you don't want to overdo it, because training's expensive. Once the agents are on the phones you do your best to monitor, coach, and program them to make them the best that they can be.

What you end up with is cheaper labor with reduced skill and motivation. As a result, while the cost of your service is low, the capability is also low. Results of this cheaper service include longer calls, less revenue generation, the need for more training, substantially higher levels of errors and callbacks, and, ultimately, dissatisfied customers who could stop doing business with you.

When the total cost of a call center agent is considered, including the impacts of wages, errors, repeat calls, turnover, absenteeism, lost customers, and revenue generated, spending more on agents can result in spending less overall.

Relocate Your Call Center

Moving your call center location is one way to have your lower-cost-labor cake and eat it too. If your call center is located in the heart of Capital City you'll have access to lots of the best-qualified people who value the job, but they'll be expensive. However, it won't cost as much for the same quality of staff in Rural City, USA; Frostbite, Canada; or Farfaraway, India.

The farther away you go, the more you can save without significantly reducing the capability of your agent group.

And you might not have to close your existing call center — you can start by sending your additional "growth" business to the remote center. Over time, rather than replace staff in Capital City lost to turnover, your might opt to grow the rural operation instead.

Appendix 1

Glossary of Key Call Center Definitions and Concepts

Abandonment rate: The percentage of callers who hang up before an agent answers their call, or before they make a selection in an IVR (interactive voice response) unit. The inverse of *Answer rate*.

Accessibility: Measures that describe the ease with which customers can access your service, the general speed of call answering, and your customers' level of acceptance with this speed of answer.

Agent availability: The amount of time that agents are available and waiting to take calls. Usually expressed as a percentage.

Agent utilization: The percentage of total agents that are logged in to the phone system, busy handling customer calls. The inverse of *Agent availability*.

Answer rate: The percentage of calls that are answered by a call center — defined by callers speaking to an agent or making a selection in the IVR — compared to the total number of calls coming in.

Automatic call distributor (ACD): A call center telephone system. Primary among its features is the ability to hold customer calls in a queue for delivery to call center agents in a designated order.

Automatic number identification (ANI): A system to identify the telephone number of a calling customer, serving a function similar to caller ID. One of the core technologies behind the 911 emergency service.

Average handle time (AHT): The average amount of time that agents spend processing customer calls — including speaking directly with customers and doing work relating to the call after the customer has hung up (like filling out customer account information). Usually expressed in seconds.

Average speed of answer (ASA): The average amount of time that customers wait in queue before being greeted by an agent.

Average talk time (ATT): The average amount of time that agents spend speaking directly with customers. Usually expressed in seconds.

Average after-call work time (AWT): The average amount of time agents spend working on customer accounts after the caller has hung up and during which they are unavailable to take another call. Also known as *not-ready* time.

Blending: Occurs when either inbound or outbound calls may be delivered by the phone system to the same agent.

Call center: You have been paying attention, haven't you? If not, have a quick glance at Chapter 1.

Call control: The act of controlling the flow of a conversation, usually by asking questions.

Call guide: A tool (or template) that outlines the natural flow of the call, providing agents with questions to ask and product information to assist them with call control. Call guides are often put online in a computer application.

Call length: How long it takes to process one customer interaction. Usually expressed as an average. See *Average handle time*.

Call-review assessment: An assessment of an agent's call-handling proficiency, usually scored and conducted by a member of your call center's quality assurance team.

Call strategy: The plan or approach that an agent will take in handling a customer call. Includes the desired outcome of the call.

Call time: See *Average handle time*.

Calls per agent: The number of calls handled by your call center divided by the total number of agents taking calls in a given period.

Cancellations per contact: The number of customers canceling service divided by the total number of calls handled in a given period.

Chat: A system that allows any number of logged-in computer users to have a typed, real-time, online conversation.

Computer–telephone integration (CTI): Communication between the call center's telephone system and its computer system. Allows the merging of information and telecommunications technologies to provide added functionality to the agents and end customers.

Contact: Any contact between a customer and an agent — could be a call, e-mail, chat, fax, or letter.

Contact center: Usually synonymous with *call center*. A contact center will handle e-mail, chat, faxes, and so on — not just "calls."

Conversion rate: A measure of agents' sales proficiency. The number of sales made divided by the number of calls taken.

Cost per call: The total costs associated with running the call center divided by the number of calls handled in a given period.

Cost–benefit analysis: The comparison of benefits and costs in decision-making, by assigning dollar values to benefits and costs.

Customer relationship management (CRM): A strategy employed by corporations for maximizing the lifetime value of their relationships with their customers. The term CRM is frequently used to describe the technology used in managing customer relationships.

Customer service: By definition, the act of assisting or working on behalf of a customer. More commonly, the level of service provided to the customer.

Customer service representative (CSR): see *Agent.*

Data warehouse: A large computer database used to store your mountains of call center statistical data.

Dialed number identification service (DNIS): Technology that identifies the number that the customer dialed and routes the call according to a specified plan.

Disaster recovery plan: A planned procedure for sending incoming calls to another site in the event that some emergency (disaster) befalls your primary site.

Drivers: Measures that impact reaching your business objectives and can be controlled by management and staff.

Dynamic network routing (DNR): A service provided by the telephone companies that allows the call center to dynamically change where customer calls are routed.

Efficiency: The use of resources, for example money, with as little waste as possible.

Efficiency metrics: Measures that gauge costs and efficiencies in the call center.

Envelope scheduling: Purposely scheduling more agents than needed to handle the forecasted number of inbound calls, then using agents who are not busy taking inbound calls to do outbound calls or other work (chat, e-mail). See also *Blending.*

Feel, felt, found: A call-handling strategy used by agents when handling difficult situations with customers. Feel, felt, found is based on the principles of empathy and understanding.

First-call resolution: The percentage of callers who do not have to call back within a certain time frame (usually a day or two) to have their issue resolved.

Idle time: The time agents spend waiting for calls; that is, not busy with customers on the line or doing after-call work. Can be expressed either as a percentage of total time logged in or in hours.

Inbound: Incoming calls (or faxes, e-mails, or chats) that are generated by customers. See also *Outbound*.

Information technology (IT): The development, installation, and implementation of computer systems and applications.

Interactive voice response (IVR): A voice-processing application that provides automated services to incoming callers and that can gather information and interact with other computer systems and databases.

ISO 9001/2000: An international standard for the creation and maintenance of a quality assurance system within a company.

LAMA: A call-handling technique that emphasizes listening and interaction with the customer for call control. Designed by Judy McKee of McKee Motivation.

Metrics: Measures of performance.

Mission statement: A statement describing an organization's goals, values, and overall plan.

Non-productive agent time: Time for which agents are being paid but are not on the phones — also called *off-phone* time. Includes time spent in meetings, training sessions, coffee breaks, and so on.

Occupancy: A measure of your call center's on-phone productivity: the time agents spend actively busy, working on customer contacts (not idle), compared to the total time logged on the phones. Expressed as a percentage.

Outbound: The calls (or faxes, e-mails, or chats) going out to customers that are generated by your agents. Telemarketing is the most common example. See also *Inbound*.

Outsourcing: The practice of sending work out to a third-party provider or manufacturer to achieve some business objective, such as reducing costs.

Performance drivers: See *Drivers*.

Predictive dialer: A piece of computer/telephone equipment that dials telephone numbers for an outbound call center.

Process management: A series of analyses, actions, and tools applied to a way of doing things so that these things will be done more effectively.

Process map: A chart that graphically represents a single business process from start to finish.

Quality analyst: A person responsible for analyzing processes and procedures.

Recruiter: A person responsible for hiring staff for the call center, reviewing résumés, setting up and conducting interviews and testing, checking references, and so on.

Reporting analyst: A person who takes the information from all the systems and produces nice reports, charts, and graphs (hopefully, with lines that go up).

Retention rate: The percentage of customers who initially called to cancel their service, but decided not to after speaking with an agent. Sometimes referred to as *Save rate*.

Revenue generation: Making money. See also *Upselling*.

Revenue metrics: Measures of revenue in the call center.

Script: The written wording and directions provided to agents to be used when talking to customers. Some are used verbatim and some are merely guides and suggestions for handling customer calls.

Server: A computer that provides some service for other computers connected to it via a network.

Service level: How fast we answer the phone, e-mail, and so on. Most commonly expressed as the percentage of incoming calls answered in a specified amount of time.

Schedule adherence: The percentage of time that agents are actually on the phones when they're supposed to be.

Scheduling: The process of assigning call center agents to weekly schedules to get the right number of people working at all times.

Single point of failure: When the success or failure of a process (or your entire call center) hinges on any one element, it's said to have a *single point of failure*.

Six Sigma: A quality improvement program developed by Motorola that focuses on gaining control of a process and attempting to drive defects, as defined by the customer, down to fewer than 3.4 per million.

Skills-based routing: Technology you can use to send calls of specific types to certain agents based on their skills.

Stakeholder: Anyone who has a share or an interest in your call center. Includes clients, customers, managers, agents, and so on.

Standard deviation: In simple (and not exactly accurate) terms, it's the average amount that a set of numbers varies from the average of the set. For you math types, it's a statistic used as a measure of the dispersion or variation in a distribution, equal to the square root of the arithmetic mean of the squares of the deviations from the arithmetic mean.

Supervisor: The first line of management, whose primary responsibility is to coach, discipline, provide feedback to, and support your call center agents. Also known as a *team leader* or *team manager.*

Telemarketing: A term typically used to describe outbound telephone sales and promotion — stereotypically used to describe the folks who call you just as you sit down to dinner.

Upselling: Attempting to increase the revenue generated per call by suggesting an increase in service or a complementary product.

Virtual call center: Created when agents are located in several locations (often their own homes) rather than an individual call center site. The Internet is used as the network to link these remote agents.

Voice recognition: Software that allows callers to speak commands instead of using their telephone keypad.

Appendix 2

Call Center Support Services

• •

*H*ere are some places to go for help when you need it.

Employee Testing and Evaluation

This is a list of companies that provide call center employee testing and evaluation tools.

BR Garrison Software Group
11525 Huggins St., Leesburg, FL 34788
Telephone: (352) 742-1769, Fax: (352) 343-0943
Web: www.plus32.com

Limra International
300 Day Hill Rd., Windsor, CT 06095
Telephone: (860) 688-3358, Fax: (860) 298-9555
Web: www.limra.com

Pearson NCS
5601 Green Valley Dr., Bloomington, MN 55437
Telephone: (800) 328-6172
Web: www.pearsonncs.com

Presenting Solutions, Inc.
55 Santa Clara Ave., Oakland, CA 94610
Telephone: (800) 547-7554, Fax: (510) 763-7599
Web: www.presol.com

SkillCheck Inc.
113 Terrace Hall Ave., Burlington, MA 01803
Telephone: (800) 648-3166, Fax: (781) 229-8108
Web: www.skillcheck.com

Thomas International Inc.
2 Robert Speck Parkway, Suite 750, Mississauga, ON L4Z 1H8
Telephone: (905) 306-2797, Fax: (905) 306-2796
Web: www.thomasinternational.net

Some specific tests you can use in your call center include

- ✔ **Plus 32-Employment Testing System** Ver. 4.0.3. Copyright 1986–2000 by BR Garrison Software Group

  This is a basic IQ test. It measures problem-solving ability.

- ✔ **TMAI (Telemarketing Aptitude Inventory) Test** NCS (National Computer Solutions) London House. Copyright 1992 NCS Pearson Inc.

  The TMAI test measures call center sales and customer service aptitude. While essentially a gauge of skill level, it also illustrates motivation, as folks who score low tend to be those less likely to enjoy a call center career.

- ✔ **MAT (Management Aptitude Test) Test** NCS London House. Copyright 1993 NCS Pearson Inc.

  This tests a person's problem-solving, logic, and people skills in various management scenarios.

- ✔ **Skill Check** Ver 4.1. Copyright Skill Check Inc. 2000

  Skill Check is a series of tests that are administered online for grammar, spelling, and vocabulary, and computer skills such as Excel, Windows, and so on.

Management Certification

These companies can provide you with call center management certification training.

Call Center Learning Solutions
44 N. Old Place Lane, Belgrade, MT 59714
Telephone: (925) 513-1010
Web: www.callcentertraining.com

The Call Center School
568 Grant Highway, Lebanon, TN 37090
Telephone: (615) 812-8400
Fax: (931) 358-3900
Web: www.thecallcenterschool.com

Customer Operations Performance Center Inc. (COPC)
500 Corporate Parkway, Suite 108, Amherst, NY 14226
Telephone: (716) 835-4455, Fax: (716) 835-4461
Web: www.copc.com

Incoming Calls Management Institute
P.O. Box 6177, Annapolis, MD 21401-0177,
Telephone: (800) 672-6177, Fax: (410) 267-0962
Web: www.incoming.com

NuComm Solutions Inc.
80 King St., Suite 300, St. Catharines, ON L2R 7G1
Telephone: (877) 637-2615, Fax: (905) 641-1456
Web: www.nucomm.net

SCInc.
600 12th St., Suite 175, Golden, CO 80401
Telephone: (877) 916-1510
Web: www.scinc.com

ISO Registration

Here's a list of a few of the larger organizations that provide ISO registration
services. (See Chapter 14 for more on ISO.) You can find many more registrars,
small and large, by searching the Internet under ISO registrar. Some registrars
also give courses in becoming certified, and most can provide you access to
a worldwide network of consultants specializing in ISO certification.

BSI Global
389 Chiswick High Rd., London, W4 4AL United Kingdom
Telephone: +44 (0)20 8996 9000
Web: www.bsi-global.com

Intertek Systems Certification
70 Codman Hill Rd.,,, Boxborough, MA 01710
Telephone: (800) 810-1195, Fax: (800) 813-9287
Web: www.intertek-sc.com

QMI Management Systems Registration
8501 E. Pleasant Valley Rd., Cleveland, OH 44131-5575
Telephone: (800) 247-0802
Web: www.qmi.com

SGS
1 Place des Alpes, P.O. Box 2152, 1211 Geneva 1, Switzerland
Telephone: +41 22 739 91 11, Fax: +41 22 739 98
Web: www.sgs.com

Call Center Consulting

You can find lots of companies that provide call center consulting services —
probably some located near you — by searching the Web. Here are a few that
I'm familiar with.

The Call Center School
568 Grant Highway, Lebanon, TN 37090
Telephone: (615) 812-8400, Fax: (931) 358-3900
Web: www.thecallcenterschool.com

The Call Center School provides standard educational programs on a variety of call center topics, customized education programs for call centers and industry vendors, and general call center consulting.

Customer Operations Performance Center Inc. (COPC)
500 Corporate Parkway, Suite 108, Amherst, NY 14226
Telephone: (716) 835-4455, Fax: (716) 835-4461
Web: www.copc.com

COPC conducts in-depth, onsite operational audits worldwide promoting best practices in call centers, and provides assistance in outsourcing contact centers as well as moving operations offshore. COPC markets a suite of monitoring systems to demonstrate return on investment. They also developed the COPC-2000(r), an industry standard certification for call centers.

Incoming Calls Management Institute (ICMI)
P.O. Box 6177, Annapolis, MD 21401-0177
Telephone: (800) 672-6177, Fax: (410) 267-0962
Web: www.incoming.com

ICMI offers training programs and educational resources for call center management. They produce the *Call Center Management Review* newsletter and authored the book *Call Center Management on Fast Forward*.

NuComm Solutions Inc.
80 King St., Suite 300, St. Catharines, ON L2R 7G1
Telephone: (877) 637-2615, Fax: (905) 641-1456
Web: www.nucomm.net

NuComm Solutions examines contact centers — from management to frontline agents — and provides consultation and operational audits from a perspective of business modeling and ISO 9001: 2000–certified processes. NuComm Solutions Inc., of which I'm the CEO, is behind the publication of *23 Steps to an Effective Call Centre*. They also develop sophisticated database applications specific to clients' customer relationship management requirements and develop customized call center training programs based on client needs. In addition, NuComm offers a suite of IVR solutions for inbound, outbound, Web-based, and e-mail applications.

Strategic Contact Inc.
9510 SW 151st Ave., Beaverton, OR 97007
Telephone: (666) 791-8560, Fax: (503) 579-8657
Web: www.strategiccontact.com

Strategic Contact provides consulting to optimize the strategic value of customer contact technology and operations through the planning and execution of projects such as call center outsourcing strategy, information technology planning, and virtual call center design.

Vanguard Communications Corp.
100 American Rd., Morris Plains, NJ 07950
Telephone: (973) 605-8000, Fax: (973) 605-8329
Web: www.vanguard.net

Vanguard provides consulting in the design, development, and implementation of effective business solutions for customer contact. Their focus is on the application of convergence technologies to contact centers.

Index

●●

• G •

• H •

• S •

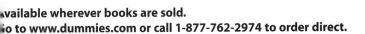